SACRED SPACE

"Inspired by one of the most successful spirituality websites around (and for good reason), *Sacred Space* offers readers short but profound meditations on the daily scriptures. Friendly, concise, and consistently thought provoking, these books are perfect for anyone who would like to pray more and be more connected to God, but may feel too busy to do so. In other words, everyone!"

James Martin, S.J.
Author of *The Jesuit Guide to (Almost) Everything*

"The *Sacred Space* website has been helping millions to pray for some years. Now Ave Maria Press makes these very helpful and easily usable prayer-helps available in handsome and accessible form, including pocket-sized booklets for the Advent/Christmas and Lenten seasons. What a great service to God's people! I hope millions more will buy the books. God is being well served."

William A. Barry, S.J.
Author of *Paying Attention to God: Discernment in Prayer*

"Powerful in its clarity and beautiful in its simplicity, *Sacred Space* is a rich and nourishing soul-companion for all of us. I am grateful for it and know that you will be, too."

Phyllis Tickle
Author of *Emergence Christianity*

"I don't know any other guides to prayer that are so direct, profound, and effective. It's no wonder that right around the world they have proved extraordinarily helpful in leading busy people to stay in touch with the presence of God."

Gerald O'Collins, S.J.
Author of *Jesus: A Portrait*

"*Sacred Space* has provided countless people with a clear and concise resource to pray alone—any time and anywhere—and yet consciously united with numerous others worldwide. This timely, unassuming aid to daily prayer is a gem."

Peter van Breemen, S.J.
Author of *The God Who Won't Let Go*

SACRED SPACE

The Prayer Book 2015

from the website www.sacredspace.ie
Prayer from the Irish Jesuits

ave maria press AmP notre dame, indiana

Acknowledgments

The publisher would like to thank Piaras Jackson, S.J., and the Sacred Space team for their kind assistance in making this book possible. Comments and suggestions relating to the site or to this book can be directed to feedback@sacredspace.ie.

Unless otherwise noted, the scripture quotations contained herein are from the *New Revised Standard Version* Bible, copyright © 1989 by the Division of Christian Education of the National Council of Churches of Christ in the United States of America. Used by permission. All rights reserved.

First published in Australia 2014 by Michelle Anderson Publishing Pty., Ltd.

Founded in 1865, Ave Maria Press is a ministry of the United States Province of Holy Cross.

www.avemariapress.com

Paperback: ISBN-13 978-1-59471-566-2

E-book: ISBN-13 978-1-59471-567-9

Cover and text design by Andy Wagoner.

Printed and bound in the United States of America.

Contents

Sacred Space Prayer

Dear Lord,

The music of our lives is meant to be a symphony of love.

Endlessly and lovingly you sustain us,

and we learn to respond as best we can.

You gaze on us and you smile, and we smile back.

You speak your life-giving Word in our hearts

and refresh us constantly through our daily prayer.

Grant that we, the Sacred Space community, may become

the "Good News in the present tense" to a needy world.

Preface

About Sacred Space: The Prayer Book and www.sacredspace.ie

The Sacred Space website began life online in 1999 and has made new content available at www.sacredspace.ie every day since then. An initiative of the Irish Jesuits, the website has developed to include many languages and various elements.

The simplicity of the user experience belies the complex and agile system which has been developed to run the website. It consistently delivers the prayer to an increasing range of mobile devices and now runs twenty languages, serving five million people annually.

In 2004, the first print publication of the daily prayer was produced by Australian publisher Michelle Anderson, Pty., Ltd. Starting in 2005, Ave Maria Press began to publish the prayer book as well.

In addition to the daily prayer, Sacred Space also publishes seasonal retreats—recently in cooperation with Pray As You Go, the prayer site run by the Jesuits in Britain. The Living Space section of the Sacred Space site offers commentaries on the daily scripture readings, its Chapel of Intentions allows visitors to offer intentions for prayer, and the Pray with the Pope pages make the intentions of the international Apostleship of Prayer available.

The small Sacred Space team in Ireland coordinates a far-flung volunteer network. They are delighted to continue Ireland's tradition of missionary outreach in the digital age and welcome you to join your prayers with the thousands of people every day who draw life from Sacred Space.

How to Use This Book

We invite you to make a sacred space in your day and spend ten minutes praying, wherever you are, with the help of a prayer guide and scripture chosen specially for each day. Every place is a sacred space, so you may wish to have this book available to be picked up and read at any time of the day: on your desk, on your bedside table, in your briefcase, or wherever is convenient. Remember that God is everywhere, all around us, constantly reaching out to us, and interested in meeting us, even in the most unlikely situations. When we know this, and with a bit of practice, we can pray anywhere.

The structure of this book is simple. At the beginning of each week, you are offered a bit of prayer advice: "something to think and pray about each day this week." A set of prayer stages follow, which will help to you focus on God:

The Presence of God
Freedom
Consciousness
The Word (daily scripture and inspiration points to help with the text)
Conversation
Conclusion

It is important to come back to these stages each day of the week, since they are all integral to the prayer of the day. The first three stages prepare our hearts to hear the Word of God in quietness, and the later stages help us to reflect on what we've read.

The stages are for *doing*, not only for reading. Each stage is an exercise or meditation to help you get in touch with God's presence in your life.

When you pray, you are not alone. We invite you to join the many people around the world who pray with us in our sacred space.

Something to think and pray about each day this week:

Mary, the Vulnerable

There is a story of a crib being banished from a Dublin hospital ward. Someone in authority, it seems, suffering from an overdose of political correctness, felt that Muslims might take offence. But Islam venerates the Virgin under her real name: Mariam.

Mind you, if Jesus' crib is a cause of offence, the original stable is scandalous, too—or it should be. Francis of Assisi never meant his model of the birth at Bethlehem to be idealised. But over-familiarity breeds contentment, and so the gospel story has lost its power to break open our comfortable imaginings. The stable has become idealised. In reality, her pregnancy must in fact have been a Calvary for Our Lady.

Let us hear the Virgin howling in the version of her ordeal that the Koran has recorded. In that holy book, she is utterly alone and afraid. "And when she felt the pain of labour she lay down against the trunk of a palm-tree and cried out: 'I wish that I were dead and my memory erased.'"

"I wish I were dead!" As well she might. Neither the Hebrew law, nor the Muslim, nor the Catholic, ever smiled on an unmarried mother. Such people always and everywhere are the single most precarious persons in the whole community. They are still massively vulnerable today in many cultures. Their comfort can be that Mary stands with them. As she promises in the Magnificat, God raises up the humble.

The Presence of God
Lord, help me to be fully alive to your holy presence.
Enfold me in your love.
Let my heart become one with yours.

Freedom
Many countries are at this moment suffering
the agonies of war.
I bow my head in thanksgiving for my freedom.
I pray for all prisoners and captives.

Consciousness
At this moment, Lord, I turn my thoughts to you.
I will leave aside my chores and preoccupations.
I will take rest and refreshment in your presence, Lord.

The Word
The Word of God comes to us through the scriptures. May the Holy
Spirit enlighten my mind and my heart to respond to the gospel
teachings. (Please turn to your scripture on the following pages.
Inspiration points are there should you need them. When you are
ready, return here to continue.)

Conversation
Sometimes I wonder what I might say
if I were to meet you in person, Lord.
I might say "Thank You, Lord" for always being there for me.
I know with certainty there were times when you carried me,
when through your strength I got through the dark times in my life.

Conclusion
Glory be to the Father, and to the Son, and to the Holy Spirit,
as it was in the beginning, is now, and ever shall be,
world without end. Amen.

December 2014

Sunday 30th November,
First Sunday of Advent
Mark 13:33—37

Jesus said, "Beware, keep alert; for you do not know when the time will come. It is like a man going on a journey, when he leaves home and puts his slaves in charge, each with his work, and commands the doorkeeper to be on the watch. Therefore, keep awake—for you do not know when the master of the house will come, in the evening, or at midnight, or at cockcrow, or at dawn, or else he may find you asleep when he comes suddenly. And what I say to you I say to all: Keep awake."

- Four times in this short passage Jesus tells me to be attentive. I would rather settle down to a comfortable life. But the world of God is breaking in everywhere, like an invasion. I ask for the grace to "seek God in all things," as St. Ignatius says.

- A new world order began with Jesus, and I have a part to play in it. Every day I review what went on, and as Gerard Manley Hopkins says, "I greet him the days I meet him, and bless when I understand."

Monday 1st December
Matthew 8:5—11

When Jesus entered Capernaum, a centurion came to him, appealing to him and saying, "Lord, my servant is lying at home paralysed, in terrible distress." And he said to him, "I will come and cure him." The centurion answered, "Lord, I am not worthy to have you come under my roof; but only speak the word, and my servant will be healed. For I also am a man under authority, with soldiers under me; and I say to one, 'Go,' and he goes, and to another, 'Come,' and he comes, and to my slave, 'Do this,' and the slave does it." When Jesus heard him, he was amazed and said to those who followed him, "Truly I tell you, in no one in Israel have I found such faith. I tell you, many will come from east and west and will eat with Abraham and Isaac and Jacob in the kingdom of heaven."

- This miracle is unusual. Jesus was not actually present when the healing took place; he spoke the word and the centurion's servant was healed. The servant did not even have to hear Jesus speak the word; it was enough that the word was spoken.

- Do we realize that when we speak God's word, someone, somewhere, may find healing?

Tuesday 2nd December
Luke 10:21—24

At that same hour Jesus rejoiced in the Holy Spirit and said, "All things have been handed over to me by my Father; and no one knows who the Son is except the Father, or who the Father is except the Son and anyone to whom the Son chooses to reveal him." Then turning to the disciples, Jesus said to them privately, "Blessed are the eyes that see what you see! For I tell you that many prophets and kings desired to see what you see, but did not see it, and to hear what you hear, but did not hear it."

- Our sense of wonder is strongest when we are children and the whole world is new. As we grow older, we become world-weary. We look without seeing and listen without hearing.

- I ask the Holy Spirit to make me sensitive to God's self-revelation in the everyday events of my life.

Wednesday 3rd December,
St. Francis Xavier
Matthew 15:32—37

Then Jesus called his disciples to him and said, "I have compassion for the crowd, because they have been with me now for three days and have nothing to eat; and I do not want to send them away hungry, for they might faint on the way." The disciples said to him, "Where are we to get enough bread in the desert to feed so great a crowd?" Jesus asked them, "How many loaves have you?" They said, "Seven, and a few small fish." Then ordering the crowd to sit down on the ground, he took the seven loaves and the fish; and after giving thanks he broke them and gave them to the disciples, and the disciples gave them to the crowds. And all of them ate and were filled; and they took up the broken pieces left over, seven baskets full.

- Mother Teresa said about Jesus, "He uses us to be his love and compassion in the world in spite of our weaknesses and frailties." In this miracle Jesus does not produce food out of nowhere. He takes the little that the apostles have, and he multiplies it a thousandfold.

- No matter how little I think I have to give, once I freely place my gifts in Jesus' service they become limitless.

Thursday 4th December
Matthew 7:21, 24–27

Jesus said to the people, "Not everyone who says to me, 'Lord, Lord,' will enter the kingdom of heaven, but only one who does the will of my Father in heaven. . . . Everyone then who hears these words of mine and acts on them will be like a wise man who built his house on rock. The rain fell, the floods came, and the winds blew and beat on that house, but it did not fall, because it had been founded on rock. And everyone who hears these words of mine and does not act on them will be like a foolish man who built his house on sand. The rain fell, and the floods came, and the winds blew and beat against that house, and it fell—and great was its fall!"

- The houses built by the wise and foolish persons probably looked very similar. The difference was in the foundations, but that was only revealed when a storm came.

- Do I relate to the foolish builder who takes shortcuts for quick results? Or to the wise builder who is content to spend time in digging hidden but secure foundations?

Friday 5th December
Matthew 9:27–31

As Jesus went on from there, two blind men followed him, crying loudly, "Have mercy on us, Son of David!" When he entered the house, the blind men came to him; and Jesus said to them, "Do you believe that I am able to do this?" They said to him, "Yes, Lord." Then he touched their eyes and said, "According to your faith let it be done to you." And their eyes were opened. Then Jesus sternly ordered them, "See that no one knows of this." But they went away and spread the news about him throughout that district.

- The blind men in the reading desperately wanted to be healed. Do I ever experience the healing power of God?

- I may be physically sighted but spiritually blind. Do I want Jesus to heal me? Or do I hold back because I don't want to give up a behaviour, an attitude, or an addiction that is keeping me in familiar and comfortable darkness?

Saturday 6th December
Matthew 9:35–38

Jesus went about all the cities and villages, teaching in their synagogues, and proclaiming the good news of the kingdom, and curing every disease and every sickness. When he saw the crowds, he had compassion for them, because they were harassed and helpless, like sheep without a shepherd. Then he said to his disciples, "The harvest is plentiful, but the labourers are few; therefore ask the Lord of the harvest to send out labourers into his harvest."

- The harvest is plentiful and ripe. I think of the people around me and ask God to enlighten me to notice where there is opportunity to reap, gather, or acknowledge goodness. I bring what is good before God, giving praise and thanks.

• There is so much good that is not noticed, so many blessings that are unacknowledged. I pray for a deeper appreciation of the rich harvest that is around me.

December 7—13

Something to think and pray about each day this week:

Christmas, as Told by St. Luke

Let's focus on the shepherds. Matthew's wise men look attractive, but the shepherds have a lot going for them. Yes, they were at the bottom of the social heap; they were tough and ignorant and probably smelled like the sheep. They didn't belong in Jewish society at that time; they were relics of Israel's nomadic past. They were lawless, because they grazed other people's lands.

But in the middle of yet another boring night, these shepherds heard a message from an angel: "The Messiah had been born in a manger in Bethlehem!" The clue was the word "manger," familiar territory for shepherds. In this humble location, God is shown to be on the side of the poor, the outcast, the despised. God had Jesus enter the human scene at the bottom of the social pyramid.

Next, it is hard to improve on a baby to indicate powerlessness and vulnerability. Tough as they were, did the shepherds feel toward him what they felt about newborn lambs? This child seemed at home with shepherds, so did they feel he was one of them? Did they later muse on what he might become—the real shepherd of Israel?

Lastly, the shepherds were the first disciples because they heard the angel, believed the Good News, searched for the Child, and found him. They were overjoyed, praised God, and then started to bear witness to him, which is what apostles do. So they're important folk, really, just like the Magi!

The Presence of God

God is with me, but more,
God is within me, giving me existence.
Let me dwell for a moment on God's life-giving presence
in my body, my mind, my heart,
and in the whole of my life.

Freedom

God is not foreign to my freedom.
Instead, the Spirit breathes life into my most intimate desires,
gently nudging me toward all that is good.
I ask for the grace to let myself be enfolded by the Spirit.

Consciousness

Help me, Lord, to be more conscious of your presence.
Teach me to recognize your presence in others.
Fill my heart with gratitude for the times your love
has been shown to me through the care of others.

The Word

I read the Word of God slowly, a few times over, and I listen to what
God is saying to me. (Please turn to your scripture on the following
pages. Inspiration points are there should you need them. When you
are ready, return here to continue.)

Conversation

How has God's Word moved me? Has it left me cold?
Has it consoled me or moved me to act in a new way?
I imagine Jesus standing or sitting beside me;
I turn and share my feelings with him.

Conclusion

Glory be to the Father, and to the Son, and to the Holy Spirit,
as it was in the beginning, is now, and ever shall be,
world without end. Amen.

December 2014

Sunday 7th December,
Second Sunday of Advent
Mark 1:4—8

John the baptizer appeared in the wilderness, proclaiming a baptism of repentance for the forgiveness of sins. And people from the whole Judean countryside and all the people of Jerusalem were going out to him, and were baptized by him in the river Jordan, confessing their sins. Now John was clothed with camel's hair, with a leather belt around his waist, and he ate locusts and wild honey. He proclaimed, "The one who is more powerful than I is coming after me; I am not worthy to stoop down and untie the thong of his sandals. I have baptized you with water; but he will baptize you with the Holy Spirit."

- I mingle with the crowds listening to John the baptizer. I know he suffered a violent death. Where is the "good news" in that?

- The good news is that he plays his part in the plan of salvation and bears steady witness to the light. In the wilderness of my life, I ask that I may always witness to light and truth and love.

Monday 8th December,
Immaculate Conception of the Blessed Virgin Mary
Luke 1:30—33

The angel said to her, "Do not be afraid, Mary, for you have found favour with God. And now, you will conceive in your womb and bear a son, and you will name him Jesus. He will be great, and will be called the Son of the Most High, and the Lord God will give to him the throne of his ancestor David. He will reign over the house of Jacob for ever, and of his kingdom there will be no end."

- Like Mary, I, too, came into the world for a purpose. That purpose will not be revealed to me as dramatically as it was to her. Perhaps she heard the word of God so clearly because of her sinlessness. And also because of her silence: there was no clamour drowning it out.

- Too often I fear the emptiness, the darkness, the silence, within me. Yet it is there that the Spirit lives and works, even when my prayer seems most arid. God, help me to go daily into the quiet of my own heart, to meet you there, in love and adoration.

Tuesday 9th December
Matthew 18:12—14

Jesus said, "What do you think? If a shepherd has a hundred sheep, and one of them has gone astray, does he not leave the ninety-nine on the mountains and go in search of the one that went astray? And if he finds it, truly I tell you, he rejoices over it more than over the ninety-nine that never went astray. So it is not the will of your Father in heaven that one of these little ones should be lost."

- If I were the only person in the world needing salvation, Jesus would still die for me. Does this thrill me or terrify me? Why?

- Jesus is telling us very clearly that every life is precious in his eyes. Every person I meet is invaluable and irreplaceable. Jesus turns conventional attitudes upside down: the "little ones," the people whom the world does not rate as important, are the most precious of all. Will my attitudes today reflect this?

Wednesday 10th December
Matthew 11:28—30

Jesus said, "Come to me, all you that are weary and are carrying heavy burdens, and I will give you rest. Take my yoke upon you, and learn from me; for I am gentle and humble in heart, and you will find rest for your souls. For my yoke is easy, and my burden is light."

- An old story describes Peter at the gates of heaven. The world has ended. The sheep have been separated from the goats; all the faithful are inside, and Peter is preparing to close the gates. Then he sees Jesus standing outside. "Master," he says, "what are you doing outside?" Jesus replies, "I'm waiting for Judas."

- In the words of today's reading, Jesus is calling directly to me: "Come to me." Jesus will wait for me beyond the end of time.

Thursday 11th December
Matthew 11:11—15

Jesus said, "Truly I tell you, among those born of women no one has arisen greater than John the Baptist; yet the least in the kingdom of heaven is greater than he. From the days of John the Baptist until now the kingdom of heaven has suffered violence, and the violent take it by force. For all the prophets and the law prophesied until John came; and if you are willing to accept it, he is Elijah who is to come. Let anyone with ears listen!"

- God does not force himself upon us. We must ourselves seize the kingdom.

- In his book *Heaven Taken by Storm*, the seventeenth-century Puritan pastor Thomas Watson asks: "Do we use violence in prayer? Is the wind of the Spirit filling our sails? Do we pray in the morning as if we were to die at night? Do we thirst for the living God? Is our desire constant? Is this spiritual pulse always beating?"

Friday 12th December
Matthew 11:16—19

Jesus spoke to the crowds, "But to what will I compare this generation? It is like children sitting in the market-places and calling to one another, 'We played the flute for you, and you did not dance; we wailed, and you did not mourn.' For John came neither eating nor drinking, and they say, 'He has a demon'; the Son of Man came eating and drinking, and they say, 'Look, a glutton and a drunkard, a friend of tax-collectors and sinners!' Yet wisdom is vindicated by her deeds."

- Very young children are completely egocentric. They cannot conceive of any point of view other than their own. Do I, like the people Jesus describes here, reduce the immensity of God to my own narrow view and criticise others for their differing perceptions?

- We can only know God by encountering him. Am I a bystander or a follower? An observer or a seeker?

Saturday 13th December
Matthew 17:10—13

And the disciples asked him, "Why, then, do the scribes say that Elijah must come first?" He replied, "Elijah is indeed coming and will restore all things; but I tell you that Elijah has already come, and they did not recognize him, but they did to him whatever they pleased. So also the Son of Man is about to suffer at their hands." Then the disciples understood that he was speaking to them about John the Baptist.

- Jesus tells his disciples that Elijah has already come in the person of John the Baptist who had "the spirit and power of Elijah" (Lk 1:17). Am I still waiting for a Messiah who has already come? Am I being left behind?

- What is preventing me from living as if my Redeemer has already come? Nietzsche remarked that Jesus' disciples should look a little more redeemed!

December 14—20

Something to think and pray about each day this week:

Christmas, as Told by St. Paul

Let's start with the opening verses of the Letter to the Ephesians. They speak of a mysterious divine plan which has just been revealed through Jesus: the "good news." This brings great joy, especially to Gentiles who felt excluded from God's concerns. At the heart of the plan is the divine decision to form an all-embracing community of love; this is the goal of God's reshaping of human history. The Christian community is already the final community in embryo, and the three divine Persons are at its core.

So now we know what God thinks about us and what God plans for us. To God we are immensely important. We are chosen before the beginning of the world, and we are showered with graces and blessings. This divine love is unconditional: it is undismayed by our failures or sinfulness. God is head-over-heels in love with us.

The plan is effective: divine resources and commitment are present from the start. Further, since we are made in God's image and likeness, deepest down we are made to want what God desires to give us. So God can orchestrate human freedom to divine purposes, somewhat as a good parent can get a child to want what the parent wants!

Jesus is the central figure in the plan, and in becoming like us he gets it started. So while Christmas is indeed a feast for the young, it has infinite depths and is already changing our world. Christmas is truly a mysterious and awesome revelation of God's wisdom and goodness.

The Presence of God

What is present to me is what has a hold on my becoming.
I reflect on the presence of God always there in love,
amidst the many things that have a hold on me.
I pause and pray that I may let God
affect my becoming in this precise moment.

Freedom

"There are very few people
who realize what God would make of them
if they abandoned themselves into his hands,
and let themselves be formed by his grace" (St. Ignatius).
I ask for the grace to trust myself totally to God's love.

Consciousness

In the presence of my loving Creator,
I look honestly at my feelings over the last day—
the highs, the lows, and the level ground.
Can I see where the Lord has been present?

The Word

God speaks to each one of us individually. I need to listen to hear what
he is saying to me. Read the text a few times, then listen. (Please turn
to your scripture on the following pages. Inspiration points are there
should you need them. When you are ready, return here to continue.)

Conversation

What is stirring in me as I pray?
Am I consoled, troubled, left cold?
I imagine Jesus himself standing or sitting at my side,
and I share my feelings with him.

Conclusion

Glory be to the Father, and to the Son, and to the Holy Spirit,
as it was in the beginning, is now, and ever shall be,
world without end. Amen.

December 2014

Sunday 14th December,
Third Sunday of Advent
John 1:6—8, 19—28

There was a man sent from God, whose name was John. He came as a witness to testify to the light, so that all might believe through him. He himself was not the light, but he came to testify to the light. . . . This is the testimony given by John when the Jews sent priests and Levites from Jerusalem to ask him, "Who are you?" He confessed and did not deny it, but confessed, "I am not the Messiah." And they asked him, "What then? Are you Elijah?" He said, "I am not." "Are you the prophet?" He answered, "No." Then they said to him, "Who are you? Let us have an answer for those who sent us. What do you say about yourself?" He said, "I am the voice of one crying out in the wilderness, 'Make straight the way of the Lord,' as the prophet Isaiah said."

Now they had been sent from the Pharisees. They asked him, "Why then are you baptizing if you are neither the Messiah, nor Elijah, nor the prophet?" John answered them, "I baptize with water. Among you stands one whom you do not know, the one who is coming after me; I am not worthy to untie the thong of his sandal." This took place in Bethany across the Jordan where John was baptizing.

- Does anyone think of me as witnessing to the light by the quality of my life? I listen to Jesus as he tells me that I am meant to be a light for the world.

- I ask humbly that he may illuminate me more. Perhaps I ask him to place his hands on my head in blessing so that I may be more lightsome.

Monday 15th December
Matthew 21:23—27

When Jesus entered the temple, the chief priests and the elders of the people came to him as he was teaching, and said, "By what authority are you doing these things, and who gave you this authority?" Jesus said to them, "I will also ask you one question; if you tell me the answer, then I will also tell you by what authority I do these things. Did the baptism of John come from heaven, or was it of human origin?" And they argued with one another, "If we say, 'From heaven,' he will say to us, 'Why then did you not believe him?' But if we say, 'Of human origin,' we are afraid of the crowd; for all regard John as a prophet." So they answered Jesus, "We do not know." And he said to them, "Neither will I tell you by what authority I am doing these things."

- Lord, you were uncovering a trap, exposing an unspoken attitude. The chief priests and elders were concerned with what was safe to say, not with the truth.

- Your eye looks into my heart, too. Do I let human respect dictate my words? Do I make decisions with a view to preserving my position and power?

- Can I talk to Jesus about this, and ask for the grace to be free, as he was?

Tuesday 16th December
Matthew 21:28—32

Jesus said, "What do you think? A man had two sons; he went to the first and said, 'Son, go and work in the vineyard today.' He answered, 'I will not'; but later he changed his mind and went. The father went to the second and said the same; and he answered, 'I go, sir'; but he did not go. Which of the two did the will of his father?" They said, "The first." Jesus said to them, "Truly I tell you, the tax-collectors and the prostitutes are going into the kingdom of God ahead of you. For John came to you in the way of righteousness and you did not believe him, but the tax-collectors and the prostitutes believed him; and even after you saw it, you did not change your minds and believe him."

- Jesus says to me, "What do you think?" Do I take time out to think about where I stand in relation to God? Do I give my soul an opportunity to catch up? I ask the Lord to help me to give time to thinking about the things that really matter.

- Am I like the Jewish leaders who sound good but perform poorly? Or am I like the tax collectors and prostitutes who know their need of God? Can I despise such people?

Wednesday 17th December
Matthew 1:1—11

An account of the genealogy of Jesus the Messiah, the son of David, the son of Abraham. Abraham was the father of Isaac, and Isaac the father of Jacob, and Jacob the father of Judah and his brothers, and Judah the father of Perez and Zerah by Tamar, and Perez the father of Hezron, and Hezron the father of Aram, and Aram the father of Aminadab, and Aminadab the father of Nahshon, and Nahshon the father of Salmon, and Salmon the father of Boaz by Rahab, and Boaz the father of Obed by Ruth, and Obed the father of Jesse, and Jesse the father of King David. And David was the father of Solomon by the wife of Uriah, and Solomon the father of Rehoboam, and Rehoboam the father of Abijah, and Abijah the father of Asaph, and Asaph the father of Jehoshaphat, and Jehoshaphat the father of Joram, and Joram the father of Uzziah, and Uzziah the father of Jotham, and Jotham the father of Ahaz, and Ahaz the father of Hezekiah, and Hezekiah the father of Manasseh, and Manasseh the father of Amos, and Amos the father of Josiah, and Josiah the father of Jechoniah and his brothers, at the time of the deportation to Babylon.

- Everyone in human history influences others. I think of people who have influenced me for good or for ill.

- Then I ask that through my prayer and my life I may be a good influence on others. With Jesus I reflect on my relationships.

Thursday 18th December
Matthew 1:18—25

Now the birth of Jesus the Messiah took place in this way. When his mother Mary had been engaged to Joseph, but before they lived together, she was found to be with child from the Holy Spirit. Her husband Joseph, being a righteous man and unwilling to expose her to public disgrace, planned to dismiss her quietly. But just when he had resolved to do this, an angel of the Lord appeared to him in a dream and said, "Joseph, son of David, do not be afraid to take Mary as your wife, for the child conceived in her is from the Holy Spirit. She will bear a son, and you are to name him Jesus, for he will save his people from their sins." All this took place to fulfil what had been spoken by the Lord through the prophet: "Look, the virgin shall conceive and bear a son, and they shall name him Emmanuel," which means, "God is with us." When Joseph awoke from sleep, he did as the angel of the Lord commanded him; he took her as his wife, but had no marital relations with her until she had borne a son; and he named him Jesus.

- Emmanuel—"God is with us." There is never an instant when he is not with me. With him, I make my own soul every day of my earthly life. I need have no fear of the changes of life. Instead, I see them for what they are—as surprising stages along my journey home with him.

- How can I be Emmanuel for the people in my life?

Friday 19th December
Luke 1:5—17

In the days of King Herod of Judea, there was a priest named Zechariah, who belonged to the priestly order of Abijah. His wife was a descendant of Aaron, and her name was Elizabeth. Both of them were righteous before God, living blamelessly according to all the commandments and regulations of the Lord. But they had no children, because Elizabeth was barren, and both were getting on in years.

Once when he was serving as priest before God and his section was on duty, he was chosen by lot, according to the custom of the priesthood, to enter the sanctuary of the Lord and offer incense. Now at the time of the incense-offering, the whole assembly of the people was praying outside. Then there appeared to him an angel of the Lord, standing at the right side of the altar of incense. When Zechariah saw him, he was terrified; and fear overwhelmed him. But the angel said to him, "Do not be afraid, Zechariah, for your prayer has been heard. Your wife Elizabeth will bear you a son, and you will name him John. You will have joy and gladness, and many will rejoice at his birth, for he will be great in the sight of the Lord. He must never drink wine or strong drink; even before his birth he will be filled with the Holy Spirit. He will turn many of the people of Israel to the Lord their God. With the spirit and power of Elijah he will go before him, to turn the hearts of parents to their children, and the disobedient to the wisdom of the righteous, to make ready a people prepared for the Lord."

- Between today and Christmas Day, the liturgy features three Old Testament women who become pregnant against all the odds—Elizabeth, mother of John the Baptist; the unnamed mother of Samson; and Hannah, mother of Samuel. They remind us that God is in control of the human story and intervenes graciously in favour of the helpless and despised.

- Gabriel was sent to bring good news to Zechariah, who did not believe his words. Have I ears to hear the good news the Lord constantly speaks to me?

Saturday 20th December
Luke 1:26—33

In the sixth month the angel Gabriel was sent by God to a town in Galilee called Nazareth, to a virgin . . . whose name was Mary. And he came to her and said, "Greetings, favoured one! The Lord is with you." But she was much perplexed by his words and pondered what sort of greeting this might be. The angel said to her, "Do not be afraid, Mary, for you have found favour with God. And now, you will conceive in your womb and bear a son, and you will name him Jesus. He will be great, and will be called the Son of the Most High, and the Lord God will give to him the throne of his ancestor David. He will reign over the house of Jacob forever, and of his kingdom there will be no end."

- Luke contrasts Jesus and John the Baptist. John will indeed be great, but Jesus will be Son of the Most High. John's role will be temporary, but Jesus' kingdom will never end.

- I ask that the contrasts may highlight the supreme importance of Jesus for me.

December 21—27

Something to think and pray about each day this week:

The Birthday Feast

Christmas is a birthday. We survive the drabness of daily life by looking forward to the bright spots, when things are special—the light at the end of the tunnel. Advent is the tunnel, and it used to have its share of fasting and repentance, sharpening the contrast between anticipation and the event.

Samuel Beckett was waiting for Godot—who never arrives. Is God different? Does he come? In Innsbruck, they reenact the arrival, putting a live baby and mother on a sleigh drawn through the lighted town. That is lovely, but imaginary. The real arrival is partly in our hearts, partly in our Eucharist. True, that happens more than once a year. But on this feast, as on a birthday, we celebrate that Bethlehem event which showed (as birthday presents show) that we are the children God wanted, that we matter to God.

The Presence of God
God is with me, but more,
God is within me.
Let me dwell for a moment on God's life-giving presence
in my body, in my mind, in my heart,
as I sit here, right now.

Freedom
"A thick and shapeless tree-trunk would never believe
that it could become a statue, admired as a miracle of sculpture,
and would never submit itself to the chisel of the sculptor,
who sees by her genius what she can make of it" (St. Ignatius).
I ask for the grace to let myself be shaped by my loving Creator.

Consciousness
Knowing that God loves me unconditionally,
I can afford to be honest about how I am.
How has the last day been, and how do I feel now?
I share my feelings openly with the Lord.

The Word
I read the Word of God slowly, a few times over, and I listen to what
God is saying to me. (Please turn to your scripture on the following
pages. Inspiration points are there should you need them. When you
are ready, return here to continue.)

Conversation
Do I notice myself reacting as I pray with the Word of God?
Do I feel challenged, comforted, angry?
Imagining Jesus sitting or standing by me,
I speak out my feelings, as one trusted friend to another.

Conclusion
Glory be to the Father, and to the Son, and to the Holy Spirit,
as it was in the beginning, is now, and ever shall be,
world without end. Amen.

December 2014

Sunday 21st December,
Fourth Sunday of Advent
Luke 1:30—38

The angel said to Mary, "Do not be afraid, Mary, for you have found favour with God. And now, you will conceive in your womb and bear a son, and you will name him Jesus. He will be great, and will be called the Son of the Most High, and the Lord God will give to him the throne of his ancestor David. He will reign over the house of Jacob forever, and of his kingdom there will be no end." Mary said to the angel, "How can this be, since I am a virgin?" The angel said to her, "The Holy Spirit will come upon you, and the power of the Most High will overshadow you; therefore the child to be born will be holy; he will be called Son of God. And now, your relative Elizabeth in her old age has also conceived a son; and this is the sixth month for her who was said to be barren. For nothing will be impossible with God." Then Mary said, "Here am I, the servant of the Lord; let it be with me according to your word." Then the angel departed from her.

- I ask for grace to believe that nothing is impossible with God. This message runs through the whole of revelation, starting with the promise to Abraham and Sarah that in their old age they will have a child.

- It ends with the picture of the new heavens and earth, where God will dwell with us and wipe away every tear from our eyes.

Monday 22nd December
Luke 1:46—56

And Mary said, "My soul magnifies the Lord, and my spirit rejoices in God my Saviour, for he has looked with favour on the lowliness of his servant. Surely, from now on all generations will call me blessed; for the Mighty One has done great things for me, and holy is his name. His mercy is for those who fear him from generation to generation. He has shown strength with his arm; he has scattered the proud in the thoughts of their hearts. He has brought down the powerful from their thrones, and lifted up the lowly; he has filled the hungry with good things, and sent the rich away empty. He has helped his servant Israel, in remembrance of his mercy, according to the promise he made to our ancestors, to Abraham and to his descendants for ever." And Mary remained with Elizabeth for about three months and then returned to her home.

- Mary praises the God who turns human history upside down. God scatters the proud, pulls down the mighty, and dismisses the rich. In their place, he exalts the unimportant ones and feeds the starving.

- Do I value the despised and downtrodden of this world above the famous and the wealthy? I talk to Mary about this.

Tuesday 23rd December
Luke 1:57—66

Now the time came for Elizabeth to give birth, and she bore a son. Her neighbours and relatives heard that the Lord had shown his great mercy to her, and they rejoiced with her. On the eighth day they came to circumcise the child, and they were going to name him Zechariah after his father. But his mother said, "No; he is to be called John." They said to her, "None of your relatives has this name." Then they began motioning to his father to find out what name he wanted to give him. He asked for a writing-tablet and wrote, "His name is John." And all of them were amazed. Immediately his mouth was opened and his tongue freed, and he began to speak, praising God. Fear came over all their neighbours, and all these things were talked about throughout the entire hill country of Judea. All who heard them pondered them and said, "What then will this child become?" For, indeed, the hand of the Lord was with him.

- How did Elizabeth know that the child was to be called John? Did a small voice tell her this? Do I listen for the small voice that tells me what to do?

- Elizabeth and Mary were "ordinary people" just as I am. God speaks to me as God spoke to them.

Wednesday 24th December
Luke 1:67—79

Then his father Zechariah was filled with the Holy Spirit and spoke this prophecy: "Blessed be the Lord God of Israel, for he has looked favourably on his people and redeemed them. He has raised up a mighty saviour for us in the house of his servant David, as he spoke through the mouth of his holy prophets from of old, that we would be saved from our enemies and from the hand of all who hate us. Thus he has shown the mercy promised to our ancestors, and has remembered his holy covenant, the oath that he swore to our ancestor Abraham, to grant us that we, being rescued from the hands of our enemies, might serve him without fear, in holiness and righteousness before him all our days. And you, child, will be called the prophet of the Most High; for you will go before the Lord to prepare his ways, to give knowledge of salvation to his people by the forgiveness of their sins. By the tender mercy of our God, the dawn from on high will break upon us, to give light to those who sit in darkness and in the shadow of death, to guide our feet into the way of peace."

- Although he was a good man, Zechariah did not believe the good news regarding the arrival of a yearned-for child. He became dumb. Now, as he names his son John, which means "God is gracious," his tongue is loosened and he bursts into this marvellous prophetic song.

- How confidently and joyfully do I proclaim the graciousness of God? Or does my lack of faith made me dumb, too?

December 2014

Thursday 25th December,
Feast of the Nativity of the Lord
John 1:1—5

In the beginning was the Word, and the Word was with God, and the Word was God. He was in the beginning with God. All things came into being through him, and without him not one thing came into being. What has come into being in him was life, and the life was the light of all people. The light shines in the darkness, and the darkness did not overcome it.

- The Light of the World has come among us. He is born in the night, with his own star blazing above him. He lies in the dimness of a stable, that same Lord who, as a pillar of cloud by day and a pillar of fire by night, led the Israelites to freedom. He has come to bring his people from darkness into light.

- As we gaze into the manger, at the tiny creature who is given to us as a light to the nations, we can only whisper, "Come, let us adore him."

Friday 26th December,
St. Stephen, the First Martyr
Matthew 10:17—22

Jesus said to his apostles, "Beware of them, for they will hand you over to councils and flog you in their synagogues; and you will be dragged before governors and kings because of me, as a testimony to them and the Gentiles. When they hand you over, do not worry about how you are to speak or what you are to say; for what you are to say will be given to you at that time; for it is not you who speak, but the Spirit of your Father speaking through you. Brother will betray brother to death, and a father his child, and children will rise against parents and have them put to death; and you will be hated by all because of my name. But the one who endures to the end will be saved."

- Following Jesus is not easy. However, we should remember that he is always with us.

- C. S. Lewis once advised a friend: "Continue seeking God with seriousness. Unless he wanted you, you would not be wanting him."

Saturday 27th December,
St. John, Evangelist
John 20:1—8

Early on the first day of the week, while it was still dark, Mary Magdalene came to the tomb and saw that the stone had been removed from the tomb. So she ran and went to Simon Peter and the other disciple, the one whom Jesus loved, and said to them, "They have taken the Lord out of the tomb, and we do not know where they have laid him." Then Peter and the other disciple set out and went towards the tomb. The two were running together, but the other disciple outran Peter and reached the tomb first. He bent down to look in and saw the linen wrappings lying there, but he did not go in. Then Simon Peter came, following him, and went into the tomb. He saw the linen wrappings lying there, and the cloth that had been on Jesus' head, not lying with the linen wrappings but rolled up in a place by itself. Then the other disciple, who reached the tomb first, also went in, and he saw and believed.

- John describes how the disciple saw and believed. However, John later points out that it is not enough for us to believe; we must spread the Good News, as he himself did: "We are writing these things so that our joy may be complete" (1 Jn 1:4).

- Notice that sharing good news brings joy to the sharer as well as to the receiver. Do I experience this?

December 28—January 3

Something to think and pray about each day this week:

Christmas, as Told by a Contemplative

The message of Christmas is simple: God is with us. "You shall call him Emmanuel, which means, 'God is with us.'" So says the angel to a bewildered Joseph, who must have spent the rest of his life pondering the implications of that statement.

If God is with us in this radical way, what is our response? Are we with God? What does it mean for us, to be with God? Is it impossible for ordinary folk? Do I want to be face-to-face with God?

Drawing from reflections in the Christian contemplative tradition, we can discern two things: first, how simple it is to be with God, and second, the world-changing power of being with God.

What about a New Year resolution for the Sacred Space community? I suggest this: that we would step out confidently into our chaotic world with the firm belief that simply by being with God we are helping to transform it. God, who sees our hearts, will bless us as we go!

The Presence of God

As I sit here, the beating of my heart,
the ebb and flow of my breathing, and the movements of my mind,
are all signs of God's ongoing creation of me.
I pause for a moment, and become aware
of this presence of God within me.

Freedom

I ask for the grace
to let go of my own concerns
and be open to what God is asking of me,
to let myself be guided and formed by my loving Creator.

Consciousness

In the presence of my loving Creator,
I look honestly at my feelings over the last day,
the highs, the lows, and the level ground.
Can I see where the Lord has been present?

The Word

I take my time to read the Word of God, slowly, a few times, allowing myself to dwell on anything that strikes me. (Please turn to your
scripture on the following pages. Inspiration points are there should
you need them. When you are ready, return here to continue.)

Conversation

Remembering that I am still in God's presence,
I imagine Jesus himself standing or sitting beside me
and say whatever is on my mind, whatever is in my heart,
speaking as one friend to another.

Conclusion

Glory be to the Father, and to the Son, and to the Holy Spirit,
as it was in the beginning, is now, and ever shall be,
world without end. Amen.

December 2014

Sunday 28th December,
The Holy Family
Luke 2:22, 25—33

When the time came for their purification according to the law of Moses, they brought him up to Jerusalem to present him to the Lord. . . . Now there was a man in Jerusalem whose name was Simeon; this man was righteous and devout, looking forward to the consolation of Israel, and the Holy Spirit rested on him. It had been revealed to him by the Holy Spirit that he would not see death before he had seen the Lord's Messiah. Guided by the Spirit, Simeon came into the temple; and when the parents brought in the child Jesus, to do for him what was customary under the law, Simeon took him in his arms and praised God, saying, "Master, now you are dismissing your servant in peace, according to your word; for my eyes have seen your salvation, which you have prepared in the presence of all peoples, a light for revelation to the Gentiles and for glory to your people Israel." And the child's father and mother were amazed at what was being said about him.

- Luke likes to pair female and male characters. Here we find the prophet Simeon, and a few verses later (in Tuesday's reading) we will meet Anna, a holy woman of great hope. They both appear just at the right moment, which is God's moment, to bear witness to the great miracle at hand.

- I ask God to liberate me from whatever holds me back in his service.

Monday 29th December
Luke 2:27—32

Guided by the Spirit, Simeon came into the temple; and when the parents brought in the child Jesus, to do for him what was customary under the law, Simeon took him in his arms and praised God, saying, "Master, now you are dismissing your servant in peace, according to your word; for my eyes have seen your salvation, which you have prepared in the presence of all peoples, a light for revelation to the Gentiles and for glory to your people Israel."

- The years of waiting did not blunt the edge of Simeon's faith. His hope and yearning kept him alive to the promptings of God, ready to hear it when it came.

- Lord, in Simeon I see hope richly rewarded. Grant that I may learn from him.

Tuesday 30th December
Luke 2:36—38

There was a prophet, Anna the daughter of Phanuel, of the tribe of Asher. She was of a great age, having lived with her husband for seven years after her marriage, then as a widow to the age of eighty-four. She never left the temple but worshipped there with fasting and prayer night and day. At that moment she came, and began to praise God and to speak about the child to all who were looking for the redemption of Jerusalem.

- Old people can seem unimportant or even problematic. But they may have great wisdom to share. God often finds them easy to work with because they are free at heart.

- I ask for the grace to respect the aged and to learn from them.

Wednesday 31st December
John 1:6—14

There was a man sent from God, whose name was John. He came as a witness to testify to the light, so that all might believe through him. He himself was not the light, but he came to testify to the light. The true light, which enlightens everyone, was coming into the world. He was in the world, and the world came into being through him; yet the world did not know him. He came to what was his own, and his own people did not accept him. But to all who received him, who believed in his name, he gave power to become children of God, who were born, not of blood or of the will of the flesh or of the will of man, but of God. And the Word became flesh and lived among us, and we have seen his glory, the glory as of a father's only son, full of grace and truth.

- Jesus brings God fully into our world. He lives among us, in our country, our city, our neighbourhood. His love and his light radiate everywhere. We are all being changed by this.

- I beg as the last grace of this year that I may let that wonderful truth sink in.

Thursday 1st January,
Solemnity of Mary, Mother of God
Luke 2:16—21

So they went with haste and found Mary and Joseph, and the child lying in the manger. When they saw this, they made known what had been told them about this child; and all who heard it were amazed at what the shepherds told them. But Mary treasured all these words and pondered them in her heart. The shepherds returned, glorifying and praising God for all they had heard and seen, as it had been told them. After eight days had passed, it was time to circumcise the child; and he was called Jesus, the name given by the angel before he was conceived in the womb.

- Loving Father of good beginnings, you start anew with us in all the stages and circumstances of our lives. We thank you for being always present for us in Jesus.

- With Jesus we look forward eagerly to being sharers throughout 2015 in a confident message of faith, of peace, and of hope for our world.

Friday 2nd January
John 1:19—28

This is the testimony given by John when the Jews sent priests and Levites from Jerusalem to ask him, "Who are you?" He confessed and did not deny it, but confessed, "I am not the Messiah." And they asked him, "What then? Are you Elijah?" He said, "I am not." "Are you the prophet?" He answered, "No." Then they said to him, "Who are you? Let us have an answer for those who sent us. What do you say about yourself?" He said, "I am the voice of one crying out in the wilderness, 'Make straight the way of the Lord,'" as the prophet Isaiah said.

Now they had been sent from the Pharisees. They asked him, "Why then are you baptizing if you are neither the Messiah, nor Elijah, nor the prophet?" John answered them, "I baptize with water. Among you stands one whom you do not know, the one who is coming after me; I am not worthy to untie the thong of his sandal." This took place in Bethany across the Jordan where John was baptizing.

- "Who are you?" I put labels on people and think I know them. But can I even fathom the mystery of my own being?

- John the Baptist is a voice in the stillness of the desert. He points beyond himself. He doesn't want to be an achiever. May he stir up in me a longing to look for the One who is coming.

Saturday 3rd January
John 1:29—34

The next day John saw Jesus coming towards him and declared, "Here is the Lamb of God who takes away the sin of the world! This is he of whom I said, 'After me comes a man who ranks ahead of me because he was before me.' I myself did not know him; but I came baptizing with water for this reason, that he might be revealed to Israel." And John testified, "I saw the Spirit descending from heaven like a dove, and it remained on him. I myself did not know him, but the one who sent me to baptize with water said to me, 'He on whom you see the Spirit descend and remain is the one who baptizes with the Holy Spirit.' And I myself have seen and have testified that this is the Son of God."

- The weak and tender child in Mary's arms stands against corrupt practices, oppression, gossip, and slander. In his gentle, forgiving way he breaks down the hardness of our hearts. In the touch of his Spirit in Baptism he heals us and makes us free.

- Loving God, open us up to the life you want for us so that we can reach out to others and help to free them from their burdens.

January 4—10

Something to think and pray about each day this week:

The Essence of Faith

The essence of Christianity is a love story between God and ourselves. The word credo (I believe) comes from cor do (I give my heart). Faith, then, is an intimate meeting between God and each individual.

The encounter of Jesus with the Samaritan woman (Jn 4:1–42) offers a perfect example. At the well, heart speaks to heart, and both persons reveal themselves. The woman comes to believe in Jesus as the Messiah, the Christ. In her joy, she hurries off to tell her neighbours, and so convincing is her witness that the whole town comes out to see Jesus. Then they tell her that they have discovered for themselves the mystery of the person she had spoken about.

It is good for us to have knowledge about God and about Jesus, but this is not enough. The witness of other believers is also helpful, but that too is not enough. Personal encounter is needed and that occurs when we meet God in personal prayer. The intention of Sacred Space is to facilitate a daily face-to-face meeting with the Jesus of the New Testament.

Like the Samaritan woman, I come privately to my well with my needs and my wonderings. Jesus welcomes me as he welcomed her. We chat. He opens his heart to me, as he did to her, and promises me true life, living water. Just as the life of that anonymous woman was transformed forever by her encounter with Jesus, mine, too, can be reconfigured around him.

The Presence of God
I pause for a moment
and reflect on God's life-giving presence
in every part of my body, in everything around me,
in the whole of my life.

Freedom
Many countries are at this moment suffering
the agonies of war.
I bow my head in thanksgiving for my freedom.
I pray for all prisoners and captives.

Consciousness
Knowing that God loves me unconditionally,
I look honestly over the last day, its events and my feelings.
Do I have something to be grateful for? Then I give thanks.
Is there something I am sorry for? Then I ask forgiveness.

The Word
God speaks to each one of us individually. I need to listen to hear
what he is saying to me. Read the text a few times, then listen.
(Please turn to your scripture on the following pages. Inspiration
points are there should you need them. When you are ready, return
here to continue.)

Conversation
How has God's Word moved me? Has it left me cold?
Has it consoled me or moved me to act in a new way?
I imagine Jesus standing or sitting beside me;
I turn and share my feelings with him.

Conclusion
Glory be to the Father, and to the Son, and to the Holy Spirit,
as it was in the beginning, is now, and ever shall be,
world without end. Amen.

Sunday 4th January,
The Epiphany of the Lord
Matthew 2:1–6

In the time of King Herod, after Jesus was born in Bethlehem of Judea, wise men from the East came to Jerusalem, asking, "Where is the child who has been born king of the Jews? For we observed his star at its rising, and have come to pay him homage." When King Herod heard this, he was frightened, and all Jerusalem with him; and calling together all the chief priests and scribes of the people, he inquired of them where the Messiah was to be born. They told him, "In Bethlehem of Judea; for so it has been written by the prophet: 'And you, Bethlehem, in the land of Judah, are by no means least among the rulers of Judah; for from you shall come a ruler who is to shepherd my people Israel.'"

- The wise men stand for all who are ready to break out of their routine and comfort zone and go in search of what they yearn for. The insignificance of the baby in the crib can draw us on more powerfully even than the majestic night sky.

- From every corner of our bustling planet Earth, we are drawn to you, Saviour and Lord, brother and companion, who touch with the healing power of love even the least valued of God's children.

Monday 5th January
Matthew 4:12–17, 23–25

Now when Jesus heard that John had been arrested, he withdrew to Galilee. He left Nazareth and made his home in Capernaum by the lake, in the territory of Zebulun and Naphtali, so that what had been spoken through the prophet Isaiah might be fulfilled: "Land of Zebulun, land of Naphtali, on the road by the sea, across the Jordan, Galilee of the Gentiles—the people who sat in darkness have seen a great light, and for those who sat in the region and shadow of death light has dawned." From that time Jesus began to proclaim, "Repent, for the kingdom of heaven has come near." . . .

Jesus went throughout Galilee, teaching in their synagogues and proclaiming the good news of the kingdom and curing every disease and every sickness among the people. So his fame spread throughout all Syria, and they brought to him all the sick, those who were afflicted with various diseases and pains, demoniacs, epileptics, and paralytics, and he cured them. And great crowds followed him from Galilee, the Decapolis, Jerusalem, Judea, and from beyond the Jordan.

- Jesus the healer applied a therapy that was his own person: his compassionate love. He accepted all sick people wholeheartedly. He suffered to see them suffering. Healing was Jesus' way of loving. He showed them that they deserved to be loved.

- Lord Jesus, a main part of your healing action was just your warmth and friendship. You drew those in need to trust in the goodness of God and to find courage to move on.

Tuesday 6th January
Mark 6:34—44

As he went ashore, he saw a great crowd; and he had compassion for them, because they were like sheep without a shepherd; and he began to teach them many things. When it grew late, his disciples came to him and said, "This is a deserted place, and the hour is now very late; send them away so that they may go into the surrounding country and villages and buy something for themselves to eat." But he answered them, "You give them something to eat." They said to him, "Are we to go and buy two hundred denarii worth of bread, and give it to them to eat?" And he said to them, "How many loaves have you? Go and see." When they had found out, they said, "Five, and two fish." Then he ordered them to get all the people to sit down in groups on the green grass. So they sat down in groups of hundreds and of fifties. Taking the five loaves and the two fish, he looked up to heaven, and blessed and broke the loaves, and gave them to his disciples to set before the people; and he divided the two fish among them all. And all ate and were filled; and they took up twelve baskets full of broken pieces and of the fish. Those who had eaten the loaves numbered five thousand men.

- The feeding of the five thousand speaks of the generosity of God and his kindness toward us. When God gives, he gives abundantly. He gives us more than we need for ourselves so that we can share with those who lack what they need.

- Jesus, you satisfy the deepest longings of our hearts. Fill me with gratitude for your blessings. Give me a generous heart, that I may freely share what you have given to me.

Wednesday 7th January
Mark 6:45—52

Immediately he made his disciples get into the boat and go on ahead to the other side, to Bethsaida, while he dismissed the crowd. After saying farewell to them, he went up on the mountain to pray. When evening came, the boat was out on the lake, and he was alone on the land. When he saw that they were straining at the oars against an adverse wind, he came towards them early in the morning, walking on the lake. He intended to pass them by. But when they saw him walking on the lake, they thought it was a ghost and cried out; for they all saw him and were terrified. But immediately he spoke to them and said, "Take heart, it is I; do not be afraid." Then he got into the boat with them and the wind ceased. And they were utterly astounded, for they did not understand about the loaves, but their hearts were hardened.

- Jesus' life was intensely active, yet he always nurtured his communication with God in silence and solitude. He needed to visit this wellspring to nourish his being. Let *Sacred Space* be a wellspring for me. From it may I draw strength to be fully alive.

- Jesus' words, "do not be afraid," surely resonate with all Christians today who often live in an indifferent or hostile world.

Thursday 8th January
Luke 4:14—21

Then Jesus, filled with the power of the Spirit, returned to Galilee, and a report about him spread through all the surrounding country. He began to teach in their synagogues and was praised by everyone. When he came to Nazareth, where he had been brought up, he went to the synagogue on the sabbath day, as was his custom. He stood up to read, and the scroll of the prophet Isaiah was given to him. He unrolled the scroll and found the place where it was written: "The Spirit of the Lord is upon me, because he has anointed me to bring good news to the poor. He has sent me to proclaim release to the captives and recovery of sight to the blind, to let the oppressed go free, to proclaim the year of the Lord's favour." And he rolled up the scroll, gave it back to the attendant, and sat down. The eyes of all in the synagogue were fixed on him. Then he began to say to them, "Today this scripture has been fulfilled in your hearing."

- God defends those whom nobody else defends. Jesus was looking at families who struggled to survive, at people dispossessed of their land, at starving children, at prostitutes and beggars. He never said they were good or virtuous; he said only that they were suffering unjustly. God takes their side! Do I?

Friday 9th January
Luke 5:12—16

Once, when Jesus was in one of the cities, there was a man covered with leprosy. When he saw Jesus, he bowed with his face to the ground and begged him, "Lord, if you choose, you can make me clean." Then Jesus stretched out his hand, touched him, and said, "I do choose. Be made clean." Immediately the leprosy left him. And he ordered him to tell no one. "Go," he said, "and show yourself to the priest, and, as Moses commanded, make an offering for your cleansing, for a testimony to them." But now more than ever the word about Jesus spread abroad; many crowds would gather to hear him and to be cured of their diseases. But he would withdraw to deserted places and pray.

- A young man called Francis met a leper on the road to Assisi. The story goes that though the leper caused him no small disgust and horror, he got off his horse and prepared to kiss him. But when the leper put out his hand as though to receive something, he received money along with a kiss.

- May I reach out with compassionate care, with love, with a touch, to those who have been rejected and mistreated.

Saturday 10th January
John 3:25—30

Now a discussion about purification arose between John's disciples and a Jew. They came to John and said to him, "Rabbi, the one who was with you across the Jordan, to whom you testified, here he is baptizing, and all are going to him." John answered, "No one can receive anything except what has been given from heaven. You yourselves are my witnesses that I said, 'I am not the Messiah, but I have been sent ahead of him.' He who has the bride is the bridegroom. The friend of the bridegroom, who stands and hears him, rejoices greatly at the bridegroom's voice. For this reason my joy has been fulfilled. He must increase, but I must decrease."

- As I grow older my question is not, "Am I qualified enough to show Jesus to people?" More and more it is: "Am I *weak* enough?"

- Do I accept my failures and the wounds of life as more important than my strengths in witnessing to Jesus? I am a wounded healer. Like my fellow human beings, I, too, am searching and struggling.

January 11—12

Something to think and pray about each day this week:

Trusting in Prayer

There's something at this time of the year about endings and beginnings. An old year ends with its memories, and a new year begins with its hope. The endings and the beginnings—past and future—are always in the present tense of Love.

Isn't that where prayer comes in? Each prayer is a moment in the day—or in the night—in which we immerse ourselves in this mystery of the divine love for us. This love brings healing of the past and trust for the future. All religion worth its name surrounds the past with a wide healing and the possibility of forgiveness and enlightens the future with the same breadth of hope and trust. No matter what our prayer and its content, its context is of healing and trust in the space of a love so large that it is the name given to God.

What I live in the ordinariness of the day forms also a context for prayer, and what I experience or think of in prayer forms a context for my life. Neither is separate from the other. Everything that this annual transition of the years evokes in me I bring to the One who is love beyond all telling.

The Presence of God

"The world is charged with the grandeur of God" (Gerard Manley Hopkins).
I dwell for a moment on the presence of God
around me, in every part of my body,
and deep within my being.

Freedom

"In these days, God taught me
as a schoolteacher teaches a pupil" (St. Ignatius).
I remind myself that there are things God has to teach me yet,
and I ask for the grace to hear them and let them change me.

Consciousness

How do I find myself today?
Where am I with God? With others?
Do I have something to be grateful for? Then I give thanks.
Is there something I am sorry for? Then I ask forgiveness.

The Word

I read the Word of God slowly, a few times over, and I listen to what
God is saying to me. (Please turn to your scripture on the following
pages. Inspiration points are there should you need them. When you
are ready, return here to continue.)

Conversation

Sometimes I wonder what I might say
if I were to meet you in person, Lord.
I might say "Thank You, Lord" for always being there for me.
I know with certainty there were times when you carried me,
when through your strength I got through the dark times in my life.

Conclusion

Glory be to the Father, and to the Son, and to the Holy Spirit,
as it was in the beginning, is now, and ever shall be,
world without end. Amen.

January 2015

Sunday 11th January,
The Baptism of the Lord
Mark 1:7—11

John proclaimed, "The one who is more powerful than I is coming after me; I am not worthy to stoop down and untie the thong of his sandals. I have baptized you with water; but he will baptize you with the Holy Spirit." In those days Jesus came from Nazareth of Galilee and was baptized by John in the Jordan. And just as he was coming up out of the water, he saw the heavens torn apart and the Spirit descending like a dove on him. And a voice came from heaven, "You are my Son, the Beloved; with you I am well pleased."

- Jesus' baptism gives us a window into a powerful religious moment. Jesus knows his identity. The imprint of the Spirit has sealed his life.

- Lord, remind me that I, too, bear your seal of approval. I am marked by your Spirit, called to participate in your mission as your beloved son or daughter.

Monday 12th January
Mark 1:14—20

Now after John was arrested, Jesus came to Galilee, proclaiming the good news of God, and saying, "The time is fulfilled, and the kingdom of God has come near; repent, and believe in the good news." As Jesus passed along the Sea of Galilee, he saw Simon and his brother Andrew casting a net into the lake—for they were fishermen. And Jesus said to them, "Follow me and I will make you fish for people." And immediately they left their nets and followed him. As he went a little farther, he saw James son of Zebedee and his brother John, who were in their boat mending the nets. Immediately he called them; and they left their father Zebedee in the boat with the hired men, and followed him.

- "Come, follow me." The ways of following Jesus are as varied as people themselves are. But they always entail breaking free from what one was before. We are true disciples when we challenge ourselves with the question: "How would Jesus act in the situation I'm in right now?"

- Lord Jesus, you are our life itself, pointing to what we can become and calling out all our power of service and devotion. We leave the frailty that is in us open to your touch. We commit the joy and the brokenness of our life to you.

Tuesday 13th January
Mark 1:21—28

Jesus entered the synagogue and taught. They were astounded at his teaching, for he taught them as one having authority, and not as the scribes. Just then there was in their synagogue a man with an unclean spirit, and he cried out, "What have you to do with us, Jesus of Nazareth? Have you come to destroy us? I know who you are, the Holy One of God." But Jesus rebuked him, saying, "Be silent, and come out of him!" And the unclean spirit, throwing him into convulsions and crying with a loud voice, came out of him. They were all amazed, and they kept on asking one another, "What is this? A new teaching—with authority! He commands even the unclean spirits, and they obey him." At once his fame began to spread throughout the surrounding region of Galilee.

- In driving out devils, Jesus shows that in the reign of God there is no room for oppressive evil forces that weigh down on God's children. No one should have to live in hell.

- Jesus is in agony until the end of the world, standing with us against all forms of addiction, exploitation, violence, and abuse.

Wednesday 14th January
Mark 1:29—34

As soon as they left the synagogue, they entered the house of Simon and Andrew, with James and John. Now Simon's mother-in-law was in bed with a fever, and they told him about her at once. He came and took her by the hand and lifted her up. Then the fever left her, and she began to serve them.

That evening, at sunset, they brought to him all who were sick or possessed with demons. And the whole city was gathered around the door. And he cured many who were sick with various diseases, and cast out many demons; and he would not permit the demons to speak, because they knew him.

- Who do you take your troubles to? Jesus heard Simon's prayer for his sick mother-in-law, and the fever left her. There is no trouble he will not face with us and for us. Put your trust in him.

- Lord Jesus, you became human for us! You brought joy to a family at Cana. You brought healing and hope to Simon Peter's mother-in-law and to the paralysed and the blind. You gave bread to the hungry. You gave us your life, your body, your spirit, your mother—everything.

Thursday 15th January
Mark 1:40—42

A leper came to Jesus begging him, and kneeling he said to him, "If you choose, you can make me clean." Moved with pity, Jesus stretched out his hand and touched him, and said to him, "I do choose. Be made clean!" Immediately the leprosy left him, and he was made clean.

- "Deeply moved, Jesus put out his hand and touched him." Jesus, the poet of God's compassion, spoke in parables, but also in actions. He healed the sick and freed people from evil, brokenness, and rejection.

- God's mercy was not just a beautiful idea. In Jesus, God is the active champion of the suffering.

Friday 16th January
Mark 2:1—12

When he returned to Capernaum after some days, it was reported that he was at home. So many gathered around that there was no longer room for them, not even in front of the door; and he was speaking the word to them. Then some people came, bringing to him a paralysed man, carried by four of them. And when they could not bring him to Jesus because of the crowd, they removed the roof above him; and after having dug through it, they let down the mat on which the paralytic lay. When Jesus saw their faith, he said to the paralytic, "Son, your sins are forgiven." Now some of the scribes were sitting there, questioning in their hearts, "Why does this fellow speak in this way? It is blasphemy! Who can forgive sins but God alone?" At once Jesus perceived in his spirit that they were discussing these questions among themselves; and he said to them, "Why do you raise such questions in your hearts? Which is easier, to say to the paralytic, 'Your sins are forgiven,' or to say, 'Stand up and take your mat and walk'? But so that you may know that the Son of Man has authority on earth to forgive sins"—he said to the paralytic—"I say to you, stand up, take your mat and go to your home." And he stood up, and immediately took the mat and went out before all of them; so that they were all amazed and glorified God, saying, "We have never seen anything like this!"

- There are those who have wronged me. But Lord, do not hold their sin against them. They remain precious to you, and I let them go to you.

- You do not hold my sins and wrongdoing against me. So, if I am to be close to you, I have no choice but to let go those who have hurt me. I must wish them well, no matter what pain I feel.

Saturday 17th January
Mark 2:13—17

Jesus went out again beside the lake; the whole crowd gathered around him, and he taught them. As he was walking along, he saw Levi son of Alphaeus sitting at the tax booth, and he said to him, "Follow me." And he got up and followed him. And as he sat at dinner in Levi's house, many tax-collectors and sinners were also sitting with Jesus and his disciples—for there were many who followed him. When the scribes of the Pharisees saw that he was eating with sinners and tax-collectors, they said to his disciples, "Why does he eat with tax-collectors and sinners?" When Jesus heard this, he said to them, "Those who are well have no need of a physician, but those who are sick; I have come to call not the righteous but sinners."

- In calling Matthew to be a disciple, Jesus picked an unlikely man. He was a tax collector, despised by the Jews. Just as a doctor visits the sick, Jesus seeks out those in greatest need. He renews their dignity and their hope.

- But the really sick are the "righteous" who despise others! Is there a touch of the "righteous" in me? If so, I ask to be healed.

January 18—24

Something to think and pray about each day this week:

The Revelation of Love

At the recent Feast of Epiphany (which means "manifestation"), the glory of God shines out for all the nations in Mary's little Child. Then, at the Feast of the Baptism of the Lord, that light is manifest once more. Heaven opens and the Spirit comes down on Jesus. A voice is heard, "You are my Son, the Beloved" (Lk 3:22). Now comes the wedding feast of Cana: Jesus transforms water into wine. He lets his glory be seen, and his disciples believe in him (see Jn 2:11). So again we have a manifestation of the heart of God.

Note the setting: a wedding feast! Why is this setting chosen? Because the prophets had already portrayed the ultimate transformation of our lives as being like a marriage union with God: "And I will take you for my wife for ever; I will take you for my wife in righteousness and in justice, in steadfast love, and in mercy" (Hos 2:19). And at the end, in God's radiant love—eternally there for us—we will shine out like the dawn. We shall be called "God's Delight" and our land will be called "The Wedded"; for the Lord takes delight in us (see Is 62:1–5). So, as we look to Jesus, and contemplate him at the wedding feast, we can reflect on all these promises which his radiant presence holds out for us. As his disciples, we can ask for the grace to believe in him, and *entrust* ourselves completely to him who is light.

The Presence of God

As I sit here, God is present,
breathing life into me and into everything around me.
For a few moments, I sit silently
and become aware of God's loving presence.

Freedom

If God were trying to tell me something, would I know?
If God were reassuring me or challenging me, would I notice?
I ask for the grace to be free of my own preoccupations
and open to what God may be saying to me.

Consciousness

In God's loving presence, I unwind the past day,
starting from now and looking back, moment by moment.
I gather in all the goodness and light in gratitude.
I attend to the shadows and what they say to me,
seeking healing, courage, forgiveness.

The Word

I take my time to read the Word of God, slowly, a few times, allowing myself to dwell on anything that strikes me. (Please turn to your scripture on the following pages. Inspiration points are there should you need them. When you are ready, return here to continue.)

Conversation

What is stirring in me as I pray?
Am I consoled, troubled, left cold?
I imagine Jesus himself standing or sitting at my side,
and I share my feelings with him.

Conclusion

Glory be to the Father, and to the Son, and to the Holy Spirit,
as it was in the beginning, is now, and ever shall be,
world without end. Amen.

January 2015

Sunday 18th January,
Second Sunday of Ordinary Time
John 1:35—42

The next day John again was standing with two of his disciples, and as he watched Jesus walk by, he exclaimed, "Look, here is the Lamb of God!" The two disciples heard him say this, and they followed Jesus. When Jesus turned and saw them following, he said to them, "What are you looking for?" They said to him, "Rabbi" (which translated means Teacher), "where are you staying?" He said to them, "Come and see." They came and saw where he was staying, and they remained with him that day. It was about four o'clock in the afternoon. One of the two who heard John speak and followed him was Andrew, Simon Peter's brother. He first found his brother Simon and said to him, "We have found the Messiah" (which is translated Anointed). He brought Simon to Jesus, who looked at him and said, "You are Simon son of John. You are to be called Cephas" (which is translated Peter).

- Spiritual awareness is highlighted today. John knows his own prophetic call. He recognizes Jesus for who he is and delights in the power of the Spirit at work. He is free to let his disciples move away to follow Jesus.

- Lord, may I grow in spiritual awareness. Bless me with a clear sense of my call. Make me sensitive to the action of your Spirit. Give me freedom to witness to you in in my current situation.

Monday 19th January
Mark 2:18—22

Now John's disciples and the Pharisees were fasting; and people came and said to him, "Why do John's disciples and the disciples of the Pharisees fast, but your disciples do not fast?" Jesus said to them, "The wedding-guests cannot fast while the bridegroom is with them, can they? As long as they have the bridegroom with them, they cannot fast. The days will come when the bridegroom is taken away from them, and then they will fast on that day.

"No one sews a piece of unshrunk cloth on an old cloak; otherwise, the patch pulls away from it, the new from the old, and a worse tear is made. And no one puts new wine into old wineskins; otherwise, the wine will burst the skins, and the wine is lost, and so are the skins; but one puts new wine into fresh wineskins."

- A wedding feast lasted an entire week in Palestine. The privilege for the closest friends of the bride and groom was to remain for the week in their company. Joy is the hallmark of the friends of the bride and groom.

- Do I find joy in knowing and being close to you, Lord?

Tuesday 20th January
Mark 2:23—28

One sabbath Jesus was going through the cornfields; and as they made their way his disciples began to pluck heads of grain. The Pharisees said to him, "Look, why are they doing what is not lawful on the sabbath?" And he said to them, "Have you never read what David did when he and his companions were hungry and in need of food? He entered the house of God, when Abiathar was high priest, and ate the bread of the Presence, which it is not lawful for any but the priests to eat, and he gave some to his companions." Then he said to them, "The sabbath was made for humankind, and not humankind for the sabbath; so the Son of Man is lord even of the sabbath."

- The sabbath is for our good. When we assemble on that day, we meet God in many ways. We encounter God in the community itself, in sharing the great story of salvation, and in the meal prepared by God. Our souls are given the chance to catch up, and we go back to our tasks refreshed.

- How do I experience God in the sabbath?

Wednesday 21st January
Mark 3:1—6

Again he entered the synagogue, and a man was there who had a withered hand. They watched him to see whether he would cure him on the sabbath, so that they might accuse him. And he said to the man who had the withered hand, "Come forward." Then he said to them, "Is it lawful to do good or to do harm on the sabbath, to save life or to kill?" But they were silent. He looked around at them with anger; he was grieved at their hardness of heart and said to the man, "Stretch out your hand." He stretched it out, and his hand was restored. The Pharisees went out and immediately conspired with the Herodians against him, how to destroy him.

- I watch Jesus in this scene. What would I have done in regard to the man with the withered hand? Is my heart hardened? Am I rightly angry when people are despised? Do I channel my anger toward healing?

- The people of power conspired how to destroy you, Jesus. I ask you to be with those who "disappear" because they are a threat to some system of injustice.

Thursday 22nd January
Mark 3:7—12

Jesus departed with his disciples to the lake, and a great multitude from Galilee followed him; hearing all that he was doing, they came to him in great numbers from Judea, Jerusalem, Idumea, beyond the Jordan, and the region around Tyre and Sidon. He told his disciples to have a boat ready for him because of the crowd, so that they would not crush him; for he had cured many, so that all who had diseases pressed upon him to touch him. Whenever the unclean spirits saw him, they fell down before him and shouted, "You are the Son of God!" But he sternly ordered them not to make him known.

- You say, Lord, that they who are not against you are with you. You are the builder of our house. Though we are imperfect disciples, we are still your living stones.

- Lord, let me risk even one initiative for unity and for a common service of love.

Friday 23rd January
Mark 3:13—19

He went up the mountain and called to him those whom he wanted, and they came to him. And he appointed twelve, whom he also named apostles, to be with him, and to be sent out to proclaim the message, and to have authority to cast out demons. So he appointed the twelve: Simon (to whom he gave the name Peter); James son of Zebedee and John the brother of James (to whom he gave the name Boanerges, that is, Sons of Thunder); and Andrew, and Philip, and Bartholomew, and Matthew, and Thomas, and James son of Alphaeus, and Thaddaeus, and Simon the Cananaean, and Judas Iscariot, who betrayed him.

- Discipleship is an important theme in the Gospel of Mark. The first disciples are not persons of consequence, yet are called by Jesus to form his first community.

- Resolute commitment in following Jesus is the necessary quality. The disciples are to identify their entire lives with him. Empowered with his message, they are heralds of the Good News.

Saturday 24th January
Mark 3:19—21

Then Jesus went home; and the crowd came together again, so that they could not even eat. When his family heard it, they went out to restrain him, for people were saying, "He has gone out of his mind."

- Jesus' family considers him imbalanced. He has left the security of Nazareth and his carpenter's business. Now he is on course for a collision with religious leaders. "He has gone out of his mind!" They totally misunderstood him.

- Lord, in choosing to live by the Gospel, I, too, run the risk of being ridiculed. You faced opposition with determination and courage. Grant me your grace to follow you resolutely, especially when opposition comes from those near to me.

January 25—31

Something to think and pray about each day this week:

The Flooding of Grace

Spiritual books do not always take account of age; but age does make a difference. One of the attractive things about our picture of Jesus is that he was, until the Passion, at the height of his manhood. This was a man whose health, strength, energy, and vitality roused admiration and love, as in the woman who cried, "Blessed is the womb that bore you and the breasts that nursed you!" (Lk 11:27).

But Jesus was never seventy. He never suffered the infirmities of age, stiff limbs, slow apprehension, failing memory, blunting of senses, tottering balance. John Henry Newman wrote from his experience of aging: "The greater part of our devotion in youth, our faith, hope, cheerfulness, perseverance, is natural—or if not natural, it is from an ease of nature which does not resist grace, and requires very little grace to illuminate. The same grace goes much further in youth as encountering less opposition—that is, in the virtues which I have mentioned. Old people are in soul as stiff, as lean, as bloodless as their bodies, except so far as grace penetrates and softens them. And it requires a flooding of grace to do this."

The Presence of God

As I sit here with these words in front of me, God is here.
He is around me, in my sensations, in my thoughts, and deep within me.
I pause for a moment, and I become aware
of God's life-giving presence.

Freedom

I need to rise above the noise—
the noise that interrupts, that separates,
the noise that isolates.
I need to listen to God again.

Consciousness

I remind myself that I am in the presence of the Lord.
I will take refuge in his loving heart.
He is my strength in times of weakness.
He is my comforter in times of sorrow.

The Word

God speaks to each one of us individually. I need to listen to what he is saying to me. (Please turn to your scripture on the following pages. Inspiration points are there should you need them. When you are ready, return here to continue.)

Conversation

Do I notice myself reacting as I pray with the Word of God?
Do I feel challenged, comforted, angry?
Imagining Jesus sitting or standing by me,
I speak out my feelings as one trusted friend to another.

Conclusion

Glory be to the Father, and to the Son, and to the Holy Spirit,
as it was in the beginning, is now, and ever shall be,
world without end. Amen.

January 2015

Sunday 25th January,
Third Sunday of Ordinary Time
Mark 1:14—20

Now after John was arrested, Jesus came to Galilee, proclaiming the good news of God, and saying, "The time is fulfilled, and the kingdom of God has come near; repent, and believe in the good news." As Jesus passed along the Sea of Galilee, he saw Simon and his brother Andrew casting a net into the lake—for they were fishermen. And Jesus said to them, "Follow me and I will make you fish for people." And immediately they left their nets and followed him. As he went a little farther, he saw James son of Zebedee and his brother John, who were in their boat mending the nets. Immediately he called them; and they left their father Zebedee in the boat with the hired men, and followed him.

- Jesus begins his ministry by calling a group to follow him. He gives his disciples a mission—to catch people for the kingdom of God. He chooses as his companions very ordinary people, people with no wealth or position. They risk all for Jesus.

- Lord, you continue to call ordinary people, like me. In all my human interactions may I bring your Good News to others.

Monday 26th January
Mark 3:22—30

And the scribes who came down from Jerusalem said, "He has Beelzebul, and by the ruler of the demons he casts out demons." And he called them to him, and spoke to them in parables, "How can Satan cast out Satan? If a kingdom is divided against itself, that kingdom cannot stand. And if a house is divided against itself, that house will not be able to stand. And if Satan has risen up against himself and is divided, he cannot stand, but his end has come. But no one can enter a strong man's house and plunder his property without first tying up the strong man; then indeed the house can be plundered.

"Truly I tell you, people will be forgiven for their sins and whatever blasphemies they utter; but whoever blasphemes against the Holy Spirit can never have forgiveness, but is guilty of an eternal sin"—for they had said, "He has an unclean spirit."

- Children learning to walk fall down often. The good parent gently urges them to get up again. The children keep their eyes fixed on the parent's loving, encouraging smile. "One more step!"

- We walk the way of Jesus like such children. The smile is always there, no matter how badly we fall.

Tuesday 27th January
Mark 3:31—35

Then Jesus' mother and brothers came; and standing outside, they sent to him and called him. A crowd was sitting around him; and they said to him, "Your mother and your brothers and sisters are outside, asking for you." And he replied, "Who are my mother and my brothers?" And looking at those who sat around him, he said, "Here are my mother and my brothers! Whoever does the will of God is my brother and sister and mother."

- The essence of being a Christian is to widen our relationships with trust, affection, commitment, loyalty, faithfulness, kindness, thoughtfulness, compassion, mercy, helpfulness, encouragement, support, strength, protection—all the qualities that bind people together in mutual love and unity.

- Lord, thank you for the gift of my parents.

Wednesday 28th January
Mark 4:2—9

Jesus began to teach them many things in parables, and in his teaching he said to them: "Listen! A sower went out to sow. And as he sowed, some seed fell on the path, and the birds came and ate it up. Other seed fell on rocky ground, where it did not have much soil, and it sprang up quickly, since it had no depth of soil. And when the sun rose, it was scorched; and since it had no root, it withered away. Other seed fell among thorns, and the thorns grew up and choked it, and it yielded no grain. Other seed fell into good soil and brought forth grain, growing up and increasing and yielding thirty and sixty and a hundredfold." And he said, "Let anyone with ears to hear listen!"

- The prophet Jeremiah has a wonderful image: "Those who trust in the Lord are blessed. They are like a tree planted near water. It sends out its roots by the stream. It does not fear when heat comes, for its leaves remain green. It is not anxious in the year of drought, and does not cease to bear fruit" (see Jer 17:7–8)

- Lord, send water to my parched roots so that I may blossom.

Thursday 29th January
Mark 4:21–25

Jesus said to them, "Is a lamp brought in to be put under the bushel basket, or under the bed, and not on the lampstand? For there is nothing hidden, except to be disclosed; nor is anything secret, except to come to light. Let anyone with ears to hear listen!" And he said to them, "Pay attention to what you hear; the measure you give will be the measure you get, and still more will be given you. For to those who have, more will be given; and from those who have nothing, even what they have will be taken away."

- "To those who have, more will be given." Lord, help me to see how much you give me. Let me see you as a lavish God who never holds back anything that might help me.

- Jesus, help me to be as generous as you are. I want to serve you beyond comfort and an easy life. I want to continue to give beyond moments of laziness and discouragement.

Friday 30th January
Mark 4:30—32

Jesus said to the crowd, "With what can we compare the kingdom of God, or what parable will we use for it? It is like a mustard seed, which, when sown upon the ground, is the smallest of all the seeds on earth; yet when it is sown it grows up and becomes the greatest of all shrubs, and puts forth large branches, so that the birds of the air can make nests in its shade."

- Like the seed in the earth, the kingdom of God does not come all at once. It arrives in stages: the stalk, the head, and the full grain. Our job is to watch and pray and to tend it.

- From even the tiniest seed planted in a soul, the kingdom of God can grow so that the person who trusts in God is a source of nourishment and care for others.

Saturday 31st January
Mark 4:35—41

On that day, when evening had come, he said to them, "Let us go across to the other side." And leaving the crowd behind, they took him with them in the boat, just as he was. Other boats were with him. A great gale arose, and the waves beat into the boat, so that the boat was already being swamped. But he was in the stern, asleep on the cushion; and they woke him up and said to him, "Teacher, do you not care that we are perishing?" He woke up and rebuked the wind, and said to the sea, "Peace! Be still!" Then the wind ceased, and there was a dead calm. He said to them, "Why are you afraid? Have you still no faith?" And they were filled with great awe and said to one another, "Who then is this, that even the wind and the sea obey him?"

- Even in the presence of Jesus, with the memory of his words fresh in their minds, the disciples doubted. Like them, I bring my doubts and questions to Jesus and listen for his answer.

- Jesus was asleep, trusting his friends to manage the boat. What confidence Jesus has in me, encouraging me to act and speak in his name!

February 1—7

Something to think and pray about each day this week:

God-Given Love

Pope Benedict XVI described Christianity as a love story between God and ourselves. What is going on deep down is that I give my heart to God who has already given his heart to me. Faith is an affair of the heart, an intimate meeting between God and each individual. This intimate encounter has both a personal and a communal expression.

The encounter between Jesus and the Samaritan woman in chapter 4 of John's Gospel illustrates the point. Jesus loves this woman; he reveals himself to her, and she trusts him and comes to love him. Finally her village becomes a little Christian community, with each person believing for themselves. This fits with one of Pope Benedict's favourite expressions, "the we-structure of faith." We come to know Jesus not through solitary exploration, but through the Christian community, which is charged with guarding the mystery of God-become-human in Jesus.

The challenge to the Church is to reveal "the art of Christian living." The Church, said Benedict, is not to be an end in itself, but a mirror reflecting Christ to the world. The Church is to be a servant of faith. Insofar as its institutions fail to make Christ known, they need critical examination. As a member of the Christian Church, I must ask myself: "How well do I and my community reflect Christ and his values to a sceptical world?"

The Presence of God
At any time of the day or night we can call on Jesus.
He is always waiting, listening for our call.
What a wonderful blessing.
No phone needed, no e-mails—just a whisper.

Freedom
I will ask God's help,
to be free from my own preoccupations,
to be open to God in this time of prayer,
to come to love and serve him more.

Consciousness
How am I feeling? Lighthearted? Heavy hearted?
I may be very much at peace, happy to be here.
Equally, I may be frustrated, worried, or angry.
I acknowledge how I really am. It is the real me that the Lord loves.

The Word
I read the Word of God slowly, a few times over, and I listen to what God is saying to me. (Please turn to your scripture on the following pages. Inspiration points are there should you need them. When you are ready, return here to continue.)

Conversation
Remembering that I am still in God's presence,
I imagine Jesus himself standing or sitting beside me,
and I say whatever is on my mind, whatever is in my heart,
speaking as one friend to another.

Conclusion
Glory be to the Father, and to the Son, and to the Holy Spirit,
as it was in the beginning, is now, and ever shall be,
world without end. Amen.

Sunday 1st February,
Fourth Sunday of Ordinary Time
Mark 1:21—28

They went to Capernaum; and when the sabbath came, Jesus entered the synagogue and taught. They were astounded at his teaching, for he taught them as one having authority, and not as the scribes. Just then there was in their synagogue a man with an unclean spirit, and he cried out, "What have you to do with us, Jesus of Nazareth? Have you come to destroy us? I know who you are, the Holy One of God." But Jesus rebuked him, saying, "Be silent, and come out of him!" And the unclean spirit, throwing him into convulsions and crying with a loud voice, came out of him. They were all amazed, and they kept on asking one another, "What is this? A new teaching—with authority! He commands even the unclean spirits, and they obey him." At once his fame began to spread throughout the surrounding region of Galilee.

• Jesus speaks the word of God as none had spoken it before. The rabbis supported their statements with quotes from authorities. But Jesus needs no human authorities to back his statements. When he speaks, God speaks. Led by the Spirit of God, Jesus confronts and destroys the power of evil.

• Lord, I struggle to believe that you have overcome evil. Help me to see that you are at work in the small signs of love, justice, and truth around me.

Monday 2nd February,
Presentation of the Lord
Luke 2:25—33

Now there was a man in Jerusalem whose name was Simeon; this man was righteous and devout, looking forward to the consolation of Israel, and the Holy Spirit rested on him. It had been revealed to him by the Holy Spirit that he would not see death before he had seen the Lord's Messiah. Guided by the Spirit, Simeon came into the temple; and when the parents brought in the child Jesus, to do for him what was customary under the law, Simeon took him in his arms and praised God, saying, "Master, now you are dismissing your servant in peace, according to your word; for my eyes have seen your salvation, which you have prepared in the presence of all peoples, a light for revelation to the Gentiles and for glory to your people Israel." And the child's father and mother were amazed at what was being said about him.

- The Holy Spirit "rested on" Simeon. Is my heart at peace and open, or am I so full of problems and requests that I have no resting space for the Spirit?

- Simeon "praised God." Praise is a particularly joyful form of prayer. There are so many things for which I can praise God, not least the wonder of my own being.

Tuesday 3rd February
Mark 5:25—34

Now there was a woman who had been suffering from haemorrhages for twelve years. She had endured much under many physicians, and had spent all that she had; and she was no better, but rather grew worse. She had heard about Jesus, and came up behind him in the crowd and touched his cloak, for she said, "If I but touch his clothes, I will be made well." Immediately her haemorrhage stopped; and she felt in her body that she was healed of her disease. Immediately aware that power had gone forth from him, Jesus turned about in the crowd and said, "Who touched my clothes?" And his disciples said to him, "You see the crowd pressing in on you; how can you say, 'Who touched me?'" He looked all round to see who had done it. But the woman, knowing what had happened to her, came in fear and trembling, fell down before him, and told him the whole truth. He said to her, "Daughter, your faith has made you well; go in peace, and be healed of your disease."

- The sick woman had "heard about Jesus." What she heard gave her the grace to believe that he would cure her if she just touched his clothes. What can I learn from her?

- How has my "hearing" about Jesus developed my faith in him?

Wednesday 4th February
Mark 6:1—6

Jesus left that place and came to his home town, and his disciples followed him. On the sabbath he began to teach in the synagogue, and many who heard him were astounded. They said, "Where did this man get all this? What is this wisdom that has been given to him? What deeds of power are being done by his hands! Is not this the carpenter, the son of Mary and brother of James and Joses and Judas and Simon, and are not his sisters here with us?" And they took offence at him. Then Jesus said to them, "Prophets are not without honour, except in their home town, and among their own kin, and in their own house." And he could do no deed of power there, except that he laid his hands on a few sick people and cured them. And he was amazed at their unbelief. Then he went about among the villages teaching.

- "Who does he think he is?" How many times have we heard, or asked, that question? It speaks of jealousy and a begrudging and small heart. Instead, the question should be, "Who am I to judge my neighbour?"

- Jesus was "amazed" at his neighbours' unbelief. He has lived among them for thirty years and all they see is "the carpenter, the son of Mary." How long have I known Jesus, and what or whom do I see? I ask for the grace to know him better.

Thursday 5th February
Mark 6:7–13

Jesus called the twelve and began to send them out two by two, and gave them authority over the unclean spirits. He ordered them to take nothing for their journey except a staff; no bread, no bag, no money in their belts; but to wear sandals and not to put on two tunics. He said to them, "Wherever you enter a house, stay there until you leave the place. If any place will not welcome you and they refuse to hear you, as you leave, shake off the dust that is on your feet as a testimony against them." So they went out and proclaimed that all should repent. They cast out many demons, and anointed with oil many who were sick and cured them.

- The disciples were allowed to take only one thing with them: a staff—something to lean on, to support them as they journeyed. Who, or what, is my "staff"? Where do I find supports in living out my life as a disciple today?

- On the other hand, what are my "demons"? Do I sometimes spoil things? Do I ever act out of a bad motive? Do I occasionally diminish people and leave them less free?

Friday 6th February
Mark 6:22–27

When his daughter Herodias came in and danced, she pleased Herod and his guests; and the king said to the girl, "Ask me for whatever you wish, and I will give it." And he solemnly swore to her, "Whatever you ask me, I will give you, even half of my kingdom." She went out and said to her mother, "What should I ask for?" She replied, "The head of John the baptizer." Immediately she rushed back to the king and requested, "I want you to give me at once the head of John the Baptist on a platter." The king was deeply grieved; yet out of regard for his oaths and for the guests, he did not want to refuse her. Immediately the king sent a soldier of the guard with orders to bring John's head. He went and beheaded him in the prison.

- Herod "liked to listen to John the Baptist," but the seed falls on stony ground. John's head is served up on a dish as if it were part of the menu.

- The appalling malice and cruelty of this feast contrasts sharply with the picture in tomorrow's gospel. There Jesus gathers his disciples and brings them away to care for them. Jesus, cleanse my heart and keep me close to you always.

Saturday 7th February
Mark 6:30—34

The apostles gathered around Jesus, and told him all that they had done and taught. He said to them, "Come away to a deserted place all by yourselves and rest a while." For many were coming and going, and they had no leisure even to eat. And they went away in the boat to a deserted place by themselves. Now many saw them going and recognized them, and they hurried there on foot from all the towns and arrived ahead of them. As he went ashore, he saw a great crowd; and he had compassion for them, because they were like sheep without a shepherd; and he began to teach them many things.

- When I give time to prayer, I am responding to the invitation of Jesus to "come away" to a quiet place. I meet God who answers my need for rest and nourishment.

- I notice that I never regret the time I give to prayer, even though for some, little seems to happen. It seems my heart is made for prayer, just as my body is made for healthy air.

February 8—14

Something to think and pray about each day this week:

Prayer Time

How do you feel about the time you dedicate to prayer? Do you feel that you are doing all the work but getting nowhere? Here your image of prayer can help or hinder you. If you have an unbalanced image, you may decide that the time "wasted in prayer" could be better used in reading a holy book or doing good somewhere. Thus you give up on prayer. Since God has his own image of what prayer is about, it helps if you can catch on to it. This will help you to cooperate better with the Holy Spirit who is at work in you.

The Holy Spirit—not yourself—is the main person in your prayer and is at work in you when you pray (see Rom 8:26). The time you spend in prayer is time for emptiness before God, being available to God.

Prayer is not "useful"; it is of a different order. What you bring to prayer is yourself, your time, and your desire to be with God. You come with your openness, to be slowly transformed by the Spirit. All of this is hard work on your part; this is your contribution to the prayer in you!

The other partner is the Spirit, who has an agenda, a divine project for you. The Spirit works deep down, forming you in the likeness of Christ. You undergo God! You are passive rather than active. Imagine yourself in a dance hall, waiting for someone to invite you onto the floor. All you can do is to be there, waiting, desiring. That is enough. The invitation is guaranteed.

The Presence of God

I pause for a moment
and think of the love and the grace that God showers on me,
creating me in his image and likeness, making me his temple.

Freedom

Lord, grant me the grace to be free from the excesses of this life.
Let me not get caught up with the desire for wealth.
Keep my heart and mind free to love and serve you.

Consciousness

In the presence of my loving Creator,
I look honestly at my feelings over the last day—
the highs, the lows, and the level ground.
Can I see where the Lord has been present?

The Word

God speaks to each one of us individually. I need to listen to what
he is saying to me. (Please turn to your scripture on the following
pages. Inspiration points are there should you need them. When you
are ready, return here to continue.)

Conversation

Sometimes I wonder what I might say
if I were to meet you in person, Lord.
I might say "Thank You, Lord" for always being there for me.
I know with certainty there were times when you carried me,
when through your strength I got through the dark times in my life.

Conclusion

Glory be to the Father, and to the Son, and to the Holy Spirit,
as it was in the beginning, is now, and ever shall be,
world without end. Amen.

February 2015

Sunday 8th February,
Fifth Sunday of Ordinary Time
Mark 1:29—39

As soon as they left the synagogue, they entered the house of Simon and Andrew, with James and John. Now Simon's mother-in-law was in bed with a fever, and they told him about her at once. He came and took her by the hand and lifted her up. Then the fever left her, and she began to serve them.

That evening, at sunset, they brought to him all who were sick or possessed with demons. And the whole city was gathered around the door. And he cured many who were sick with various diseases, and cast out many demons; and he would not permit the demons to speak, because they knew him.

In the morning, while it was still very dark, he got up and went out to a deserted place, and there he prayed. And Simon and his companions hunted for him. When they found him, they said to him, "Everyone is searching for you." He answered, "Let us go on to the neighbouring towns, so that I may proclaim the message there also; for that is what I came out to do." And he went throughout Galilee, proclaiming the message in their synagogues and casting out demons.

- Jesus, this gospel portrays a very busy day in your life. My days, as you know, can be busy, too. But you find time to pray, and I must try to do the same. You bless the time I give to prayer, and my life becomes more fruitful.

- When Simon's mother-in-law is cured, she does what Jesus himself does. She serves those in need. She becomes a disciple. Well-being of spirit involves a willingness to serve. I ask the Lord to make me truly well.

Monday 9th February
Mark 6:53—56

When Jesus and the disciples had crossed over, they came to land at Gennesaret and moored the boat. When they got out of the boat, people at once recognized him, and rushed about that whole region and began to bring the sick on mats to wherever they heard he was. And wherever he went, into villages or cities or farms, they laid the sick in the market-places, and begged him that they might touch even the fringe of his cloak; and all who touched it were healed.

- Jesus, you loved to cure people. You taught the disciples to show compassion to the needy. I am your disciple now.

- May I spread your love and compassion to the needy around me today. May I be a healing presence for those I meet.

Tuesday 10th February
Mark 7:1—2, 5—8

Now when the Pharisees and some of the scribes who had come from Jerusalem gathered around him, they noticed that some of his disciples were eating with defiled hands, that is, without washing them. . . . So the Pharisees and the scribes asked him, "Why do your disciples not live according to the tradition of the elders, but eat with defiled hands?" He said to them, "Isaiah prophesied rightly about you hypocrites, as it is written, 'This people honours me with their lips, but their hearts are far from me; in vain do they worship me, teaching human precepts as doctrines.' You abandon the command-ment of God and hold to human tradition."

- The Pharisees and scribes who challenged Jesus "had come from Jerusalem." They had come with authority. And all that they found to criticise was that the disciples had not washed their hands before eating!

- How often do we choose to be distracted by little things in order to avoid or admit to the real problem? Lord, help me to focus on "the one thing needed." Let nothing get in the way of love.

Wednesday 11th February
Mark 7:14—19

Then Jesus called the crowd again and said to them, "Listen to me, all of you, and understand: there is nothing outside a person that by going in can defile, but the things that come out are what defile." When he had left the crowd and entered the house, his disciples asked him about the parable. He said to them, "Then do you also fail to understand? Do you not see that whatever goes into a person from outside cannot defile, since it enters, not the heart but the stomach, and goes out into the sewer?"

- Jewish tradition held that some foods were clean and others unclean. Jesus says that all foods are clean. What matters, he says, is the heart! By "the heart," he meant what is inside us: moods, thoughts, plans, attitudes, choices, conscience, knowledge, and love. All these must be kept clean.

- Lord, you see into my heart. A pure heart create in me. Take away my heart of stone and give me a heart of flesh, so that I may become as compassionate as you are.

Thursday 12th February
Mark 7:24—30

From there Jesus set out and went away to the region of Tyre. He entered a house and did not want anyone to know he was there. Yet he could not escape notice, but a woman whose little daughter had an unclean spirit immediately heard about him, and she came and bowed down at his feet. Now the woman was a Gentile, of Syrophoenician origin. She begged him to cast the demon out of her daughter. He said to her, "Let the children be fed first, for it is not fair to take the children's food and throw it to the dogs." But she answered him, "Sir, even the dogs under the table eat the children's crumbs." Then he said to her, "For saying that, you may go—the demon has left your daughter." So she went home, found the child lying on the bed, and the demon gone.

- This is a brave and determined woman! She risks her self-respect and dignity to save her sick daughter. She is the only woman in this gospel to win an argument against Jesus. She got him to change his mind about the scope of his ministry.

- Lord, may I have courage to do what I can so that the gifts which women bring to the Church may be more fully appreciated. Without the full engagement of women, the Church is like a bird on one wing.

Friday 13th February
Mark 7:31—37

Then Jesus returned from the region of Tyre, and went by way of Sidon towards the Sea of Galilee, in the region of the Decapolis. They brought to him a deaf man who had an impediment in his speech; and they begged him to lay his hand on him. He took him aside in private, away from the crowd, and put his fingers into his ears, and he spat and touched his tongue. Then looking up to heaven, he sighed and said to him, "Ephphatha," that is, "Be opened." And immediately his ears were opened, his tongue was released, and he spoke plainly. Then Jesus ordered them to tell no one; but the more he ordered them, the more zealously they proclaimed it. They were astounded beyond measure, saying, "He has done everything well; he even makes the deaf to hear and the mute to speak."

- Deep inside me, I, too, can be deaf and dumb. I allow Jesus to take me by the hand and bring me to a quiet place. Can I let him touch my ears and tongue? Until I am cured, I can't hear his sigh or what he says, but I guess that he is praying for me. When I am cured, each word and sound is precious to me, like sweet music.

- Can I hug him in gratitude for his goodness to me?

Saturday 14th February
Mark 8:1—8

In those days when there was again a great crowd without anything to eat, Jesus called his disciples and said to them, "I have compassion for the crowd, because they have been with me now for three days and have nothing to eat. If I send them away hungry to their homes, they will faint on the way—and some of them have come from a great distance." His disciples replied, "How can one feed these people with bread here in the desert?" He asked them, "How many loaves do you have?" They said, "Seven." Then he ordered the crowd to sit down on the ground; and he took the seven loaves, and after giving thanks he broke them and gave them to his disciples to distribute; and they distributed them to the crowd. They had also a few small fish; and after blessing them, he ordered that these too should be distributed. They ate and were filled; and they took up the broken pieces left over, seven baskets full.

- The disciples have plenty of common sense, but they have little faith that God can do extraordinary things. They do not yet see that with God all things are possible, even though Jesus performed a similar miracle a little while earlier.

- In what ways am I like those disciples?

February 15—21

Something to think and pray about each day this week:

Into the Wilderness

If the Spirit is to take over in our prayer, we need to be in something like a wilderness, where nothing much is happening. In Hosea 2:14, God says of his people Israel: "I will now persuade her, and bring her into the wilderness, and speak tenderly to her."

It is good to draw back from the noise and chatter that imprisons you on the surface of yourself, to create those wilderness conditions that heighten your sensitivity to God's word. You will be allured by God's attractiveness, and God will speak to your heart.

The promise of God in Hosea is played out in chapter 3 of Exodus, the story of Moses. Moses has led his flock "beyond the wilderness, and come to Horeb, the mountain of God" (Ex 3:1). He has slowed down and is quiet. He is ideally placed now for God to catch his attention. Next, Moses notices a steadily blazing bush and is fascinated. Here God is captivating Moses. God then calls him by name: "Moses! Moses!" This intimate meeting touches Moses to his depths. God is speaking to his heart.

God is active in your prayer, too. Your wilderness is a graced place. Be still and let the things of God touch your heart. Invite God to whisper your name, to light a little flame in your heart, and to tell you how he loves you.

The Presence of God

"I stand at the door and knock," says the Lord.
What a wonderful privilege
that the Lord of all creation desires to come to me.
I welcome his presence.

Freedom

Lord, grant me the grace to be free from the excesses of this life.
Let me not get caught up with the desire for wealth.
Keep my heart and mind free to love and serve you.

Consciousness

"There is a time and place for everything," as the saying goes.
Lord, grant that I may always desire
to spend time in your presence, to hear your call.

The Word

God speaks to each one of us individually. I need to listen to what
he is saying to me. (Please turn to your scripture on the following
pages. Inspiration points are there should you need them. When you
are ready, return here to continue.)

Conversation

The gift of speech is a wonderful gift.
May I use this gift with kindness.
May I be slow to utter harsh words,
hurtful words, and words spoken in anger.

Conclusion

Glory be to the Father, and to the Son, and to the Holy Spirit,
as it was in the beginning, is now, and ever shall be,
world without end. Amen.

Sunday 15th February,
Sixth Sunday of Ordinary Time
Mark 1:40—45

A leper came to Jesus begging him, and kneeling he said to him, "If you choose, you can make me clean." Moved with pity, Jesus stretched out his hand and touched him, and said to him, "I do choose. Be made clean!" Immediately the leprosy left him, and he was made clean. After sternly warning him he sent him away at once, saying to him, "See that you say nothing to anyone; but go, show yourself to the priest, and offer for your cleansing what Moses commanded, as a testimony to them." But he went out and began to proclaim it freely, and to spread the word, so that Jesus could no longer go into a town openly, but stayed out in the country; and people came to him from every quarter.

- Leprosy was a term which covered a variety of skin diseases. In Jewish law, any or all of them made the victim unclean. Lepers were often banished from society lest they might infect others. For Jesus to touch a leper was shocking. But in this way, Jesus shows his closeness to us in our need. I thank him for this.

- The leper becomes a disciple—he spreads the word. He witnesses to Jesus' goodness. Can I let him take me by the hand so that I, too, may become a witness to what God is doing in my life?

Monday 16th February
Mark 8:11—13

The Pharisees came and began to argue with Jesus, asking him for a sign from heaven, to test him. And he sighed deeply in his spirit and said, "Why does this generation ask for a sign? Truly I tell you, no sign will be given to this generation." And he left them, and getting into the boat again, he went across to the other side.

- All the wonders that Jesus is doing are the "sign from heaven" that the Pharisees are demanding. But their hearts are closed. If a new sign came, they would look for yet another. Earlier, it was Satan who demanded a sign from Jesus when tempting him in the desert.

• Lord, what about me? Am I always looking for something more from you? You reveal yourself as being totally on my side, through your passion and resurrection. Let me accept these great signs. Let me trust that you are on my side even when smaller things do not go well.

Tuesday 17th February
Mark 8:14–17

Now the disciples had forgotten to bring any bread; and they had only one loaf with them in the boat. And he cautioned them, saying, "Watch out—beware of the yeast of the Pharisees and the yeast of Herod." They said to one another, "It is because we have no bread." And becoming aware of it, Jesus said to them, "Why are you talking about having no bread? Do you still not perceive or understand?"

• The disciples took things at face value, missing Jesus' meaning. I take the time I need to listen deeply.

• Jesus sometimes refers to yeast as positive, asking us to be like leaven. Is there a negative image of yeast that I need to be aware of?

Wednesday 18th February,
Ash Wednesday
Matthew 6:1–6

Beware of practising your piety before others in order to be seen by them; for then you have no reward from your Father in heaven. So whenever you give alms, do not sound a trumpet before you, as the hypocrites do in the synagogues and in the streets, so that they may be praised by others. Truly I tell you, they have received their reward. But when you give alms, do not let your left hand know what your right hand is doing, so that your alms may be done in secret; and your Father who sees in secret will reward you.

And whenever you pray, do not be like the hypocrites; for they love to stand and pray in the synagogues and at the street corners, so that they may be seen by others. Truly I tell you, they have received their reward. But whenever you pray, go into your room and shut the door and pray to your Father who is in secret; and your Father who sees in secret will reward you.

- Today, Ash Wednesday, Christians all over the world begin the penitential but joyous season of Lent. Whatever we do in Lent should bring us ever closer to Jesus and prepare us to celebrate his resurrection at Easter.

- Lent is a personal journey in the company of Jesus. Whatever I agree with Jesus to do or not to do remains between him and me. It does not concern anyone else.

Thursday 19th February
Luke 9:22—25

Jesus said to his disciples, "The Son of Man must undergo great suffering, and be rejected by the elders, chief priests, and scribes, and be killed, and on the third day be raised." Then he said to them all, "If any want to become my followers, let them deny themselves and take up their cross daily and follow me. For those who want to save their life will lose it, and those who lose their life for my sake will save it. What does it profit them if they gain the whole world, but lose or forfeit themselves?"

- Much of what we want to hold onto in life can be swiftly taken away—our good health, our security of wealth, even our good name.

- What we share in love and in God cannot be taken away. Ask in prayer to value love and to offer your life now and always in love and for love.

Friday 20th February
Matthew 9:14—15

Then the disciples of John came to him, saying, "Why do we and the Pharisees fast often, but your disciples do not fast?" And Jesus said to them, "The wedding guests cannot mourn as long as the bridegroom is with them, can they? The days will come when the bridegroom is taken away from them, and then they will fast."

- People say, "Why do you not do as I do?" But each of us has our own path to Jesus. We should not force others along our path, nor allow them to make us follow them. Each of us has the Holy Spirit to guide our steps.

- Finding our own path with Jesus is not easy. It may involve trial and error. It takes time, effort, and prayer. But on our path, we find peace—the peace which the world cannot give.

Saturday 21st February
Luke 5:27—32

After this he went out and saw a tax-collector named Levi, sitting at the tax booth; and he said to him, "Follow me." And he got up, left everything, and followed him. Then Levi gave a great banquet for him in his house; and there was a large crowd of tax-collectors and others sitting at the table with them. The Pharisees and their scribes were complaining to his disciples, saying, "Why do you eat and drink with tax-collectors and sinners?" Jesus answered, "Those who are well have no need of a physician, but those who are sick; I have come to call not the righteous but sinners to repentance."

- For Levi the tax collector, following Jesus meant leaving "everything"—job, home, security. Jesus does not ask this of everyone. What does "following him" mean for me?

- Those who are satisfied with the way they are do not need Jesus. They feel no need of repentance or change. They are not listening to his call, "Follow me." Am I?

February 22—28

Something to think and pray about each day this week:

Embracing the Season

The season of Lent has begun. Lent originally meant "springtime," and so we can view it as a springtime for the spirit. It is a time also to spring-clean the cave of our hearts!

Whatever the variations in the practice of Lent over the last two thousand years, the main issue is whether Lent helps me to become more aware of how I stand in relation to God and my neighbour. The ancient practices designed to achieve these goals were fasting, almsgiving, and prayer. The call to fast makes me focus on the affairs of the spirit rather than of the body. The call to almsgiving makes me more alert to my neighbour's needs. The call to prayer nourishes my bond with God, especially with Jesus in his passion.

Why forty days for Lent? This period called to mind the time Jesus spent in the desert. For some it was also a reminder of the forty hours he spent on the Cross.

The Sacred Space community is at home with the calls to prayer and almsgiving. But what about fasting? There are many little things I can perhaps do without—the spring vacation, the hairdo, the fattening muffin, the extra hour watching TV, the purchase of things I don't need. The point is that the shock to the system should lead to a deeper sense of what God may want of me!

The Presence of God

Jesus waits silent and unseen to come into my heart.
I will respond to his call.
He comes with his infinite power and love.
May I be filled with joy in his presence.

Freedom

I ask for the grace
to let go of my own concerns
and be open to what God is asking of me,
to let myself be guided and formed by my loving Creator.

Consciousness

Knowing that God loves me unconditionally,
I can afford to be honest about how I am.
How has the last day been, and how do I feel now?
I share my feelings openly with the Lord.

The Word

I read the Word of God slowly, a few times over, and I listen to what
God is saying to me. (Please turn to your scripture on the following
pages. Inspiration points are there should you need them. When you
are ready, return here to continue.)

Conversation

Remembering that I am still in God's presence,
I imagine Jesus himself standing or sitting beside me,
and I say whatever is on my mind, whatever is in my heart,
speaking as one friend to another.

Conclusion

Glory be to the Father, and to the Son, and to the Holy Spirit,
as it was in the beginning, is now, and ever shall be,
world without end. Amen.

February 2015

Sunday 22nd February,
First Sunday of Lent
Mark 1:12—15

And the Spirit immediately drove him out into the wilderness. He was in the wilderness for forty days, tempted by Satan; and he was with the wild beasts; and the angels waited on him. Now after John was arrested, Jesus came to Galilee, proclaiming the good news of God, and saying, "The time is fulfilled, and the kingdom of God has come near; repent, and believe in the good news."

- Mark's gospel depicts Jesus as divine but also deeply human. He enters the wilderness for one purpose only: to find God, to seek God, and to belong to him totally. Only then does he come into Galilee and proclaim the good news.

- Lord, come with me into my wilderness. Speak to my preoccupied heart. Reveal to me where addiction to power, possession, and gratification choke my path. Only when I am free from these can I be good news to others.

Monday 23rd February
Matthew 25:34—40

Jesus said, "The king will say to those at his right hand, 'Come, you that are blessed by my Father, inherit the kingdom prepared for you from the foundation of the world; for I was hungry and you gave me food, I was thirsty and you gave me something to drink, I was a stranger and you welcomed me, I was naked and you gave me clothing, I was sick and you took care of me, I was in prison and you visited me.' Then the righteous will answer him, 'Lord, when was it that we saw you hungry and gave you food, or thirsty and gave you something to drink? And when was it that we saw you a stranger and welcomed you, or naked and gave you clothing? And when was it that we saw you sick or in prison and visited you?' And the king will answer them, 'Truly I tell you, just as you did it to one of the least of these who are members of my family, you did it to me.'"

February 2015

- Those on the king's right hand have in their lifetime provided for the most basic of human needs in God's family. Not only that, but they have done it for "the least." Am I selective in my giving of time, money, material, or spiritual goods?

- Love is shown in action. Prayer is not always enough. The prayer which does not lead to action is not real prayer.

Tuesday 24th February
Matthew 6:7—15

Jesus said, "When you are praying, do not heap up empty phrases as the Gentiles do; for they think that they will be heard because of their many words. Do not be like them, for your Father knows what you need before you ask him. Pray then in this way: Our Father in heaven, hallowed be your name. Your kingdom come. Your will be done, on earth as it is in heaven. Give us this day our daily bread. And forgive us our debts, as we also have forgiven our debtors. And do not bring us to the time of trial, but rescue us from the evil one. For if you forgive others their trespasses, your heavenly Father will also forgive you; but if you do not forgive others, neither will your Father forgive your trespasses."

- Jesus, the petitions in this prayer put God at the centre of everything. That is how you lived. You always forgive me. May I rejoice at this and be generous in forgiving others. Let me be known as a forgiving person who holds no grudges.

Wednesday 25th February
Luke 11:29—32

When the crowds were increasing, he began to say, "This generation is an evil generation; it asks for a sign, but no sign will be given to it except the sign of Jonah. For just as Jonah became a sign to the people of Nineveh, so the Son of Man will be to this generation. The queen of the South will rise at the judgement with the people of this generation and condemn them, because she came from the ends of the earth to listen to the wisdom of Solomon, and see, something greater than Solomon is here! The people of Nineveh will rise up at the judgement with this generation and condemn it, because they repented at the proclamation of Jonah, and see, something greater than Jonah is here!"

- Jesus tells it as it is. When "the crowds were increasing," he challenged them to ask themselves why they were coming to see and listen to him. Why do I come to Sacred Space each day?

- "Something greater is here." He challenges the crowd to consider the question he put to his apostles: "Who do you think I am?" He asks us the same question.

Thursday 26th February
Matthew 7:7—8

Jesus said to the disciples, "Ask, and it will be given you; search, and you will find; knock, and the door will be opened for you. For everyone who asks receives, and everyone who searches finds, and for everyone who knocks, the door will be opened."

- Jesus says that we will not ask without receiving what God knows is best for us. We will not seek without finding what God knows we most need. We will not knock without having the most worthwhile way opened to us.

- Can I trust in this radical goodness of God?

Friday 27th February
Matthew 5:20—24

Jesus said to his disciples, "For I tell you, unless your righteousness exceeds that of the scribes and Pharisees, you will never enter the kingdom of heaven. You have heard that it was said to those of ancient times, 'You shall not murder'; and 'whoever murders shall be liable to judgement.' But I say to you that if you are angry with a brother or sister, you will be liable to judgement; and if you insult a brother or sister, you will be liable to the council; and if you say, 'You fool,' you will be liable to the hell of fire. So when you are offering your gift at the altar, if you remember that your brother or sister has something against you, leave your gift there before the altar and go; first be reconciled to your brother or sister, and then come and offer your gift."

- Jesus, you set me very high standards of conduct! You want my relationships to mirror those of God. Not only is murder forbidden me, but even angry thoughts and insults. Purify my wayward heart of all that is unworthy of a child of God.

- Reconciliation must be a first priority among the People of God. God will always be on my side when I try to mend a quarrel. Am I known as a peacemaker who takes the first step when a quarrel occurs?

Saturday 28th February
Matthew 5:43—48

Jesus said to the disciples, "You have heard that it was said, 'You shall love your neighbour and hate your enemy.' But I say to you, Love your enemies and pray for those who persecute you, so that you may be children of your Father in heaven; for he makes his sun rise on the evil and on the good, and sends rain on the righteous and on the unrighteous. For if you love those who love you, what reward do you have? Do not even the tax-collectors do the same? And if you greet only your brothers and sisters, what more are you doing than others? Do not even the Gentiles do the same? Be perfect, therefore, as your heavenly Father is perfect."

- Why should we love our enemies and pray for our persecutors? We are to do this because God does it, and we are called to be God's children.

- As his children, we are commanded to be "perfect." Perfection consists in loving as God loves, without exceptions or conditions. I beg for the grace to do this.

March 1—7

Something to think and pray about each day this week:

Searching for God

Two little children look up at the stars on a dark, clear night. One child says: "I bet you those stars are five miles away." The other says: "No, they're not—they're ten miles away." The first child says: "Don't be stupid. If they were ten miles away, you wouldn't be able to see them."

We can laugh at the children. But we adults also disagree and dispute with one another—over our understandings of God! These children are trying to express a truth on which they both agree, namely, that the stars are a very, very long way away. They use the only concepts they have; they are doing their best to express a truth. The reality is beyond their comprehension.

Likewise, God is beyond our understanding. But like the children, we, too, make the mistake of trying to "capture" God with our minds. We can claim to know God while thinking that those who disagree with us are wrong. In fact, we can never know God; we must only search for God. To search for God is to acknowledge that we are not there yet. Were we to stop searching, we might start claiming that we have found him. And then, of course, we would miss God, who is too big to understand.

So when we have differing views about God, let us disagree gracefully and always be alert to the possibility that others may have an insight which we have missed. One thing we can hold fast: that God is the Giver of all the good things in our life.

The Presence of God

For a few moments, I think of God's veiled presence in things:
in the elements, giving them existence;
in plants, giving them life; in animals, giving them sensation;
and finally, in me, giving me all this and more,
making me a temple, a dwelling-place of the Spirit.

Freedom

God is not foreign to my freedom.
Instead, the Spirit breathes life into my most intimate desires,
gently nudging me toward all that is good.
I ask for the grace to let myself be enfolded by the Spirit.

Consciousness

Knowing that God loves me unconditionally,
I can afford to be honest about how I am.
How has the last day been, and how do I feel now?
I share my feelings openly with the Lord.

The Word

The Word of God comes to us through the scriptures. May the Holy
Spirit enlighten my mind and my heart to respond to the Gospel
teachings. (Please turn to your scripture on the following pages.
Inspiration points are there should you need them. When you are
ready, return here to continue.)

Conversation

How has God's Word moved me? Has it left me cold?
Has it consoled me or moved me to act in a new way?
I imagine Jesus standing or sitting beside me;
I turn and share my feelings with him.

Conclusion

Glory be to the Father, and to the Son, and to the Holy Spirit,
as it was in the beginning, is now, and ever shall be,
world without end. Amen.

March 2015

Sunday 1st March,
Second Sunday of Lent
Mark 9:2—10

Six days later, Jesus took with him Peter and James and John, and led them up a high mountain apart, by themselves. And he was transfigured before them, and his clothes became dazzling white, such as no one on earth could bleach them. And there appeared to them Elijah with Moses, who were talking with Jesus. Then Peter said to Jesus, "Rabbi, it is good for us to be here; let us make three dwellings, one for you, one for Moses, and one for Elijah." He did not know what to say, for they were terrified. Then a cloud over-shadowed them, and from the cloud there came a voice, "This is my Son, the Beloved; listen to him!" Suddenly when they looked around, they saw no one with them any more, but only Jesus. As they were coming down the mountain, he ordered them to tell no one about what they had seen, until after the Son of Man had risen from the dead. So they kept the matter to themselves, questioning what this rising from the dead could mean.

- Jesus, you needed this deep experience of transfiguration to strengthen you before your passion. Life is hard, so help me to believe that, like you, I, too, am "the beloved of God" as St. Paul says (see Rom 1:7). This will steady me in times of trial.

- The divine is hidden within each of us. Sometimes my goodness shines out, and sometimes it is hidden. But everyone I meet, at home, on the streets, at work, in the hospital, and at the supermarket, is a daughter or son of God. Lord, help me in this Lenten season to see that everyone is a divine mystery in motion!

Monday 2nd March
Luke 6:36—38

Jesus said to the disciples, "Be merciful, just as your Father is merciful. Do not judge, and you will not be judged; do not con-demn, and you will not be condemned. Forgive, and you will be forgiven; give, and it will be given to you. A good measure, pressed down, shaken together, running over, will be put into your lap; for the measure you give will be the measure you get back."

- Lord, my poor heart is very small, and it can also be very hard. Your heart is large and also very tender and compassionate.

- When I try to forgive others, my heart becomes a bit more like yours, and you swamp me with your overflowing generosity. I like that!

Tuesday 3rd March
Matthew 23:1—12

Then Jesus said to the crowds and to his disciples, "The scribes and the Pharisees sit on Moses' seat; therefore, do whatever they teach you and follow it; but do not do as they do, for they do not practise what they teach. They tie up heavy burdens, hard to bear, and lay them on the shoulders of others; but they themselves are unwilling to lift a finger to move them. They do all their deeds to be seen by others; for they make their phylacteries broad and their fringes long. They love to have the place of honour at banquets and the best seats in the synagogues, and to be greeted with respect in the market-places, and to have people call them rabbi. But you are not to be called rabbi, for you have one teacher, and you are all students. And call no one your father on earth, for you have one Father—the one in heaven. Nor are you to be called instructors, for you have one instructor, the Messiah. The greatest among you will be your servant. All who exalt themselves will be humbled, and all who humble themselves will be exalted."

- Jesus' criticisms are valid for religious leaders anywhere who lose sight of the ideal of service of their people.

- "They do all their deeds to be seen by others." What motivates my actions, especially my charitable actions? Does my left hand know what my right hand is doing? Is it all about how it looks, or about how it is? Do I ensure that my good deeds get known in the right places?

Wednesday 4th March
Matthew 20:17—23

While Jesus was going up to Jerusalem, he took the twelve disciples aside by themselves, and said to them on the way, "See, we are going up to Jerusalem, and the Son of Man will be handed over to the chief priests and scribes, and they will condemn him to death; then they will hand him over to the Gentiles to be mocked and flogged and crucified; and on the third day he will be raised."

Then the mother of the sons of Zebedee came to him with her sons, and kneeling before him, she asked a favour of him. And he said to her, "What do you want?" She said to him, "Declare that these two sons of mine will sit, one at your right hand and one at your left, in your kingdom." But Jesus answered, "You do not know what you are asking. Are you able to drink the cup that I am about to drink?" They said to him, "We are able." He said to them, "You will indeed drink my cup, but to sit at my right hand and at my left, this is not mine to grant, but it is for those for whom it has been prepared by my Father."

- The apostles had spent a few years with Jesus. They had slept rough and gone hungry; they were condemned and ostracized, even by their own families. No wonder they did not want to hear that, after all that, Jesus was going to suffer a shameful death.

- The mother of James and John did not want to hear it either. Her request is very human. Jesus did not condemn her or her sons. He understood. That's the kind of person he is. Instead, he spells out a lesson for everyone, the lesson of self-sacrificing service.

Thursday 5th March
Luke 16:19—31

Jesus said to the Pharisees, "There was a rich man who was dressed in purple and fine linen and who feasted sumptuously every day. And at his gate lay a poor man named Lazarus, covered with sores, who longed to satisfy his hunger with what fell from the rich man's table; even the dogs would come and lick his sores. The poor man died and was carried away by the angels to be with Abraham. The rich man also died and was buried. In Hades, where he was being tormented, he looked up and saw Abraham far away with Lazarus by his side. He called out, 'Father Abraham, have mercy on me, and send Lazarus to dip the tip of his finger in water and cool my tongue; for I am in agony in these flames.' But Abraham said, 'Child, remember that during your lifetime you received your good things, and Lazarus in like manner evil things; but now he is comforted here, and you are in agony. Besides all this, between you and us a great chasm has been fixed, so that those who might want to pass from here to you cannot do so, and no one can cross from there to us.' He said, 'Then, father, I beg you to send him to my father's house—for I have five brothers—that he may warn them, so that they will not also come into this place of torment.' Abraham replied, 'They have Moses and the prophets; they should listen to them.' He said, 'No, father Abraham; but if someone goes to them from the dead, they will repent.' He said to him, 'If they do not listen to Moses and the prophets, neither will they be convinced even if someone rises from the dead.'"

- This parable is addressed to the religious leaders of the time. But it applies to each of us, especially those who have been blessed with privilege, money, talent, or education. There's nothing wrong with being rich in any of these ways. It's how we use our riches that matters eternally.

- In the modern world, we all know Lazarus and his millions of companions. The hungry, deprived, dispossessed, and exploited are lying at our gates in the First World. We are uncomfortably aware of them and their needs. Like the rich man in the parable, we have no excuse.

Friday 6th March
Matthew 21:33—41

Jesus said, "Listen to another parable. There was a landowner who planted a vineyard, put a fence around it, dug a wine press in it, and built a watch-tower. Then he leased it to tenants and went to another country. When the harvest time had come, he sent his slaves to the tenants to collect his produce. But the tenants seized his slaves and beat one, killed another, and stoned another. Again he sent other slaves, more than the first; and they treated them in the same way. Finally he sent his son to them, saying, 'They will respect my son.' But when the tenants saw the son, they said to themselves, 'This is the heir; come, let us kill him and get his inheritance.' So they seized him, threw him out of the vineyard, and killed him. Now when the owner of the vineyard comes, what will he do to those tenants?" They said to him, "He will put those wretches to a miserable death, and lease the vineyard to other tenants who will give him the produce at the harvest time."

- We are the tenants in the parable. God provides us with everything we need to make our vineyard prosper. God gives us the freedom to run the vineyard as we choose—but it is God's. We need to be sensitive to what God desires of us. This is what prayer is about—coming to know the mind of God about our lives.

- What fruits will I produce for the Lord?

Saturday 7th March
Luke 15:25—32

Jesus told them a parable: "Now his elder son was in the field; and when he came and approached the house, he heard music and dancing. He called one of the slaves and asked what was going on. He replied, 'Your brother has come, and your father has killed the fatted calf, because he has got him back safe and sound.' Then he became angry and refused to go in. His father came out and began to plead with him. But he answered his father, 'Listen! For all these years I have been working like a slave for you, and I have never disobeyed your command; yet you have never given me even a young goat so that I might celebrate with my friends. But when this son of yours came back, who has devoured your property with prostitutes, you killed the fatted calf for him!' Then the father said to him, 'Son, you are always with me, and all that is mine is yours. But we had to celebrate and rejoice, because this brother of yours was dead and has come to life; he was lost and has been found.'"

- Forgiveness is rarely deserved. If we rejoice in knowing that we are ourselves forgiven despite our unworthiness, we will be much more ready to forgive others, even when they do not deserve it.

- Forgiveness is a gift. Do I give this gift generously?

March 8—14

Something to think and pray about each day this week:

Union with God

In traditional spirituality, union with God is found solely in contemplative prayer. In that tradition, it was understood that we can only unite ourselves with God through uniting our spirit with God, who is Spirit. This means leaving behind this material, sometimes chaotic, world and climbing the mountain, as Jesus did with Peter, James, and John. There, at the top of the mountain, far distant from the cares of this world, in contemplative prayer we enter into an intimate relationship with God.

However, St. Ignatius had a more complex view of how some of us may find union with God. Yes, he would say, climb the mountain; yes, enter into that intimate relationship with God at the highest levels of contemplative prayer; yes, experience the joy of that intimacy. You may be invited to stay there and become a contemplative. But you may be told to go back down the mountain, to this material, messy, violent world, and to find union with God through union of your will with God's will. God, he would say, labours in our world and can be found there as fully as on the mountain.

If, however, we work in the world, we must, again and again, climb to the top of the mountain, to be alone with God, with ourselves, our memories and desires—but always returning back down to the bottom of the mountain.

The Presence of God

Dear Jesus, today I call on you in a special way.
Mostly I come asking for favours.
Today I'd like just to be in your presence.
Let my heart respond to your love.

Freedom

"I am free."
When I look at these words in writing,
they seem to create in me a feeling of awe—
yes, a wonderful feeling of freedom.
Thank you, God.

Consciousness

Lord, you gave me the night to rest in sleep.
In my waking hours may I not forget your goodness to me.
Guide me to share your blessings with others.

The Word

I read the Word of God slowly, a few times over, and I listen to what
God is saying to me. (Please turn to your scripture on the following
pages. Inspiration points are there should you need them. When you
are ready, return here to continue.)

Conversation

Dear Jesus, I can open up my heart to you.
I can tell you everything that troubles me.
I know you care about all the concerns in my life.
Teach me to live in the knowledge
that you, who care for me today,
will care for me tomorrow and all the days of my life.

Conclusion

Glory be to the Father, and to the Son, and to the Holy Spirit,
as it was in the beginning, is now, and ever shall be,
world without end. Amen.

March 2015

Sunday 8th March,
Third Sunday of Lent
John 2:13—17

The Passover of the Jews was near, and Jesus went up to Jerusalem. In the temple he found people selling cattle, sheep, and doves, and the money-changers seated at their tables. Making a whip of cords, he drove all of them out of the temple, both the sheep and the cattle. He also poured out the coins of the money-changers and overturned their tables. He told those who were selling the doves, "Take these things out of here! Stop making my Father's house a market-place!" His disciples remembered that it was written, "Zeal for your house will consume me."

- Jesus loved the temple. He felt at home there because it was his father's house. It was a sacred space for him. Yet he could also meet God anywhere, because he carried God within.

- I can think of my workplace or kitchen as my temple, and when I read *Sacred Space*, I can think of myself as being drawn into the world of God. This will make me happy.

Monday 9th March
Luke 4:24—30

And he said, "Truly I tell you, no prophet is accepted in the prophet's home town. But the truth is, there were many widows in Israel in the time of Elijah, when the heaven was shut up for three years and six months, and there was a severe famine over all the land; yet Elijah was sent to none of them except to a widow at Zarephath in Sidon. There were also many lepers in Israel in the time of the prophet Elisha, and none of them was cleansed except Naaman the Syrian." When they heard this, all in the synagogue were filled with rage. They got up, drove him out of the town, and led him to the brow of the hill on which their town was built, so that they might hurl him off the cliff. But he passed through the midst of them and went on his way.

March 2015

- The people in Jesus' home town thought they knew him so well that there was nothing new he had to say to them.

- How often do I fail to pay real attention to those close to me? Might I be missing something very important in another person and not know it?

Tuesday 10th March
Matthew 18:21—22

Then Peter came and said to him, "Lord, if another member of the church sins against me, how often should I forgive? As many as seven times?" Jesus said to him, "Not seven times, but, I tell you, seventy-seven times."

- Peter must have been shocked to know that the path of forgiveness knows no end. But later he is glad, because Jesus forgives him even though Peter has denied his Master. The apostle saw that if God never stops forgiving him, he must try to forgive others.

- Only those who forgive belong in God's kingdom.

Wednesday 11th March
Matthew 5:17—19

Jesus said to his disciples, "Do not think that I have come to abolish the law or the prophets; I have come not to abolish but to fulfil. For truly I tell you, until heaven and earth pass away, not one letter, not one stroke of a letter, will pass from the law until all is accomplished. Therefore, whoever breaks one of the least of these commandments, and teaches others to do the same, will be called least in the kingdom of heaven; but whoever does them and teaches them will be called great in the kingdom of heaven."

- The commandments to which Jesus is referring here were given to Moses on Mount Sinai. They were valid when Jesus spoke, fourteen hundred years after Moses. They are still valid today.

- Can I list the Ten Commandments? To which do I need to attend right now?

Thursday 12th March
Luke 11:14—20

Jesus was casting out a demon that was mute; when the demon had gone out, the one who had been mute spoke, and the crowds were amazed. But some of them said, "He casts out demons by Beelzebul, the ruler of the demons." Others, to test him, kept demanding from him a sign from heaven. But he knew what they were thinking and said to them, "Every kingdom divided against itself becomes a desert, and house falls on house. If Satan also is divided against himself, how will his kingdom stand?—for you say that I cast out the demons by Beelzebul. Now if I cast out the demons by Beelzebul, by whom do your exorcists cast them out? Therefore they will be your judges. But if it is by the finger of God that I cast out the demons, then the kingdom of God has come to you."

- With whom do I identify in the crowd that witnesses Jesus' miracle? With those who watch in amazed belief? With those who reject him? Or with those who hedge their bets, looking for further signs?

- Jesus forces us off the middle ground. We cannot be neutral; we are either with him or against him.

Friday 13th March
Mark 12:28—34

One of the scribes came near and heard them disputing with one another, and seeing that he answered them well, he asked him, "Which commandment is the first of all?" Jesus answered, "The first is, 'Hear, O Israel: the Lord our God, the Lord is one; you shall love the Lord your God with all your heart, and with all your soul, and with all your mind, and with all your strength.' The second is this,

'You shall love your neighbour as yourself.' There is no other commandment greater than these." Then the scribe said to him, "You are right, Teacher; you have truly said that 'he is one, and besides him there is no other'; and 'to love him with all the heart, and with all the understanding, and with all the strength,' and 'to love one's neighbour as oneself,'—this is much more important than all whole burnt-offerings and sacrifices." When Jesus saw that he answered wisely, he said to him, "You are not far from the kingdom of God." After that no one dared to ask him any question.

- If we don't sufficiently accept and love ourselves, we can never really enter into communion with others and with God. Was this what St. Augustine meant when he cried to God, "And look, you were within me and I was outside, and there I sought for you"?

- I need to find the God who is within, hidden in the depths of my heart.

Saturday 14th March
Luke 18:9—14

He also told this parable to some who trusted in themselves that they were righteous and regarded others with contempt: "Two men went up to the temple to pray, one a Pharisee and the other a tax-collector. The Pharisee, standing by himself, was praying thus, 'God, I thank you that I am not like other people: thieves, rogues, adulterers, or even like this tax-collector. I fast twice a week; I give a tenth of all my income.' But the tax-collector, standing far off, would not even look up to heaven, but was beating his breast and saying, 'God, be merciful to me, a sinner!' I tell you, this man went down to his home justified rather than the other; for all who exalt themselves will be humbled, but all who humble themselves will be exalted."

- The Pharisee derives his satisfaction from the fact that he does not commit the sins that other people do. But what matters is not avoiding this and doing that, but rather handing oneself over to God's mercy.

- Whom do I consider beyond God's mercy? How does this passage speak to me in that regard?

March 15—21

Something to think and pray about each day this week:

Giving Thanks

Why should Christians struggle for justice, as Jesus did? After all, it can be difficult, self-sacrificing, and problematic.

Is it for fear of being punished if we fail to show love? No. The unconditional love of God always forgives us our failings. I can go off to Bermuda and lie on the beach, sipping brandy for the rest of my life, and not care about anyone—and I will still be loved unconditionally by God.

Is it for the sake of reward? No, because the reward has already been given! The moment we were created, we were given the gift of God's unconditional and infinite love, and that gift is ours to keep forever.

For a Christian, the only motivation to do good is gratitude, gratitude for God's many gifts to us, and above all for his infinite and unconditional love. The Eucharistic Prefaces say that it is right always and everywhere to give God thanks for all God's gifts. The deeper my awareness of these gifts, the deeper my gratitude, and this makes me more committed to reaching out to God's children on the margins. And the more I reach out to them, the closer they lead me to contemplate the Giver of the gifts. To work for social justice, I have to be contemplative.

The Presence of God

I pause for a moment
and think of the love and the grace that God showers on me,
creating me in his image and likeness, making me his temple.

Freedom

Everything has the potential to draw forth from me a fuller love
and life.
Yet my desires are often fixed, caught, on illusions of fulfillment.
I ask that God, through my freedom, may orchestrate
my desires in a vibrant, loving melody rich in harmony.

Consciousness

In the presence of my loving Creator,
I look honestly at my feelings over the last day—
the highs, the lows, and the level ground.
Can I see where the Lord has been present?

The Word

God speaks to each one of us individually. I need to listen to what
he is saying to me. (Please turn to your scripture on the following
pages. Inspiration points are there should you need them. When you
are ready, return here to continue.)

Conversation

What feelings are rising in me
as I pray and reflect on God's Word?
I imagine Jesus himself sitting or standing beside me,
and I open my heart to him.

Conclusion

Glory be to the Father, and to the Son, and to the Holy Spirit,
as it was in the beginning, is now, and ever shall be,
world without end. Amen.

March 2015

Sunday 15th March,
Fourth Sunday of Lent
John 3:14—21

Jesus said to Nicodemus, "And just as Moses lifted up the serpent in the wilderness, so must the Son of Man be lifted up, that whoever believes in him may have eternal life. For God so loved the world that he gave his only Son, so that everyone who believes in him may not perish but may have eternal life. Indeed, God did not send the Son into the world to condemn the world, but in order that the world might be saved through him. Those who believe in him are not condemned; but those who do not believe are condemned already, because they have not believed in the name of the only Son of God. And this is the judgement, that the light has come into the world, and people loved darkness rather than light because their deeds were evil. For all who do evil hate the light and do not come to the light, so that their deeds may not be exposed. But those who do what is true come to the light, so that it may be clearly seen that their deeds have been done in God."

- "God so loved the world that he gave his only Son." Someone has said that if all the scriptures had been lost except these eleven words, we would have enough to give us hope. God, I thank you for this statement of your love for us all.

- Jesus, the Light of the World, enlightens everyone, often in mysterious ways that others cannot understand. An early-Church writer says: "Sinners, deprived of the light, worship in the dark." Lord, let me live in the light that streams from you.

Monday 16th March
John 4:46—50

Now there was a royal official whose son lay ill in Capernaum. When he heard that Jesus had come from Judea to Galilee, he went and begged him to come down and heal his son, for he was at the point of death. Then Jesus said to him, "Unless you see signs and wonders you will not believe." The official said to him, "Sir, come down before my little boy dies." Jesus said to him, "Go; your son will live." The man believed the word that Jesus spoke to him and started on his way.

- Jesus reproaches the people who are looking for something sensational. Yet the words of Jesus pack as mighty a punch as any action. The royal official hears the word of Jesus and believes it.

- Do I believe that the word of Jesus is enough to conquer death and lead to eternal life? I give thanks for the attention I pay to God's Word through *Sacred Space*.

Tuesday 17th March,
St. Patrick
Matthew 13:24—30

He put before them another parable: "The kingdom of heaven may be compared to someone who sowed good seed in his field; but while everybody was asleep, an enemy came and sowed weeds among the wheat, and then went away. So when the plants came up and bore grain, then the weeds appeared as well. And the slaves of the householder came and said to him, 'Master, did you not sow good seed in your field? Where, then, did these weeds come from?' He answered, 'An enemy has done this.' The slaves said to him, 'Then do you want us to go and gather them?' But he replied, 'No; for in gathering the weeds you would uproot the wheat along with them. Let both of them grow together until the harvest; and at harvest time I will tell the reapers, Collect the weeds first and bind them in bundles to be burned, but gather the wheat into my barn.'"

- Lord, is the field of my heart a dreadful mix of wheat and weeds? Some of my weeds have deep roots, such as my personality defects. Teach me to be patient with these.

- Make me patient with the weeds I notice in others. Don't let me start tearing them up, lest I do more harm than good.

Wednesday 18th March
John 5:17—23

Jesus said to the Jews, "My Father is still working, and I also am working." For this reason the Jews were seeking all the more to kill him, because he was not only breaking the sabbath, but was also calling God his own Father, thereby making himself equal to God.

Jesus said to them, "Very truly, I tell you, the Son can do nothing on his own, but only what he sees the Father doing; for whatever the Father does, the Son does likewise. The Father loves the Son and shows him all that he himself is doing; and he will show him greater works than these, so that you will be astonished. Indeed, just as the Father raises the dead and gives them life, so also the Son gives life to whomsoever he wishes. The Father judges no one but has given all judgement to the Son, so that all may honour the Son just as they honour the Father. Anyone who does not honour the Son does not honour the Father who sent him."

- Jesus is utterly attentive to the Father. This attention allows the Father's creative, life-giving love to flow through Christ to those around him. Perfect love demands perfect attention. How attentive will I be to the people in my life today?

- The relationship between the Father and Son is perfect. The Father is reflected in all that the Son does. Do I bear witness to God's work in what I say and do?

Thursday 19th March,
St. Joseph
Matthew 1:18—25

Now the birth of Jesus the Messiah took place in this way. When his mother Mary had been engaged to Joseph, but before they lived together, she was found to be with child from the Holy Spirit. Her husband Joseph, being a righteous man and unwilling to expose her to public disgrace, planned to dismiss her quietly. But just when he had resolved to do this, an angel of the Lord appeared to him in a dream and said, "Joseph, son of David, do not be afraid to take Mary as your wife, for the child conceived in her is from the Holy Spirit. She will bear a son, and you are to name him Jesus, for he will save his people from their sins." All this took place to fulfil what had been spoken by the Lord through the prophet: "Look, the virgin shall conceive and bear a son, and they shall name him Emmanuel," which means, "God is with us." When Joseph awoke from sleep, he did as the angel of the Lord commanded him; he took her as his wife, but had no marital relations with her until she had borne a son; and he named him Jesus.

- Lord, when my problems seem heavy and impenetrable, may I recall that you are watching to help me even in the most unexpected circumstances. I must be still enough to hear the angel's voice and courageous enough to act on it.

- God, you give your help and guidance to those who trust in you. Where do I need your help and guidance today?

Friday 20th March
John 7:1—2, 10, 25—30

Jesus went about in Galilee. He did not wish to go about in Judea because the Jews were looking for an opportunity to kill him. Now the Jewish festival of Booths was near. . . . But after his brothers had gone to the festival, then he also went, not publicly but as it were in secret. . . . Now some of the people of Jerusalem were saying, "Is not this the man whom they are trying to kill? And here he is, speaking openly, but they say nothing to him! Can it be that the authorities really know that this is the Messiah? Yet we know where this man is from; but when the Messiah comes, no one will know where he is from." Then Jesus cried out as he was teaching in the temple, "You know me, and you know where I am from. I have not come on my own. But the one who sent me is true, and you do not know him. I know him, because I am from him, and he sent me." Then they tried to arrest him, but no one laid hands on him, because his hour had not yet come.

- The people think they know who Jesus is and where he comes from. We make snap judgements about others all the time, not realizing how our own limitations blind us to their truth.

- Today, Lord, open my eyes to see the extraordinary people with whom I deal with daily. And let me see myself thus also.

Saturday 21st March
John 7:40—49

When they heard these words, some in the crowd said, "This is really the prophet." Others said, "This is the Messiah." But some asked, "Surely the Messiah does not come from Galilee, does he? Has not the scripture said that the Messiah is descended from David and comes from Bethlehem, the village where David lived?" So there was a division in the crowd because of him. Some of them wanted to arrest him, but no one laid hands on him.

Then the temple police went back to the chief priests and Pharisees, who asked them, "Why did you not arrest him?" The police answered, "Never has anyone spoken like this!" Then the Pharisees replied, "Surely you have not been deceived too, have you? Has any one of the authorities or of the Pharisees believed in him? But this crowd, which does not know the law—they are accursed."

- The police were sent to Jesus to arrest him, but they came back empty-handed, exclaiming, "Never has anyone spoken like this!" Familiarity can blunt us to the revolutionary power of Christ's words.

- Lord, grant that I may hear your words as if for the first time.

March 22—28

Something to think and pray about each day this week:

Gospel Values

I work with homeless kids. They're tough, but sometimes one will sit down in front of me and say: "Can I ask you something?" "Sure," I reply. He admits he has seriously offended society in some way, then says: "You won't give up on me, will you?" What shall I say?

The conviction that everyone is to be loved infinitely and unconditionally is the basis of a commitment to justice. Starting with myself, I believe that I am loved infinitely. I am also valued beyond price. My value comes from the infinite love which the Giver of the gifts has for me. So I am of infinite value.

Such a notion is countercultural in Western culture. But if we value people by Gospel values, the person who is paralysed from the neck down and incapable of lifting a finger has the same value as the person who employs a thousand people. All are loved infinitely by God.

I am valued and loved unconditionally. Nothing can separate me from the love of God. The one thing in this world that never changes is God's love. Nothing, not even my own sinfulness, can take away the value and dignity that God's love bestows on me. Again, this is countercultural; society devalues evildoers, those who kill, rob, and rape. But our faith reminds us that no one ever forfeits the love of God or their dignity as a human being, no matter what they do.

So what shall I say?

The Presence of God

I reflect for a moment on God's presence around me and in me.
The creator of the universe is in the sun and the moon, the earth,
every molecule, every atom, everything that is:
God is in every beat of my heart. God is with me now.

Freedom

"A thick and shapeless tree-trunk would never believe
that it could become a statue, admired as a miracle of sculpture,
and would never submit itself to the chisel of the sculptor,
who sees by her genius what she can make of it" (St. Ignatius).
I ask for the grace to let myself be shaped by my loving Creator.

Consciousness

Knowing that God loves me unconditionally,
I look honestly over the last day, its events and my feelings.
Do I have something to be grateful for? Then I give thanks.
Is there something I am sorry for? Then I ask forgiveness.

The Word

I read the Word of God slowly, a few times over, and I listen to what
God is saying to me. (Please turn to your scripture on the following
pages. Inspiration points are there should you need them. When you
are ready, return here to continue.)

Conversation

What is stirring in me as I pray?
Am I consoled, troubled, left cold?
I imagine Jesus himself standing or sitting at my side,
and I share my feelings with him.

Conclusion

Glory be to the Father, and to the Son, and to the Holy Spirit,
as it was in the beginning, is now, and ever shall be,
world without end. Amen.

March 2015

Sunday 22nd March,
Fifth Sunday of Lent
John 12:20—26

Now among those who went up to worship at the festival were some Greeks. They came to Philip, who was from Bethsaida in Galilee, and said to him, "Sir, we wish to see Jesus." Philip went and told Andrew; then Andrew and Philip went and told Jesus. Jesus answered them, "The hour has come for the Son of Man to be glorified. Very truly, I tell you, unless a grain of wheat falls into the earth and dies, it remains just a single grain; but if it dies, it bears much fruit. Those who love their life lose it, and those who hate their life in this world will keep it for eternal life. Whoever serves me must follow me, and where I am, there will my servant be also. Whoever serves me, the Father will honour."

- Jesus, in this time of prayer, I imagine you putting a grain of wheat into my hand. You and I chat about what it can mean.

- When I next eat bread, it will have a deeper significance for me. When I share in the Eucharist, I will try to be aware that it means your own life, which is blessed, broken, shared out, and consumed for the life of the world.

Monday 23rd March
John 8:7—11

When they kept on questioning him, he straightened up and said to them, "Let anyone among you who is without sin be the first to throw a stone at her." And once again he bent down and wrote on the ground. When they heard it, they went away, one by one, beginning with the elders; and Jesus was left alone with the woman standing before him. Jesus straightened up and said to her, "Woman, where are they? Has no one condemned you?" She said, "No one, sir." And Jesus said, "Neither do I condemn you. Go your way, and from now on do not sin again."

- In prayer we often feel condemned or shamed for our past. We condemn ourselves for past meanness or for using other people. We may also feel ashamed for certain feelings or for aspects of our personalities.

- We can do nothing better than come before the Lord with our shame and sin and allow the words of mercy, "I do not condemn you," to fill the emptiness inside us.

Tuesday 24th March
John 8:28—30

Jesus said to the disciples, "When you have lifted up the Son of Man, then you will realize that I am he, and that I do nothing on my own, but I speak these things as the Father instructed me. And the one who sent me is with me; he has not left me alone, for I always do what is pleasing to him." As he was saying these things, many believed in him.

- "I always do what is pleasing to the Father." This reveals the heart of Jesus' spirituality.

- I pray that this same phrase may become the truth of my life, too, because God is so good to me.

Wednesday 25th March,
Annunciation of the Lord
Luke 1:26—35

In the sixth month the angel Gabriel was sent by God to a town in Galilee called Nazareth, to a virgin . . . whose name was Mary. And he came to her and said, "Greetings, favoured one! The Lord is with you." But she was much perplexed by his words and pondered what sort of greeting this might be. The angel said to her, "Do not be afraid, Mary, for you have found favour with God. And now, you will conceive in your womb and bear a son, and you will name him Jesus. He will be great, and will be called the Son of the Most High, and the Lord God will give to him the throne of his ancestor David. He will reign over the house of Jacob for ever, and of his kingdom there will be no end." Mary said to the angel, "How can this be, since I am a virgin?" The angel said to her, "The Holy Spirit will come upon you, and the power of the Most High will overshadow you; therefore the child to be born will be holy; he will be called Son of God."

• A young woman feels the touch of God. Rooted in this personal encounter, Mary entrusts her life, her reputation, and her entire being to the divine plan for the good of the world.

• Lord, nothing is impossible to you. Overshadow me with your presence, so that I may not limit your power to my small and narrow boundaries. Enable me to entrust my life to you and to your plans for me.

Thursday 26th March
John 8:51—56

Jesus said, "Very truly, I tell you, whoever keeps my word will never see death." The Jews said to him, "Now we know that you have a demon. Abraham died, and so did the prophets; yet you say, 'Whoever keeps my word will never taste death.' Are you greater than our father Abraham, who died? The prophets also died. Who do you claim to be?" Jesus answered, "If I glorify myself, my glory is nothing. It is my Father who glorifies me, he of whom you say, 'He is our God,' though you do not know him. But I know him; if I were to say that I do not know him, I would be a liar like you. But I do know him and I keep his word. Your ancestor Abraham rejoiced that he would see my day; he saw it and was glad."

• At an advanced age, Abraham answered God's call to undertake an immense journey toward the Promised Land. He believed in God's promises to him. Four thousand years later, we are still a pilgrim people, and the promises are still being made to each one of us.

- "Whoever keeps my word will not taste death." Lord, do I truly believe this? Then, like Abraham, let me hear each word of yours and keep it. I am to be "a keeper of the word."

Friday 27th March
John 10:31—38

The Jews took up stones again to stone him. Jesus replied, "I have shown you many good works from the Father. For which of these are you going to stone me?" The Jews answered, "It is not for a good work that we are going to stone you, but for blasphemy, because you, though only a human being, are making yourself God." Jesus answered, "Is it not written in your law, 'I said, you are gods'? If those to whom the word of God came were called 'gods'—and the scripture cannot be annulled—can you say that the one whom the Father has sanctified and sent into the world is blaspheming because I said, 'I am God's Son'? If I am not doing the works of my Father, then do not believe me. But if I do them, even though you do not believe me, believe the works, so that you may know and understand that the Father is in me and I am in the Father."

- Jesus often impresses upon us the need to act upon his word. One can argue with words, but deeds cannot be contradicted. They speak for themselves.

- The Word is planted deep in me, and I pray in the words of the apostle James, Let me be a doer of the word, and not a forgetful hearer (see Jas 1:22). The world watches the deeds of Christians and is often not impressed.

Saturday 28th March
John 11:45—56

Many of the Jews therefore, who had come with Mary and had seen what Jesus did, believed in him. But some of them went to the Pharisees and told them what he had done. So the chief priests and the Pharisees called a meeting of the council, and said, "What are we to do? This man is performing many signs. If we let him go on like this, everyone will believe in him, and the Romans will come and destroy both our holy place and our nation." But one of them, Caiaphas, who was high priest that year, said to them, "You know nothing at all! You do not understand that it is better for you to have one man die for the people than to have the whole nation destroyed." He did not say this on his own, but being high priest that year he prophesied that Jesus was about to die for the nation, and not for the nation only, but to gather into one the dispersed children of God. So from that day on they planned to put him to death. Jesus therefore no longer walked about openly among the Jews, but went from there to a town called Ephraim in the region near the wilderness; and he remained there with the disciples. Now the Passover of the Jews was near, and many went up from the country to Jerusalem before the Passover to purify themselves. They were looking for Jesus and were asking one another as they stood in the temple, "What do you think? Surely he will not come to the festival, will he?"

- Caiaphas is afraid that the popularity of Jesus will draw down the wrath of Rome and destroy both the Temple—the holy place—and the nation. In his blindness, he cannot see that the Jewish people are themselves the temple.

- Do I appreciate that I, too, am a temple of the living God? Lord, take away my blindness so that I can see myself as you see me.

March 29—April 4

Something to think and pray about each day this week:

The Mystery of God's Compassion

Imagine John, a boy of twelve who has been abused by his father all his life. I ask myself: "How does God see this young man?" Surely our God of compassion must have a special place in his heart for him, for his innocent suffering.

Now imagine Gerry. He's eighteen, and he robs defenceless people to feed a drug habit. Why? Because the only way he can cope with having been sexually abused as a child is to take drugs. How does a God of compassion see Gerry? I don't pretend to know. I doubt there is some tidy solution somewhere. But love does strange things.

A mother once came to me and said: "Father, I don't know what to do. My son is a drug user. He has often come into the house demanding money, and if I didn't have it to give him, he'd smash all the windows in the room. Sometimes he has even beaten me, because I didn't have the money for his drugs. I don't know what to do. Declan's in jail, Father, and now I have my first bit of peace in five years."

"And do you ever go to visit him?" I asked.

"Ah, Father, I go up to see him every Saturday afternoon without fail. Sure, isn't he still my son?" Declan had never said sorry to her, but she could still say: "Sure, isn't he still my son?" I learned a lot from her about love, and about God, and about how I should love. What should I have said to her?

The Presence of God

In the silence of my innermost being,
in the fragments of my yearned-for wholeness,
can I hear the whispers of God's presence?
Can I remember when I felt God's nearness,
when we walked together and I let myself be embraced by God's love?

Freedom

"There are very few people
who realize what God would make of them
if they abandoned themselves into his hands,
and let themselves be formed by his grace" (St. Ignatius).
I ask for the grace to trust myself totally to God's love.

Consciousness

How do I find myself today?
Where am I with God? With others?
Do I have something to be grateful for? Then I give thanks.
Is there something I am sorry for? Then I ask forgiveness.

The Word

I take my time to read the Word of God, slowly, a few times, allowing myself to dwell on anything that strikes me. (Please turn to your scripture on the following pages. Inspiration points are there should you need them. When you are ready, return here to continue.)

Conversation

Do I notice myself reacting as I pray with the Word of God?
Do I feel challenged, comforted, angry?
Imagining Jesus sitting or standing by me,
I speak out my feelings, as one trusted friend to another.

Conclusion

Glory be to the Father, and to the Son, and to the Holy Spirit,
as it was in the beginning, is now, and ever shall be,
world without end. Amen.

March 2015

Sunday 29th March,
Palm Sunday of the Lord's Passion
Mark 14:17—25

When it was evening, he came with the twelve. And when they had taken their places and were eating, Jesus said, "Truly I tell you, one of you will betray me, one who is eating with me." They began to be distressed and to say to him one after another, "Surely, not I?" He said to them, "It is one of the twelve, one who is dipping bread into the bowl with me. For the Son of Man goes as it is written of him, but woe to that one by whom the Son of Man is betrayed! It would have been better for that one not to have been born."

While they were eating, he took a loaf of bread, and after blessing it he broke it, gave it to them, and said, "Take; this is my body." Then he took a cup, and after giving thanks he gave it to them, and all of them drank from it. He said to them, "This is my blood of the covenant, which is poured out for many. Truly I tell you, I will never again drink of the fruit of the vine until that day when I drink it new in the kingdom of God."

- The betrayal of Jesus by Judas was dramatic and obvious. Do I join the disciples in saying "Surely, not I?" My betrayals may not be so dramatic or so obvious. What are my little, hidden, daily betrayals of Jesus? Of others?

- Jesus blessed and gave thanks for the food laid before them. The custom of saying grace before and after meals is not widely practised now. Perhaps I could revive it for myself and in my home.

Monday 30th March
John 12:1—6

Six days before the Passover Jesus came to Bethany, the home of Lazarus, whom he had raised from the dead. There they gave a dinner for him. Martha served, and Lazarus was one of those at the table with him. Mary took a pound of costly perfume made of pure nard, anointed Jesus' feet, and wiped them with her hair. The house

124

was filled with the fragrance of the perfume. But Judas Iscariot, one of his disciples (the one who was about to betray him), said, "Why was this perfume not sold for three hundred denarii and the money given to the poor?" (He said this not because he cared about the poor, but because he was a thief; he kept the common purse and used to steal what was put into it.)

- Shortly after Mary's action, Jesus will himself wash his disciples' feet, in a similar act of love and humility.

- The mystery of salvation is whether we will accept absolute and unconditional love and allow it to envelop us wholly.

Tuesday 31st March
John 13:21–24, 26–27, 30

Jesus was troubled in spirit, and declared, "Very truly, I tell you, one of you will betray me." The disciples looked at one another, uncertain of whom he was speaking. One of his disciples—the one whom Jesus loved—was reclining next to him; Simon Peter therefore motioned to him to ask Jesus of whom he was speaking. . . . Jesus answered, "It is the one to whom I give this piece of bread when I have dipped it in the dish." So when he had dipped the piece of bread, he gave it to Judas son of Simon Iscariot. After he received the piece of bread, Satan entered into him. Jesus said to him, "Do quickly what you are going to do." . . . So, after receiving the piece of bread, he immediately went out. And it was night.

- "And it was night" is not simply a description of the time of day; it is a stark image of the gloom of sin and rejection.

- Judas walks into the darkness—away from Jesus, the true light that the darkness cannot overcome. He will die in despair, in a pride so stiff-necked that it selects the misery of damnation rather than the happiness offered by a kindly God.

Wednesday 1st April
Matthew 26:14—19

Then one of the twelve, who was called Judas Iscariot, went to the chief priests and said, "What will you give me if I betray him to you?" They paid him thirty pieces of silver. And from that moment he began to look for an opportunity to betray him.

On the first day of Unleavened Bread the disciples came to Jesus, saying, "Where do you want us to make the preparations for you to eat the Passover?" He said, "Go into the city to a certain man, and say to him, 'The Teacher says, My time is near; I will keep the Passover at your house with my disciples.'" So the disciples did as Jesus had directed them, and they prepared the Passover meal.

- Is Judas motivated by anger and disappointment? Had he a different vision of the messianic kingdom than Jesus? Did he resent that Jesus saw through him when he protested at the waste of Mary's costly ointment at the feast?

- One thing is clear: he refused to accept Jesus as he was. He refused to see that he, not God, must change. Are we willing to accept our need to change as well?

Thursday 2nd April,
Holy Thursday
John 13:2—15

During supper Jesus, knowing that the Father had given all things into his hands, and that he had come from God and was going to God, got up from the table, took off his outer robe, and tied a towel around himself. Then he poured water into a basin and began to wash the disciples' feet and to wipe them with the towel that was tied around him. He came to Simon Peter, who said to him, "Lord, are you going to wash my feet?" Jesus answered, "You do not know now what I am doing, but later you will understand." Peter said to him, "You will never wash my feet." Jesus answered, "Unless I wash you, you have no share with me." Simon Peter said to him, "Lord, not my feet only but also my hands and my head!" Jesus said to him, "One who has bathed does not need to wash, except for the feet, but is entirely clean. And you are clean, though not all of you." For he knew who was to betray him; for this reason he said, "Not all of you are clean." After he had washed their feet, had put on his robe, and had returned to the table, he said to them, "Do you know what I have done to you? You call me Teacher and Lord—and you are right, for that is what I am. So if I, your Lord and Teacher, have washed your feet, you also ought to wash one another's feet. For I have set you an example, that you also should do as I have done to you."

- Do I feel like Peter, when Jesus kneels at my feet? Let me hear him whisper to me: "Unless I wash you, you have no share with me." Have I the courage and the generosity to accept his humble service and unconditional love?

- Jesus' instruction—to do to others what he does to us—was not intended to stop at the church door. How can I bear witness as a servant of God in my life today?

Friday 3rd April,
Good Friday
John 19:16—25

So they took Jesus; and carrying the cross by himself, he went out to what is called The Place of the Skull, which in Hebrew is called Golgotha. There they crucified him, and with him two others, one on either side, with Jesus between them. Pilate also had an inscription written and put on the cross. It read, "Jesus of Nazareth, the King of the Jews." Many of the Jews read this inscription, because the place where Jesus was crucified was near the city; and it was written in Hebrew, in Latin, and in Greek. Then the chief priests of the Jews said to Pilate, "Do not write, 'The King of the Jews,' but, 'This man said, I am King of the Jews.'" Pilate answered, "What I have written I have written." When the soldiers had crucified Jesus, they took his clothes and divided them into four parts, one for each soldier. They also took his tunic; now the tunic was seamless, woven in one piece from the top. So they said to one another, "Let us not tear it, but cast lots for it to see who will get it." This was to fulfil what the scripture says, "They divided my clothes among themselves, and for my clothing they cast lots." And that is what the soldiers did.

- We can only dimly imagine the love Jesus had for his mother. He now shows exquisite care for her and also commits to her the task of caring for the early Church.

- Later, we find her praying with the disciples before Pentecost (see Acts 1:14). Surely she prays with us and guides us toward her Son.

Saturday 4th April,
Holy Saturday
Luke 24:1—12

On the first day of the week, at early dawn, they came to the tomb, taking the spices that they had prepared. They found the stone rolled away from the tomb, but when they went in, they did not find the body. While they were perplexed about this, suddenly two men in dazzling clothes stood beside them. The women were terrified and bowed their faces to the ground, but the men said to them, "Why do you look for the living among the dead? He is not here, but has risen. Remember how he told you, while he was still in Galilee, that the Son of Man must be handed over to sinners, and be crucified, and on the third day rise again." Then they remembered his words, and returning from the tomb, they told all this to the eleven and to all the rest. Now it was Mary Magdalene, Joanna, Mary the mother of James, and the other women with them who told this to the apostles. But these words seemed to them an idle tale, and they did not believe them. But Peter got up and ran to the tomb; stooping and looking in, he saw the linen cloths by themselves; then he went home, amazed at what had happened.

- We can picture the women moving through the garden with heavy hearts, oblivious to the dawning spring morning. They are oblivious, above all, to the glorious presence of the risen Christ not a stone's throw away.

- Lord, help me to realize that when I am weighed down with sorrow, anxiety, or hopelessness, you are no further from me than you were to the women in that dawn garden.

April 5—11

Something to think and pray about each day this week:

Passionate in Prayer

The great mystic St. Teresa of Avila says that in the Song of Songs the Lord is teaching the soul how to pray. We can, she tells us, make the bride's prayer our own.

My own reaction to the experience of praying the Song of Songs was a revelation to me. I have to say it felt completely alien to me—almost shocking in its loving, desiring, tactile imagery:

> "I am faint with love.
> O that his left hand were under my head.
> and that his right hand embraced me!" (Sg 2:5–6)

But perhaps Teresa was right, and this is the kind of language God longs to hear the soul speak. This would mean that we might have to radically shift our perception of what it truly is to love and be loved by God. Ecstatic delight in God's presence is not the preserve of mystics, inaccessible to people living among the commonplace realities of everyday life. Prayer as passionate seeking, as desolation in the absence of the beloved and rapture in finding him—this kind of prayer is not only possible for all of us, but it is the kind of prayer that God, himself passionately in love with us, wants to hear.

The Presence of God

God is with me, but more,
God is within me, giving me existence.
Let me dwell for a moment on God's life-giving presence
in my body, my mind, my heart,
and in the whole of my life.

Freedom

Many countries are at this moment suffering
the agonies of war.
I bow my head in thanksgiving for my freedom.
I pray for all prisoners and captives.

Consciousness

I remind myself that I am in the presence of the Lord.
I will take refuge in his loving heart.
He is my strength in times of weakness.
He is my comforter in times of sorrow.

The Word

I read the Word of God slowly, a few times over, and I listen to what
God is saying to me. (Please turn to your scripture on the following
pages. Inspiration points are there should you need them. When you
are ready, return here to continue.)

Conversation

How has God's Word moved me? Has it left me cold?
Has it consoled me or moved me to act in a new way?
I imagine Jesus standing or sitting beside me;
I turn and share my feelings with him.

Conclusion

Glory be to the Father, and to the Son, and to the Holy Spirit,
as it was in the beginning, is now, and ever shall be,
world without end. Amen.

April 2015

Sunday 5th April,
Easter Sunday
John 20:1—9

Early on the first day of the week, while it was still dark, Mary Magdalene came to the tomb and saw that the stone had been removed from the tomb. So she ran and went to Simon Peter and the other disciple, the one whom Jesus loved, and said to them, "They have taken the Lord out of the tomb, and we do not know where they have laid him." Then Peter and the other disciple set out and went towards the tomb. The two were running together, but the other disciple outran Peter and reached the tomb first. He bent down to look in and saw the linen wrappings lying there, but he did not go in. Then Simon Peter came, following him, and went into the tomb. He saw the linen wrappings lying there, and the cloth that had been on Jesus' head, not lying with the linen wrappings but rolled up in a place by itself. Then the other disciple, who reached the tomb first, also went in, and he saw and believed; for as yet they did not understand the scripture, that he must rise from the dead.

- What were their thoughts, Peter and John, as they went running to the tomb? Mary Magdalene did not think Jesus was risen. She said "they" had taken the Lord out of the tomb. Peter, impulsive as ever, went straight into the tomb. John lingered. What would I have done? How might I have reacted?

- One of the things that convinces Peter and John that Jesus is risen is that the cloth which had been over his head is "rolled up in a place by itself." This is no hasty, secretive departure. It is calm, and ordered, and glorious.

Monday 6th April
Matthew 28:8—10

The women left the tomb quickly with fear and great joy, and ran to tell his disciples. Suddenly Jesus met them and said, "Greetings!" And they came to him, took hold of his feet, and worshipped him. Then Jesus said to them, "Do not be afraid; go and tell my brothers to go to Galilee; there they will see me."

- Lord, you fill me with confident joy and tell me not to be afraid. Strengthened by encountering you, you send me to the "Galilees" of my world, where you are often disguised in the poor, the deprived, the oppressed.

- Let me be a witness to you, an agent of hope and encouragement to all whom I meet.

Tuesday 7th April
John 20:11—18

Mary stood weeping outside the tomb. As she wept, she bent over to look into the tomb; and she saw two angels in white, sitting where the body of Jesus had been lying, one at the head and the other at the feet. They said to her, "Woman, why are you weeping?" She said to them, "They have taken away my Lord, and I do not know where they have laid him." When she had said this, she turned round and saw Jesus standing there, but she did not know that it was Jesus. Jesus said to her, "Woman, why are you weeping? For whom are you looking?" Supposing him to be the gardener, she said to him, "Sir, if you have carried him away, tell me where you have laid him, and I will take him away." Jesus said to her, "Mary!" She turned and said to him in Hebrew, "Rabbouni!" (which means Teacher). Jesus said to her, "Do not hold on to me, because I have not yet ascended to the Father. But go to my brothers and say to them, 'I am ascending to my Father and your Father, to my God and your God.'" Mary Magdalene went and announced to the disciples, "I have seen the Lord"; and she told them that he had said these things to her.

- There is a journey here from the darkness of unfaith, to partial faith, and finally to perfect faith. Mary's seeing is clouded by disappointment, grief, and unspeakable loss. But the sound of

Jesus' voice and the use of her name gives her new vision. She recognizes him and is filled with hope and joy.

- Lord, the Easter event bids me to leave my tomb of self-absorption and hopelessness. I am called to walk with Easter eyes. Let me bear witness to your risen presence in our shadowed and fractured world. May my humble efforts of advocacy and solidarity enable others to rise from their tombs and live.

Wednesday 8th April
Luke 24:13, 15—17, 19, 22—23, 25—29

Two of the disciples were going to a village called Emmaus. While they were talking and discussing, Jesus himself came near and went with them, but their eyes were kept from recognizing him. And he said to them, "What are you discussing with each other while you walk along?" . . . They replied, "The things about Jesus of Nazareth. . . . Moreover, some women of our group astounded us. They were at the tomb early this morning, and when they did not find his body there, they came back and told us that they had indeed seen a vision of angels who said that he was alive." . . . Then he said to them, "Oh, how foolish you are. . . . Was it not necessary that the Messiah should suffer these things and then enter into his glory?" Then . . . he interpreted to them the things about himself in all the scriptures. As they came near the village to which they were going, he walked ahead as if he were going on. But they urged him strongly, saying, "Stay with us, because it is almost evening and the day is now nearly over." So he went in to stay with them.

- This story of shattered hopes and loss of dreams is familiar to us. Jesus' gentle accompaniment and listening presence enables two downcast disciples to express their story. Only then does he offer them a more life-giving interpretation of recent events. As recognition dawns, their hearts are ablaze.

- Jesus, in times of disillusionment and faded dreams, you stand at the door of my life waiting for me to invite you in. May the experience of your risen presence bring about a transformation in my daily engagement with others. Teach me how to listen well, both to my own story and theirs.

Thursday 9th April
Luke 24:35—40

Then the disciples told what had happened on the road, and how he had been made known to them in the breaking of the bread. While they were talking about this, Jesus himself stood among them and said to them, "Peace be with you." They were startled and terrified, and thought that they were seeing a ghost. He said to them, "Why are you frightened, and why do doubts arise in your hearts? Look at my hands and my feet; see that it is I myself. Touch me and see; for a ghost does not have flesh and bones as you see that I have." And when he had said this, he showed them his hands and his feet.

- Jesus comes as consoler, with words of peace, to the fearful and doubt-filled disciples. Their world had been turned upside down. They were terrified when confronted with the living presence of him whom they knew to be dead.

- Jesus uses many means to strengthen their fragile faith. He shows his wounds; they can touch him; he eats with them. How does he strengthen my faith?

Friday 10th April
John 21:1—7

After these things Jesus showed himself again to the disciples by the Sea of Tiberias; and he showed himself in this way. Gathered there together were Simon Peter, Thomas called the Twin, Nathanael of Cana in Galilee, the sons of Zebedee, and two others of his disciples. Simon Peter said to them, "I am going fishing." They said to him, "We will go with you." They went out and got into the boat, but that night they caught nothing. Just after daybreak, Jesus stood on the beach; but the disciples did not know that it was Jesus. Jesus said to them, "Children, you have no fish, have you?" They answered him, "No." He said to them, "Cast the net to the right side of the boat, and you will find some." So they cast it, and now they were not able to haul it in because there were so many fish. That disciple whom Jesus loved said to Peter, "It is the Lord!"

- A night of futile fishing leaves empty nets and empty hearts. Jesus takes the initiative and meets them in the early morning light. He invites them to eat: "Breakfast is ready!"

- In the Eucharist, there is an abundant table ready for us as well—of food, love, warmth, and great joy. Here fractured relationships are healed.

Saturday 11th April
Mark 16:9—15

Now after he rose early on the first day of the week, he appeared first to Mary Magdalene, from whom he had cast out seven demons. She went out and told those who had been with him, while they were mourning and weeping. But when they heard that he was alive and had been seen by her, they would not believe it. After this he appeared in another form to two of them, as they were walking into the country. And they went back and told the rest, but they did not believe them. Later he appeared to the eleven themselves as they were sitting at the table; and he upbraided them for their lack of faith and stubbornness, because they had not believed those who saw him after he had risen. And he said to them, "Go into all the world and proclaim the good news to the whole creation."

- Mark's gospel highlights the way of discipleship, where the cross and resurrection are intertwined. Jesus takes the initiative by challenging the disciples' incredulity and obstinacy.

- Jesus, before I ever go searching for you, you already search for me. But do I recognize you and do I respond? Help me to practise what I believe and to live in the liberating truth that you are indeed risen!

April 12—18

Something to think and pray about each day this week:

God's Delight

Wisdom, the first of all creation and God's endless delight, is described as follows:

> I was beside him, like a master worker,
> and I was daily his delight,
> rejoicing before him always,
> rejoicing in his inhabited world
> and delighting in the human race. (Prv 8:30–31)

If we are indeed created in God's image, then our human play is rooted in divine play. Every creature plays, especially the young—from kittens and puppies to bullocks and tiger cubs. As children, we play with joyful abandon, delighting our parents as Wisdom delighted God day after day. But in our prayer, the child in us is often stifled. Without a child's sense of wonder, our praise of God becomes sterile.

Yet it is the child in us who can most truly live in a state of becoming—untrammelled by the past, always open to growth and change. It is the child in us who can truly be open to God's constant invitation to be born again, to be part of the creation which is itself constantly being re-created. It is the child in us who can thrill to a sense of closeness to the source of all creation.

I am God's delight. I can play spontaneously before my Creator and take joy in the human story, despite its disasters. I can also become a "master worker" collaborating with God in the shaping of the future.

The Presence of God
To be present is to arrive as one is and open up to the other.
At this instant, as I arrive here, God is present waiting for me.
God always arrives before me, desiring to connect with me
even more than my most intimate friend.
I take a moment and greet my loving God.

Freedom
"In these days, God taught me
as a schoolteacher teaches a pupil" (St. Ignatius).
I remind myself that there are things God has to teach me yet,
and I ask for the grace to hear them and let them change me.

Consciousness
How am I really feeling? Lighthearted? Heavy hearted?
I may be very much at peace, happy to be here.
Equally, I may be frustrated, worried, or angry.
I acknowledge how I really am. It is the real me that the Lord loves.

The Word
I take my time to read the Word of God, slowly, a few times, allowing myself to dwell on anything that strikes me. (Please turn to your
scripture on the following pages. Inspiration points are there should
you need them. When you are ready, return here to continue.)

Conversation
What feelings are rising in me
as I pray and reflect on God's Word?
I imagine Jesus himself sitting or standing beside me,
and I open my heart to him.

Conclusion
Glory be to the Father, and to the Son, and to the Holy Spirit,
as it was in the beginning, is now, and ever shall be,
world without end. Amen.

April 2015

Sunday 12th April,
Second Sunday of Easter
John 20:19–21

When it was evening on that day, the first day of the week, and the doors of the house where the disciples had met were locked for fear of the Jews, Jesus came and stood among them and said, "Peace be with you." After he said this, he showed them his hands and his side. Then the disciples rejoiced when they saw the Lord. Jesus said to them again, "Peace be with you. As the Father has sent me, so I send you."

- Are the doors of my heart locked? Do I not expect Jesus to show up and visit me? Am I afraid—afraid that my well-ordered ways of thinking and doing things might be turned upside down if I let Jesus in?

- Jesus, batter my unyielding heart and break down my defences and come in.

Monday 13th April
John 3:1–6

Now there was a Pharisee named Nicodemus, a leader of the Jews. He came to Jesus by night and said to him, "Rabbi, we know that you are a teacher who has come from God; for no one can do these signs that you do apart from the presence of God." Jesus answered him, "Very truly, I tell you, no one can see the kingdom of God without being born from above." Nicodemus said to him, "How can anyone be born after having grown old? Can one enter a second time into the mother's womb and be born?" Jesus answered, "Very truly, I tell you, no one can enter the kingdom of God without being born of water and Spirit. What is born of the flesh is flesh, and what is born of the Spirit is spirit."

- When I let the Good Spirit guide me, life takes on a new dimension. I am no longer stuck in a groove, living a flat, dull life. I begin to notice God more. I see people freshly as images of God and as extraordinary immortals.

- Lord, help me to see myself as a carrier and sharer of God's great love. Let me become a freer spirit and a happier person.

Tuesday 14th April
John 3:7—15

Jesus said to Nicodemus, "Do not be astonished that I said to you, 'You must be born from above.' The wind blows where it chooses, and you hear the sound of it, but you do not know where it comes from or where it goes. So it is with everyone who is born of the Spirit." Nicodemus said to him, "How can these things be?" Jesus answered him, "Are you a teacher of Israel, and yet you do not understand these things? Very truly, I tell you, we speak of what we know and testify to what we have seen; yet you do not receive our testimony. If I have told you about earthly things and you do not believe, how can you believe if I tell you about heavenly things? No one has ascended into heaven except the one who descended from heaven, the Son of Man. And just as Moses lifted up the serpent in the wilderness, so must the Son of Man be lifted up, that whoever believes in him may have eternal life."

- Although Nicodemus is a Pharisee, a Jewish leader, he is in the dark. He knows the Law. Yet this very knowledge and certainty prevents him from being open to the ways of God, and it stifles the activity of the Holy Spirit.

- Lord, help me to change, to leave behind previous certainties that stifled the activity of your Holy Spirit in me. Grace me with a disciple's ear. Let me be born again to a new way of being and a new mode of living. May I move more sensitively each day, guided by the gentle wind of your Spirit.

Wednesday 15th April
John 3:16—21

Jesus said, "For God so loved the world that he gave his only Son, so that everyone who believes in him may not perish but may have eternal life. Indeed, God did not send the Son into the world to condemn the world, but in order that the world might be saved through him. Those who believe in him are not condemned; but those who do not believe are condemned already, because they have not believed in the name of the only Son of God. And this is the judgement, that the light has come into the world, and people loved darkness rather than light because their deeds were evil. For all who do evil hate the light and do not come to the light, so that their deeds may not be exposed. But those who do what is true come to the light, so that it may be clearly seen that their deeds have been done in God."

- To live the message of John's gospel requires that one move from the shadows of darkness into the light. To stake our life on Jesus—the promised gift of God—is to know now this life of God, moving, living, and acting in us today.

- Jesus, you are the face of God revealed, a light shining out in our darkened world. I move between the shadow lands of darkness and light. With each daily encounter, may the relationship between us deepen.

Thursday 16th April
John 3:31—36

The one who comes from above is above all; the one who is of the earth belongs to the earth and speaks about earthly things. The one who comes from heaven is above all. He testifies to what he has seen and heard, yet no one accepts his testimony. Whoever has accepted his testimony has certified this, that God is true. He whom God has sent speaks the words of God, for he gives the Spirit without measure. The Father loves the Son and has placed all things in his hands. Whoever believes in the Son has eternal life; whoever disobeys the Son will not see life, but must endure God's wrath.

- Giving and receiving—the deepest relationship of love—shines out in this text. The reciprocal love of Father and Son, a love without limits, is poured out on us through the Holy Spirit. May I give to others what I am constantly receiving.

- Lord, you alone can satisfy the longing of my heart and its many contradictions. In this year of faith, confirm my personal faith and commitment to you. May the example of my life invite others to believe in you.

Friday 17th April
John 6:1—14

After this Jesus went to the other side of the Sea of Galilee, also called the Sea of Tiberias. A large crowd kept following him, because they saw the signs that he was doing for the sick. Jesus went up the mountain and sat down there with his disciples. Now the Passover, the festival of the Jews, was near. When he looked up and saw a large crowd coming towards him, Jesus said to Philip, "Where are we to buy bread for these people to eat?" He said this to test him, for he himself knew what he was going to do. Philip answered him, "Six months' wages would not buy enough bread for each of them to get a little." One of his disciples, Andrew, Simon Peter's brother, said to him, "There is a boy here who has five barley loaves and two fish. But what are they among so many people?" Jesus said, "Make the people sit down." Now there was a great deal of grass in the place; so they sat down, about five thousand in all. Then Jesus took the loaves, and when he had given thanks, he distributed them to those who were seated; so also the fish, as much as they wanted. When they were satisfied, he told his disciples, "Gather up the fragments left over, so that nothing may be lost." So they gathered them up, and from the fragments of the five barley loaves, left by those who had eaten, they filled twelve baskets. When the people saw the sign that he had done, they began to say, "This is indeed the prophet who is to come into the world."

- Jesus, you do not want to be "king." You dream of a community where everyone is equal. You want no one dominating. You want everyone to feel accepted and respected.

- Reveal to me ways in which I dominate. Do I think I am better than others? Can I admit when I'm wrong? Don't let me play at being "king"!

Saturday 18th April
John 6:16—21

When evening came, his disciples went down to the lake, got into a boat, and started across the lake to Capernaum. It was now dark, and Jesus had not yet come to them. The lake became rough because a strong wind was blowing. When they had rowed about three or four miles, they saw Jesus walking on the lake and coming near the boat, and they were terrified. But he said to them, "It is I; do not be afraid." Then they wanted to take him into the boat, and immediately the boat reached the land towards which they were going.

- The disciples travel without Jesus, but without him they will be lost. With him they arrive "immediately." What does this teach me about staying close to Jesus? Do I take him into my boat every day?

- Human beings cannot control storms and waves. So the disciples are given here a revelation of the mysterious power of Jesus. He is indeed human, but divine, too! He uses his power for our good.

April 19—25

Something to think and pray about each day this week:

Refreshed in Christ

If we are to nourish faith for tomorrow, we are challenged today to imagine a different quality of Christian commitment than existed before. This will involve a rediscovery of Christ as "disturbing freshness."

Sixty years ago, Henri de Lubac described Christ as "the great disturber," but also as the new image of God and of humanity, who brings refreshing novelty into a tired world. He was asking how we had arrived at a situation where Christianity was seen either as the enemy of full humanity, or, worse still, as a boring and empty legend. These same accusations are alive today, though in a different cultural context.

Our lived culture is nine-tenths invisible; we live by unstated and unexamined perceptions. But this world of images and values has immense, if often unconscious, impact on our capacity for life decisions, including, of course, the decision about faith in God.

When science claims a monopoly on truth, spiritual wisdom is ignored and even despised. It is a liberation to realize, with Cardinal Newman, that existential truth can only be found when the whole person is involved; some forms of knowledge are accessible only through love.

Many are now seeking for a spiritual consciousness beyond the confusion and fragmentation of our day. There is a hunger, less shy or silent than a generation back, for something more, which Christians may identify as the "disturbing freshness of Christ."

The Presence of God

What is present to me is what has a hold on my becoming.
I reflect on the presence of God always there in love,
amidst the many things that have a hold on me.
I pause and pray that I may let God
affect my becoming in this precise moment.

Freedom

If God were trying to tell me something, would I know?
If God were reassuring me or challenging me, would I notice?
I ask for the grace to be free of my own preoccupations
and open to what God may be saying to me.

Consciousness

Knowing that God loves me unconditionally,
I can afford to be honest about how I am.
How has the last day been, and how do I feel now?
I share my feelings openly with the Lord.

The Word

God speaks to each one of us individually. I need to listen to what
he is saying to me. (Please turn to your scripture on the following
pages. Inspiration points are there should you need them. When you
are ready, return here to continue.)

Conversation

What is stirring in me as I pray?
Am I consoled, troubled, left cold?
I imagine Jesus himself standing or sitting at my side,
and I share my feelings with him.

Conclusion

Glory be to the Father, and to the Son, and to the Holy Spirit,
as it was in the beginning, is now, and ever shall be,
world without end. Amen.

April 2015

Sunday 19th April,
Third Sunday of Easter
Luke 24:35—48

Then they told what had happened on the road, and how he had been made known to them in the breaking of the bread. While they were talking about this, Jesus himself stood among them and said to them, "Peace be with you." They were startled and terrified, and thought that they were seeing a ghost. He said to them, "Why are you frightened, and why do doubts arise in your hearts? Look at my hands and my feet; see that it is I myself. Touch me and see; for a ghost does not have flesh and bones as you see that I have." And when he had said this, he showed them his hands and his feet. While in their joy they were disbelieving and still wondering, he said to them, "Have you anything here to eat?" They gave him a piece of broiled fish, and he took it and ate in their presence. Then he said to them, "These are my words that I spoke to you while I was still with you—that everything written about me in the law of Moses, the prophets, and the psalms must be fulfilled." Then he opened their minds to understand the scriptures, and he said to them, "Thus it is written, that the Messiah is to suffer and to rise from the dead on the third day, and that repentance and forgiveness of sins is to be proclaimed in his name to all nations, beginning from Jerusalem. You are witnesses of these things."

- The Greeks thought that only the soul survived after death. But Luke emphasises that the risen Jesus is the same as the man who walked our earth. His wounds are still showing. The real Jesus is indeed back with his friends, and doing all he can to help them to believe. Only then can they be "witnesses of these things."

- The faith of the disciples is based on the fact that Jesus is with them again. But he seems to have forgotten their sins! Now they must forget the wrongdoing of others against themselves. The world would be transformed if we all did this.

Monday 20th April
John 6:22—27

The next day the crowd that had stayed on the other side of the lake saw that there had been only one boat there. They also saw that Jesus had not got into the boat with his disciples, but that his disciples had gone away alone. Then some boats from Tiberias came near the place where they had eaten the bread after the Lord had given thanks. So when the crowd saw that neither Jesus nor his disciples were there, they themselves got into the boats and went to Capernaum looking for Jesus. When they found him on the other side of the lake, they said to him, "Rabbi, when did you come here?" Jesus answered them, "Very truly, I tell you, you are looking for me, not because you saw signs, but because you ate your fill of the loaves. Do not work for the food that perishes, but for the food that endures for eternal life, which the Son of Man will give you."

- Lord, I can be like the crowd, seeking only to satisfy my immediate hungers. Forgive the times when I have used you to serve my interests.

- Remind me that the Father's seal is imprinted within me. Let this truth nourish my hungering spirit.

Tuesday 21st April
John 6:30—35

So they said to him, "What sign are you going to give us then, so that we may see it and believe you? What work are you performing? Our ancestors ate the manna in the wilderness; as it is written, 'He gave them bread from heaven to eat.'" Then Jesus said to them, "Very truly, I tell you, it was not Moses who gave you the bread from heaven, but it is my Father who gives you the true bread from heaven. For the bread of God is that which comes down from heaven and gives life to the world." They said to him, "Sir, give us this bread always." Jesus said to them, "I am the bread of life.

Whoever comes to me will never be hungry, and whoever believes in me will never be thirsty."

- Jesus points out to the crowd that it was God rather than Moses who provided the hungry Israelites with manna. Now he himself is God's divine intervention in our world. He is the once-and-for-all gift of God to us.

- Lord, today you hold out to me the same words you held out to those Galileans so long ago. In every Eucharist, you bring me life, even if I do not understand how. By partaking of the bread of life, let me become your hands, your feet, your heart in the world.

Wednesday 22nd April
John 6:37—40

Jesus said to them, "Everything that the Father gives me will come to me, and anyone who comes to me I will never drive away; for I have come down from heaven, not to do my own will, but the will of him who sent me. And this is the will of him who sent me, that I should lose nothing of all that he has given me, but raise it up on the last day. This is indeed the will of my Father, that all who see the Son and believe in him may have eternal life; and I will raise them up on the last day."

- Jesus seeks to draw those who listened to him into a profound relationship. He asks them to believe in his wonderful promises about eternal life.

- Jesus, you invite me to partake in a life that is indestructible. I am to share in the very life of God. This sharing has already begun. May my life and prayer witness that I belong where you are. Bring me—and all others—home to you.

Thursday 23rd April
John 6:47—51

Jesus said to the people, "Very truly, I tell you, whoever believes has eternal life. I am the bread of life. Your ancestors ate the manna in the wilderness, and they died. This is the bread that comes down from heaven, so that one may eat of it and not die. I am the living bread that came down from heaven. Whoever eats of this bread will live for ever; and the bread that I will give for the life of the world is my flesh."

- Jesus reveals to the people how they will obtain eternal life. They are to allow him to be the nourishment of their inner lives. This will call for faith in him and also for a change in lifestyle. Love must inform their every word and deed.

- Lord, you are a magnetic force forever drawing me into life and love. I am reminded of St. Augustine's words about the Eucharist: "Become what you receive." May all that is you flow into me. Help me to change in order to become like you.

Friday 24th April
John 6:52—57

The Jews then disputed among themselves, saying, "How can this man give us his flesh to eat?" So Jesus said to them, "Very truly, I tell you, unless you eat the flesh of the Son of Man and drink his blood, you have no life in you. Those who eat my flesh and drink my blood have eternal life, and I will raise them up on the last day; for my flesh is true food and my blood is true drink. Those who eat my flesh and drink my blood abide in me, and I in them. Just as the living Father sent me, and I live because of the Father, so whoever eats me will live because of me."

- The Jews were disputing about "this man." They reject what they cannot understand.

- Jesus, I don't understand you either; you are so mysterious! Give me a stronger faith in you so that I may believe what I cannot understand. Make me more like a child who trusts a parent without needing to know why.

Saturday 25th April,
St. Mark, Evangelist
Mark 16:15—20

And Jesus said to the disciples, "Go into all the world and proclaim the good news to the whole creation. The one who believes and is baptized will be saved; but the one who does not believe will be condemned. And these signs will accompany those who believe: by using my name they will cast out demons; they will speak in new tongues; they will pick up snakes in their hands, and if they drink any deadly thing, it will not hurt them; they will lay their hands on the sick, and they will recover." So then the Lord Jesus, after he had spoken to them, was taken up into heaven and sat down at the right hand of God. And they went out and proclaimed the good news everywhere, while the Lord worked with them and confirmed the message by the signs that accompanied it.

- Do I ever refer the Good News to myself? The good news about me is that I am massively loved and cared for by God. Jesus has died for me. I am promised eternal life. God is with me always, so I need not be afraid. Good news indeed!

- Lord, the goodness that I find in life comes from you. Good things don't just happen; it is you who make them happen. I am showered with your gifts. Let me then be a grateful and joyous person.

April 26—May 2

Something to think and pray about each day this week:

Growing into Faith

While scripture, the sacraments, and Church teaching are at the heart of faith, they may not always be the best point of departure for the faith journey of the young. The seed of faith must be allowed to take root and grow at its own pace.

So we need to cultivate first an open *disposition* in young people; it will be the "good soil" for the things of the spirit. This openness is evident in curiosity and wonder. Its simple expression can be the request, "Tell me more!" Jesus invented his parables to surprise and to open the imagination. The gospels tell a story of slow learners whose imaginations were closed against seeing God in the man Jesus. But when imagination blossomed in the Resurrection, the unthinkable became thinkable, and faith emerged as living conviction.

Next comes *decision*. Today faith has to be a free and personal decision, where an individual states his or her belief in Christ. Past generations may have made such a decision only implicitly and socially, but now it has to be explicit and personal.

Lastly comes *difference*. In the past, it took courage to be an unbeliever; now it takes a high level of courage to be a believer. To be a Christian means resisting dominant but ambiguous values. This does not mean being negative or fundamentalist, but courageous and wise in discerning good from bad.

The Presence of God

At any time of the day or night, we can call on Jesus.
He is always waiting, listening for our call.
What a wonderful blessing.
No phone needed, no e-mails—just a whisper.

Freedom

I need to rise above the noise—
the noise that interrupts and separates,
the noise that isolates.
I need to listen to God again.

Consciousness

Help me, Lord, to be more conscious of your presence.
Teach me to recognize your presence in others.
Fill my heart with gratitude for the times your love
has been shown to me through the care of others.

The Word

I read the Word of God slowly, a few times over, and I listen to what
God is saying to me. (Please turn to your scripture on the following
pages. Inspiration points are there should you need them. When you
are ready, return here to continue.)

Conversation

Do I notice myself reacting as I pray with the Word of God?
Do I feel challenged, comforted, angry?
Imagining Jesus sitting or standing by me,
I speak out my feelings, as one trusted friend to another.

Conclusion

Glory be to the Father, and to the Son, and to the Holy Spirit,
as it was in the beginning, is now, and ever shall be,
world without end. Amen.

April 2015

Sunday 26th April,
Fourth Sunday of Easter
John 10:11—18

Jesus said, "I am the good shepherd. The good shepherd lays down his life for the sheep. The hired hand, who is not the shepherd and does not own the sheep, sees the wolf coming and leaves the sheep and runs away—and the wolf snatches them and scatters them. The hired hand runs away because a hired hand does not care for the sheep. I am the good shepherd. I know my own and my own know me, just as the Father knows me and I know the Father. And I lay down my life for the sheep. I have other sheep that do not belong to this fold. I must bring them also, and they will listen to my voice. So there will be one flock, one shepherd. For this reason the Father loves me, because I lay down my life in order to take it up again. No one takes it from me, but I lay it down of my own accord. I have power to lay it down, and I have power to take it up again. I have received this command from my Father."

- "One flock, one shepherd." God thinks big. The divine project is to gather in everyone at the close of human history.

- This makes me look at awkward people in a new way—they are to be my eternal companions! Does it make me look at myself in a new way? Would I make a pleasant eternal companion if I died today?

Monday 27th April
John 10:7—10

So again Jesus said to them, "Very truly, I tell you, I am the gate for the sheep. All who came before me are thieves and bandits; but the sheep did not listen to them. I am the gate. Whoever enters by me will be saved, and will come in and go out and find pasture. The thief comes only to steal and kill and destroy. I came that they may have life, and have it abundantly."

- We live in a world of discordant voices.

- Lord, let me hear your voice, so that I may open the gate of my heart for you. Draw me to the pathways of life. May others then see me as a safe gateway leading to abundant life.

Tuesday 28th April
John 10:22—30

At that time the festival of the Dedication took place in Jerusalem. It was winter, and Jesus was walking in the temple, in the portico of Solomon. So the Jews gathered around him and said to him, "How long will you keep us in suspense? If you are the Messiah, tell us plainly." Jesus answered, "I have told you, and you do not believe. The works that I do in my Father's name testify to me; but you do not believe, because you do not belong to my sheep. My sheep hear my voice. I know them, and they follow me. I give them eternal life, and they will never perish. No one will snatch them out of my hand. What my Father has given me is greater than all else, and no one can snatch it out of the Father's hand. The Father and I are one."

- The festival of Dedication was a celebration of light. But the Jews remain in the dark, blind to the mystery of Jesus. Like them, I have my blind spots; the truth may be confronting me on some issue, but I close my eyes to it.

- Jesus, if I am to be your true disciple, I need to listen to your words. Draw me into the loving intimacy that you so long for me to experience.

Wednesday 29th April
John 12:44—50

Then Jesus cried aloud: "Whoever believes in me believes not in me but in him who sent me. And whoever sees me sees him who sent me. I have come as light into the world, so that everyone who believes in me should not remain in the darkness. I do not judge anyone who hears my words and does not keep them, for I came not to judge the world, but to save the world. The one who rejects me and does not receive my word has a judge; on the last day the word that I have spoken will serve as judge, for I have not spoken on my own, but the Father who sent me has himself given me a commandment about what to say and what to speak. And I know that his commandment is eternal life. What I speak, therefore, I speak just as the Father has told me."

- Jesus has come as light into the world. In this time of prayer, I allow myself to be bathed in this light.

- Just as natural light reveals what is hidden in the dark, God's Word reveals to us what is otherwise hidden from us. And just as natural light enables growth in living things, so exposure to the light of the Gospel brings growth to our spirits. My time of prayer brings growth in me, even though I may not notice it until later.

Thursday 30th April
John 13:16—17

Jesus said to them, "Very truly, I tell you, servants are not greater than their master, nor are messengers greater than the one who sent them. If you know these things, you are blessed if you do them."

- Jesus allows that there is a difference between knowing and doing. I take this time to let my knowing deepen, to become part of me.

- I am like a courier with a message, like a servant with a task; I do not sit with an idea but am blessed as I express God's love in my life.

Friday 1st May
John 14:1—6

Jesus said to his disciples, "Do not let your hearts be troubled. Believe in God, believe also in me. In my Father's house there are many dwelling-places. If it were not so, would I have told you that I go to prepare a place for you? And if I go and prepare a place for you, I will come again and will take you to myself, so that where I am, there you may be also. And you know the way to the place where I am going." Thomas said to him, "Lord, we do not know where you are going. How can we know the way?" Jesus said to him, "I am the way, and the truth, and the life. No one comes to the Father except through me."

- This is Jesus' farewell discourse. He speaks with words of encouragement, kindness, and promise to the disturbed disciples.

- In Jesus' words, there are no maps, no compasses, only Jesus. He promises to be the lodestar, the true guide. He will be our gateway into loving communion with the Father.

Saturday 2nd May
John 14:7—11

Jesus said to Thomas, "If you know me, you will know my Father also. From now on you do know him and have seen him." Philip said to him, "Lord, show us the Father, and we will be satisfied." Jesus said to him, "Have I been with you all this time, Philip, and you still do not know me? Whoever has seen me has seen the Father. How can you say, 'Show us the Father'? Do you not believe that I am in the Father and the Father is in me? The words that I say to you I do not speak on my own; but the Father who dwells in me does his works. Believe me that I am in the Father and the Father is in me; but if you do not, then believe me because of the works themselves."

- Jesus reveals the depth of relationship between Father and Son. To know the Son is to know the Father. For John, "knowing" is an affair of the heart, a felt-knowledge born of mutual love. It is not simply head-knowledge.

- I ask to know God deeply.

May 3—9

Something to think and pray about each day this week:

Being with Mary

Not everyone finds poetry manageable. I invite you, however, to let some lines of this beautiful poem by Gerard Manley Hopkins charm you. It hints at the intimate relationship between Mary and ourselves. I have abbreviated it considerably, but those who are caught by it can get the full text on the Internet. Note the short words and lines, and within them a richness of imagery. Think of the poem as a verbal sculpture, to be appreciated for its beauty and religious sensitivity.

"The Blessed Virgin Compared to the Air We Breathe"

Wild air, world-mothering air,
Nestling me everywhere, . . .
Minds me in many ways
Of her who not only
Gave God's infinity
Dwindled to infancy
Welcome in womb and breast,
Birth, milk, and all the rest
But mothers each new grace
That does now reach our race . . .
And makes, O marvellous!
New Nazareths in us,
Where she shall yet conceive
Him, morning, noon, and eve . . .

The Presence of God
As I sit here, the beating of my heart,
the ebb and flow of my breathing, the movements of my mind
are all signs of God's ongoing creation of me.
I pause for a moment and become aware
of this presence of God within me.

Freedom
I ask God's help,
to be free from my own preoccupations,
to be open to God in this time of prayer,
to come to love and serve him more.

Consciousness
Knowing that God loves me unconditionally,
I look honestly over the last day, its events and my feelings.
Do I have something to be grateful for? Then I give thanks.
Is there something I am sorry for? Then I ask forgiveness.

The Word
I take my time to read the Word of God, slowly, a few times, allowing myself to dwell on anything that strikes me. (Please turn to your
scripture on the following pages. Inspiration points are there should
you need them. When you are ready, return here to continue.)

Conversation
Remembering that I am still in God's presence,
I imagine Jesus himself standing or sitting beside me,
and I say whatever is on my mind, whatever is in my heart,
speaking as one friend to another.

Conclusion
Glory be to the Father, and to the Son, and to the Holy Spirit,
as it was in the beginning, is now, and ever shall be,
world without end. Amen.

May 2015

Sunday 3rd May,
Fifth Sunday of Easter
John 15:1—8

Jesus said to his disciples, "I am the true vine, and my Father is the vine-grower. He removes every branch in me that bears no fruit. Every branch that bears fruit he prunes to make it bear more fruit. You have already been cleansed by the word that I have spoken to you. Abide in me as I abide in you. Just as the branch cannot bear fruit by itself unless it abides in the vine, neither can you unless you abide in me. I am the vine, you are the branches. Those who abide in me and I in them bear much fruit, because apart from me you can do nothing. Whoever does not abide in me is thrown away like a branch and withers; such branches are gathered, thrown into the fire, and burned. If you abide in me, and my words abide in you, ask for whatever you wish, and it will be done for you. My Father is glorified by this, that you bear much fruit and become my disciples."

- I picture a grapevine with its branches, large and small.

- Which branch mirrors me? Is my branch healthy or a bit withered and tired? Can I accept the attention of the vine-grower as he prunes this branch? Can I trust that my branch can then bear much fruit at harvest time?

Monday 4th May
John 14:21—26

Jesus said to his disciples, "They who have my commandments and keep them are those who love me; and those who love me will be loved by my Father, and I will love them and reveal myself to them." Judas (not Iscariot) said to him, "Lord, how is it that you will reveal yourself to us, and not to the world?" Jesus answered him, "Those who love me will keep my word, and my Father will love them, and we will come to them and make our home with them. Whoever does not love me does not keep my words; and the word that you hear is not mine, but is from the Father who sent me. I have said these things to you while I am still with you. But the Advocate, the Holy Spirit, whom the Father will send in my name, will teach you everything, and remind you of all that I have said to you."

- Jesus, you repeatedly emphasise the importance of hearing the Word and completing it in a life that reflects servant love. Make your home now in my heart, and please bring your Father!

- Lord, thank you for the gift of the great Spirit of God, who is by my side, defending me, consoling me, and teaching me the ways of love.

Tuesday 5th May
John 14:27—31

Jesus said to his disciples, "Peace I leave with you; my peace I give to you. I do not give to you as the world gives. Do not let your hearts be troubled, and do not let them be afraid. You heard me say to you, 'I am going away, and I am coming to you.' If you loved me, you would rejoice that I am going to the Father, because the Father is greater than I. And now I have told you this before it occurs, so that when it does occur, you may believe. I will no longer talk much with you, for the ruler of this world is coming. He has no power over me; but I do as the Father has commanded me, so that the world may know that I love the Father. Rise, let us be on our way."

- Throughout the Old and New Testament, there are echoes of the words "Do not let your hearts be troubled." The evil forces of this world have no power over Jesus and need have no power over us as his disciples. We need not be afraid.

- Do I rejoice in the peace which Jesus gives me? Love changes everything, and my troubles and fears are to be put in their place within the limitless love that God has for me. This is the peace Jesus offers, not a life free of challenges or suffering.

162

Wednesday 6th May
John 15:5—8

J esus said to his disciples, "I am the vine, you are the branches. Those who abide in me and I in them bear much fruit, because apart from me you can do nothing. Whoever does not abide in me is thrown away like a branch and withers; such branches are gathered, thrown into the fire, and burned. If you abide in me, and my words abide in you, ask for whatever you wish, and it will be done for you. My Father is glorified by this, that you bear much fruit and become my disciples."

- "Ask for whatever you wish." If I abide in Jesus, heart to heart, I will want only what he wants.

- Jesus wants divine love to flow like a river in the world; this is the background to true prayer. "Thy will be done on earth."

Thursday 7th May
John 15:9—11

J esus said to his disciples, "As the Father has loved me, so I have loved you; abide in my love. If you keep my commandments, you will abide in my love, just as I have kept my Father's commandments and abide in his love. I have said these things to you so that my joy may be in you, and that your joy may be complete."

- If we could grasp God's unconditional love for us, life would be a radical journey of joy. Joy can be present in the midst of hardship. Jesus' joy is profound and deep, even in his passion. It is the joy of being loved by the Father.

- Lord, I do not know why you should care that my joy may be complete. But you do, so let me give time now to savour this and to praise and thank you.

Friday 8th May
John 15:12—17

J esus said to his disciples, "This is my commandment, that you love one another as I have loved you. No one has greater love than this, to lay down one's life for one's friends. You are my friends if you do what I command you. I do not call you servants any longer, because the servant does not know what the master is doing; but I have called you friends, because I have made known to you everything that I have heard from my Father. You did not choose me but I chose you. And I appointed you to go and bear fruit, fruit that will last, so that the Father will give you whatever you ask him in my name. I am giving you these commands so that you may love one another."

- Throughout the scriptures, a mark of the greatest favour is to be called the friend of God, as Abraham was (see Jas 2:23). In the secret scripture of my life I, too, am called the friend of God. This is my truth. I am highly favoured; I am unique and very special.

- Jesus models true friendship by sharing with me everything he has. I must not hoard this love but reach out in my turn to others who are starved of love. Because he chooses to love others through me, I have much to do.

Saturday 9th May
John 15:18—20

J esus said to his disciples, "If the world hates you, be aware that it hated me before it hated you. If you belonged to the world, the world would love you as its own. Because you do not belong to the world, but I have chosen you out of the world—therefore the world hates you. Remember the word that I said to you, 'Servants are not greater than their master.' If they persecuted me, they will persecute you; if they kept my word, they will keep yours also."

- Jesus gives us advance warning of tough times. Which of us wants to be hated? Instead we want to be affirmed for what we are and for the choices we make.

- But he tells us that the experience of rejection is an opportunity for us to live his passion in our own lives. In facing this, companionship with the suffering Christ strengthens us.

May 10—16

Something to think and pray about each day this week:

The Power of the Word

In his message for the forty-seventh World Communications Day, Pope Benedict XVI said that social media provides "portals of truth and faith, and new spaces for evangelisation." They are "new languages" which enable the infinite riches of the gospel to reach the hearts of all. Happily, Sacred Space has been developing its own Facebook presence on these lines. It invites people to enter into meditation, to form community, and to link with the Sacred Space site itself.

Benedict asked us to engage the questions and doubts of people searching for meaning in life. This requires that we be authentic. Further, visitors are to be enabled to encounter God's love through the use of symbols. Christian tradition offers a rich resource of these: the cross, icons, images of the Blessed Virgin, cribs, stained glass, statues, and paintings.

The pope observed that we can trust the power of the Word to touch hearts, far beyond our own efforts, and here we find this to be true. It happens because a deep desire for love and truth has been placed in the human heart by God, which opens us to the "kindly light" of faith. Benedict stresses that the most radical response to the questions of humankind is found in the person of Jesus Christ. This leads to practical charity and to an experience of Christian community. Benedict's is a heartening message for which we are grateful.

The Presence of God

Dear Jesus, today I call on you in a special way.
Mostly I come asking for favours.
Today I'd like just to be in your presence.
Let my heart respond to your love.

Freedom

"I am free."
When I look at these words in writing,
they seem to create in me a feeling of awe—
yes, a wonderful feeling of freedom.
Thank you, God.

Consciousness

Lord, you gave me the night to rest in sleep.
In my waking hours, may I not forget your goodness to me.
Guide me to share your blessings with others.

The Word

I read the Word of God slowly, a few times over, and I listen to what God is saying to me. (Please turn to your scripture on the following pages. Inspiration points are there should you need them. When you are ready, return here to continue.)

Conversation

Dear Jesus, I can open up my heart to you.
I can tell you everything that troubles me.
I know you care about all the concerns in my life.
Teach me to live in the knowledge
that you, who care for me today,
will care for me tomorrow and all the days of my life.

Conclusion

Glory be to the Father, and to the Son, and to the Holy Spirit,
as it was in the beginning, is now, and ever shall be,
world without end. Amen.

May 2015

Sunday 10th May,
Sixth Sunday of Easter
John 15:9—14

Jesus said to his disciples, "As the Father has loved me, so I have loved you; abide in my love. If you keep my commandments, you will abide in my love, just as I have kept my Father's commandments and abide in his love. I have said these things to you so that my joy may be in you, and that your joy may be complete. This is my commandment, that you love one another as I have loved you. No one has greater love than this, to lay down one's life for one's friends. You are my friends if you do what I command you."

- My love for others must not be conditioned by how they respond. Jesus loves me totally, whether I am good or bad or indifferent. My love must have that quality, too. This is costly love—it could demand my very life!

- This costly love will bear rich fruit, whether I see it or not. Just so, Jesus' love bears fruit only after his death. I must not be discouraged when my love seems to be wasted. True love never comes to an end (see 1 Cor 13:8). Loving actions are the building blocks of eternal life.

Monday 11th May
John 15:26—16:4

Jesus said to his disciples, "When the Advocate comes, whom I will send to you from the Father, the Spirit of truth who comes from the Father, he will testify on my behalf. You also are to testify because you have been with me from the beginning. I have said these things to you to keep you from stumbling. They will put you out of the synagogues. Indeed, an hour is coming when those who kill you will think that by doing so they are offering worship to God. And they will do this because they have not known the Father or me. But I have said these things to you so that when their hour comes you may remember that I told you about them. I did not say these things to you from the beginning, because I was with you."

- Terrible things have been done in God's name. But God's way is love, and Jesus assures us that those who do such things are misled.

- We ask to "know" him more closely so that we will not make the same mistakes. We pray for others who act without the motivation of love and yet think they are pleasing God.

Tuesday 12th May
John 16:5—11

Jesus said to his disciples, "But now I am going to him who sent me; yet none of you asks me, 'Where are you going?' But because I have said these things to you, sorrow has filled your hearts. Nevertheless, I tell you the truth: it is to your advantage that I go away, for if I do not go away, the Advocate will not come to you; but if I go, I will send him to you. And when he comes, he will prove the world wrong about sin and righteousness and judgement: about sin, because they do not believe in me; about righteousness, because I am going to the Father and you will see me no longer; about judgement, because the ruler of this world has been condemned."

- It is hard to lose someone we love, and so the disciples grieve. How much would I miss Jesus if he were no longer in my life?

- The gift of the Holy Spirit means we don't have to rely on our own resources to reach God. Our call is to become better attuned to the wavelength of the Spirit so that our lives are shaped by the Spirit.

Wednesday 13th May
John 16:12—15

Jesus said, "I still have many things to say to you, but you cannot bear them now. When the Spirit of truth comes, he will guide you into all the truth; for he will not speak on his own, but will speak whatever he hears, and he will declare to you the things that are to come. He will glorify me, because he will take what is mine and declare it to you. All that the Father has is mine. For this reason I said that he will take what is mine and declare it to you."

- Jesus is sensitive to his followers' limited understanding. By telling them he has more to tell them, he is in a gentle way preparing them! I ask his wisdom to know when it is good to speak and when it is better to wait and be silent.

- Jesus knows how anxious we can be both to let go of the past and to trust what the future will bring. Can I speak to him about my anxieties?

Thursday 14th May
St. Mathias, Apostle
John 15:15—17

Jesus said to his disciples, "I do not call you servants any longer, because the servant does not know what the master is doing; but I have called you friends, because I have made known to you everything that I have heard from my Father. You did not choose me but I chose you. And I appointed you to go and bear fruit, fruit that will last, so that the Father will give you whatever you ask him in my name. I am giving you these commands so that you may love one another."

- "Nothing is more practical than finding God, that is, than falling in love in a quite absolute, final way. What you are in love with, what seizes your imagination, will affect everything. It will decide what will get you out of bed in the mornings, what you will do with your evenings, how you spend your weekends, what you read, who you know, what breaks your heart, and what amazes you with joy and gratitude. Fall in love, stay in love, and it will decide everything" (Fr. Pedro Arrupe, S.J.).

- "You did not choose me but I chose you." Jesus' choosing of me gives me a sense of my place in the world, a sense of purpose. What fruit am I called on to bear?

Friday 15th May
John 16:20—23

Jesus said to his disciples, "Very truly, I tell you, you will weep and mourn, but the world will rejoice; you will have pain, but your pain will turn into joy. When a woman is in labour, she has pain, because her hour has come. But when her child is born, she no longer remembers the anguish because of the joy of having brought a human being into the world. So you have pain now; but I will see you again, and your hearts will rejoice, and no one will take your joy from you. On that day you will ask nothing of me. Very truly, I tell you, if you ask anything of the Father in my name, he will give it to you."

- Mary, Mother of God, experienced the heights and depths of human experience. In her "Yes" to the angel, she opened herself in trust. She experienced the joys and sorrows of any one who makes their way, step by step, on the dark road of faith.

- In this the month of Mary, can I find comfort and wisdom pondering what similarities exist between the experiences of Mary and my own?

Saturday 16th May
John 16:24—28

Jesus said to his disciples, "Ask and you will receive, so that your joy may be complete. I have said these things to you in figures of speech. The hour is coming when I will no longer speak to you in figures, but will tell you plainly of the Father. On that day you will ask in my name. I do not say to you that I will ask the Father on your behalf; for the Father himself loves you, because you have loved me and have believed that I came from God. I came from the Father and have come into the world; again, I am leaving the world and am going to the Father."

- A request for something in "Jesus' name" is to ask for something that will help to bring about God's reign on earth. So I pray, "Thy kingdom come. Thy will be done on earth."

- While God's kingdom is not "of this world," in the sense of sharing this world's values, it is certainly present wherever people live the Beatitudes and listen to and practise what Jesus teaches.

May 17—23

Something to think and pray about each day this week:

Embracing Forgiveness

In James Joyce's first novel, *A Portrait of the Artist as a Young Man*, a schoolboy's soul is tortured by sins of lust; he is convinced that his sins are beyond forgiveness because God is great and stern. He has, however, a glimmer of hope: his failure has not offended Our Lady. So he prays, in the words of Cardinal Newman:

> God once had meant to come on earth in heavenly glory, but we sinned; and then he could not safely visit us but with a shrouded majesty and a bedimmed radiance, for he was God. So he came himself in weakness, not in power, and he sent thee, a creature, in his stead, with a creature's comeliness and lustre, suited to our state. And now thy very face and form, dear Mother, speak to us of the eternal: not like earthly beauty, dangerous to look upon, but like the morning star which is thy emblem, bright and musical, breathing purity, telling of heaven and infusing peace. O harbinger of day! O light of the pilgrim! Lead us still as thou hast led. In the dark night, across the bleak wilderness, guide us on to our Lord Jesus, guide us home.

His eyes dimmed with tears, he looks humbly up to heaven, and weeps for the innocence he has lost. Later he finds a chapel and emerges from the confessional, a contrite young man of sixteen now at peace with God.

The Presence of God

I remind myself that, as I sit here now,
God is gazing on me with love and holding me in being.
I pause for a moment and think of this.

Freedom

I need to rise above the noise—
the noise that interrupts and separates,
the noise that isolates.
I need to listen to God again.

Consciousness

In God's loving presence, I unwind the past day,
starting from now and looking back, moment by moment.
I gather in all the goodness and light in gratitude.
I attend to the shadows and what they say to me,
seeking healing, courage, forgiveness.

The Word

I take my time to read the Word of God, slowly, a few times, allowing myself to dwell on anything that strikes me. (Please turn to your
scripture on the following pages. Inspiration points are there should
you need them. When you are ready, return here to continue.)

Conversation

Do I notice myself reacting as I pray with the Word of God?
Do I feel challenged, comforted, angry?
Imagining Jesus sitting or standing by me,
I speak out my feelings, as one trusted friend to another.

Conclusion

Glory be to the Father, and to the Son, and to the Holy Spirit,
as it was in the beginning, is now, and ever shall be,
world without end. Amen.

May 2015

Sunday 17th May,
Ascension of the Lord
Mark 16:15—20

And Jesus said to the disciples, "Go into all the world and proclaim the good news to the whole creation. The one who believes and is baptized will be saved; but the one who does not believe will be condemned. And these signs will accompany those who believe: by using my name they will cast out demons; they will speak in new tongues; they will pick up snakes in their hands, and if they drink any deadly thing, it will not hurt them; they will lay their hands on the sick, and they will recover." So then the Lord Jesus, after he had spoken to them, was taken up into heaven and sat down at the right hand of God. And they went out and proclaimed the good news everywhere, while the Lord worked with them and confirmed the message by the signs that accompanied it.

- Jesus commissions his disciples to bring the good news that God is on the side of the poor, the sick, the outcasts, and all those who suffer injustice. Those who cannot bear to have beggars, former prostitutes, servants, women, and children as their equals would simply not be at home in God's kingdom.

- Jesus, help me to be inclusive in my love. Open my narrow heart to include those who injure me or differ from me in so many ways.

Monday 18th May
John 16:29—33

His disciples said to Jesus, "Yes, now you are speaking plainly, not in any figure of speech! Now we know that you know all things, and do not need to have anyone question you; by this we believe that you came from God." Jesus answered them, "Do you now believe? The hour is coming, indeed it has come, when you will be scattered, each one to his home, and you will leave me alone. Yet I am not alone because the Father is with me. I have said this to you, so that in me you may have peace. In the world you face persecution. But take courage; I have conquered the world!"

- Peace and courage are two gifts that Jesus wants to leave with us. Peace comes from knowing he will be with us always. Courage comes from knowing that when we try to live in the light of the gospel, God's strength will shine out through our weakness.

- In what areas of my life do I need peace and courage at the present time?

Tuesday 19th May
John 17:1—3

After Jesus had spoken these words, he looked up to heaven and said, "Father, the hour has come; glorify your Son so that the Son may glorify you, since you have given him authority over all people, to give eternal life to all whom you have given him. And this is eternal life, that they may know you, the only true God, and Jesus Christ whom you have sent."

- The letters AMDG are an invitation to live *Ad Majorem Dei Gloriam,* "to the greater glory of God." I think of how my words, actions, and talents reflect God's glory and imagine myself signing them, AMDG.

- As I grow in the knowledge of God, I experience a taste of this glorious eternal life Christ promises us.

Wednesday 20th May
John 17:11—19

Jesus looked up to heaven and said, "And now I am no longer in the world, but they are in the world, and I am coming to you. Holy Father, protect them in your name that you have given me, so that they may be one, as we are one. While I was with them, I protected them in your name that you have given me. I guarded them, and not one of them was lost except the one destined to be lost, so that the scripture might be fulfilled. But now I am coming to you, and I speak these things in the world so that they may have my joy made complete in themselves. I have given them your word, and the world has hated them because they do not belong to the world, just as I do not belong to the world. I am not asking you to take them out of the world, but I ask you to protect them from the evil one. They do not belong to the world, just as I do not belong to the world. Sanctify them in the truth; your word is truth. As you have sent me into the world, so I have sent them into the world. And for their sakes I sanctify myself, so that they also may be sanctified in truth."

- Jesus' love for his disciples does not fade. It endures eternally.

- He asks the Father to protect and guide his followers. He entrusts us, his friends and companions, to the loving care of his Father.

Thursday 21st May
John 17:20—23

Jesus looked up to heaven and said, "Father, I ask not only on behalf of these, but also on behalf of those who will believe in me through their word, that they may all be one. As you, Father, are in me and I am in you, may they also be in us, so that the world may believe that you have sent me. The glory that you have given me I have given them, so that they may be one, as we are one, I in them and you in me, that they may become completely one, so that the world may know that you have sent me and have loved them even as you have loved me."

- That Jesus was and is the Son of God is the underlying theme in the Gospel of John. In turn, Jesus calls us to oneness with each other and with God.

- Does the life that I lead reflect my innermost truth—that I am the focus of intense divine loving?

Friday 22nd May
John 21:15—17

When they had finished breakfast, Jesus said to Simon Peter, "Simon son of John, do you love me more than these?" He said to him, "Yes, Lord; you know that I love you." Jesus said to him, "Feed my lambs." A second time he said to him, "Simon son of John, do you love me?" He said to him, "Yes, Lord; you know that I love you." Jesus said to him, "Tend my sheep." He said to him the third time, "Simon son of John, do you love me?" Peter felt hurt because he said to him the third time, "Do you love me?" And he said to him, "Lord, you know everything; you know that I love you." Jesus said to him, "Feed my sheep."

- Three times Peter answers Jesus that he loves him. He means it. Yet, gripped by fear and confusion during the passion of the Lord, Peter was unable to admit even to knowing Jesus. Could this happen to him again?

- Jesus understands and forgives our human frailties, but he never ceases to say to us, "Follow me."

Saturday 23rd May
John 21:20—25

Peter turned and saw the disciple whom Jesus loved following them; he was the one who had reclined next to Jesus at the supper and had said, "Lord, who is it that is going to betray you?" When Peter saw him, he said to Jesus, "Lord, what about him?" Jesus said to him, "If it is my will that he remain until I come, what is that to you? Follow me!" So the rumour spread in the community that this disciple would not die. Yet Jesus did not say to him that he would not die, but, "If it is my will that he remain until I come, what is that to you?"

This is the disciple who is testifying to these things and has written them, and we know that his testimony is true. But there are also many other things that Jesus did; if every one of them were written down, I suppose that the world itself could not contain the books that would be written.

- "The rumour spread!" In one of the stories of C. S. Lewis, the lead character—who is a Christ figure—is challenged about the way he has dealt with another. He replies, "I tell no one any story but their own!"

- Let me not interfere with what is going on between others and God.

May 24—30

Something to think and pray about each day this week:

In Our Lady's Care

Our Lady still keeps watch outside an empty monastery in Algeria. Nearly twenty years ago, its occupants—seven Trappist monks— were abducted and murdered. Their story was later made into the film *Of Gods and Men*.

Today we need examples of humble courage and dedication such as these monks provide. Despite the death threats issued to foreigners, they remained out of solidarity with their Muslim neighbours. Their choice was made with pain, soul-searching, and disagreement.

They were ordinary people, not very different from ourselves. They got on one another's nerves; they wavered in their decision. "Perhaps it would be better to go home to France and serve God in a quieter way? What good would our deaths bring? In a wave of violent deaths, the murder of a few monks would be nothing special." These men did not choose death—rather, it came their way and they had to adjust to it or feel that they had betrayed a silent God who was the love of their lives.

In his last testament, the abbot addresses his final sentence to his prospective killer: "Thank you, my friend of the last moment, who will not know what you are doing. . . . May we meet in heaven, like happy thieves, if it pleases God, our common Father." Our Lady surely approved of that prayer and welcomed the monks home after their final ordeal.

The Presence of God

What is present to me is what has a hold on my becoming.
I reflect on the presence of God always there in love,
amidst the many things that have a hold on me.
I pause and pray that I may let God
affect my becoming in this precise moment.

Freedom

"There are very few people
who realize what God would make of them
if they abandoned themselves into his hands,
and let themselves be formed by his grace" (St. Ignatius).
I ask for the grace to trust myself totally to God's love.

Consciousness

In the presence of my loving Creator,
I look honestly at my feelings over the last day—
the highs, the lows, and the level ground.
Can I see where the Lord has been present?

The Word

God speaks to each one of us individually. I need to listen to what
he is saying to me. (Please turn to your scripture on the following
pages. Inspiration points are there should you need them. When you
are ready, return here to continue.)

Conversation

What is stirring in me as I pray?
Am I consoled, troubled, left cold?
I imagine Jesus himself standing or sitting at my side,
and I share my feelings with him.

Conclusion

Glory be to the Father, and to the Son, and to the Holy Spirit,
as it was in the beginning, is now, and ever shall be,
world without end. Amen.

May 2015

Sunday 24th May,
Feast of Pentecost
John 20:19—23

When it was evening on that day, the first day of the week, and the doors of the house where the disciples had met were locked for fear of the Jews, Jesus came and stood among them and said, "Peace be with you." After he said this, he showed them his hands and his side. Then the disciples rejoiced when they saw the Lord. Jesus said to them again, "Peace be with you. As the Father has sent me, so I send you." When he had said this, he breathed on them and said to them, "Receive the Holy Spirit. If you forgive the sins of any, they are forgiven them; if you retain the sins of any, they are retained."

- In the Book of Genesis, God breathes on human beings to bring them life. Now Jesus breathes his Spirit into his disciples to give them new life. They will have power over sin, which otherwise deadens the human heart.

- Holy Spirit, I welcome you now into my small heart. Let today be "the first day of the week" for me, which means the first day of my renewed creation. Let us celebrate this together.

Monday 25th May
Mark 10:17—23

As he was setting out on a journey, a man ran up and knelt before him, and asked him, "Good Teacher, what must I do to inherit eternal life?" Jesus said to him, "Why do you call me good? No one is good but God alone. You know the commandments: 'You shall not murder; You shall not commit adultery; You shall not steal; You shall not bear false witness; You shall not defraud; Honour your father and mother.'" He said to him, "Teacher, I have kept all these since my youth." Jesus, looking at him, loved him and said, "You lack one thing; go, sell what you own, and give the money to the poor, and you will have treasure in heaven; then come, follow me."

When he heard this, he was shocked and went away grieving, for he had many possessions. Then Jesus looked around and said to his disciples, "How hard it will be for those who have wealth to enter the kingdom of God!"

- Jesus looked at the man and loved him. It is good to be reminded that before Jesus makes a judgement on what we say or do, he loves us. He loves us unconditionally for who we are and as we are. He also loves every effort that we make to live more lovingly.

- His "many possessions" were in fact enslaving this rich man. They gave him his sense of worth. It is disordered attachment to things, not the things themselves, that keep us from Jesus.

Tuesday 26th May
Mark 10:28—30

Peter began to say to Jesus, "Look, we have left everything and followed you." Jesus said, "Truly I tell you, there is no one who has left house or brothers or sisters or mother or father or children or fields, for my sake and for the sake of the good news, who will not receive a hundredfold now in this age—houses, brothers and sisters, mothers and children, and fields, with persecutions—and in the age to come eternal life."

- Jesus does not ask that we turn our back on our responsibilities. Rather he invites us to cultivate a freedom and generosity of spirit that is centered on the greater good.

- Can I ask Jesus to help me face, with courage and generosity, any responsibilities I might be running away from?

Wednesday 27th May
Mark 10:42—45

Jesus called the disciples and said to them, "You know that among the Gentiles those whom they recognize as their rulers lord it over them, and their great ones are tyrants over them. But it is not so among you; but whoever wishes to become great among you must be your servant, and whoever wishes to be first among you must be slave of all. For the Son of Man came not to be served but to serve, and to give his life a ransom for many."

- Being a servant or slave seems repulsive to the modern mind.

- I think of how I might give quiet, unrecognized, or unrewarded service to those around me, not announcing it or seeking recognition.

Thursday 28th May
Mark 10:46—52

They came to Jericho. As he and his disciples and a large crowd were leaving Jericho, Bartimaeus son of Timaeus, a blind beggar, was sitting by the roadside. When he heard that it was Jesus of Nazareth, he began to shout out and say, "Jesus, Son of David, have mercy on me!" Many sternly ordered him to be quiet, but he cried out even more loudly, "Son of David, have mercy on me!" Jesus stood still and said, "Call him here." And they called the blind man, saying to him, "Take heart; get up, he is calling you." So throwing off his cloak, he sprang up and came to Jesus. Then Jesus said to him, "What do you want me to do for you?" The blind man said to him, "My teacher, let me see again." Jesus said to him, "Go; your faith has made you well." Immediately he regained his sight and followed him on the way.

- It can be hard to stand up and be counted in society. We are conditioned not to make spectacles of ourselves. But unless we stand up for truth and justice, we fail others and condemn ourselves to mediocrity.

- What do you say to Jesus when he turns to you and says, "What do you want me to do for you"?

Friday 29th May
Mark 11:15—17

They came to Jerusalem. And Jesus entered the temple and began to drive out those who were selling and those who were buying in the temple, and he overturned the tables of the money-changers and the seats of those who sold doves; and he would not allow anyone to carry anything through the temple. He was teaching and saying, "Is it not written, 'My house shall be called a house of prayer for all the nations'? But you have made it a den of robbers."

- It is easy for my time of prayer to become a time of reflection, pondering, figuring things out. My prayer time can become like the Temple—seeming to be given to God but in fact committed to other activities, preoccupied with the affairs of the day.

- I ask God to help me to bring these concerns for blessing but not to seek to control them now.

Saturday 30th May
Mark 11:27—33

Again they came to Jerusalem. As he was walking in the temple, the chief priests, the scribes, and the elders came to him and said, "By what authority are you doing these things? Who gave you this authority to do them?" Jesus said to them, "I will ask you one question; answer me, and I will tell you by what authority I do these things. Did the baptism of John come from heaven, or was it of human origin? Answer me." They argued with one another, "If we say, 'From heaven,' he will say, 'Why then did you not believe him?' But shall we say, 'Of human origin'?"—they were afraid of the crowd, for all regarded John as truly a prophet. So they answered Jesus, "We do not know." And Jesus said to them, "Neither will I tell you by what authority I am doing these things."

- The opponents of Jesus question the source of his authority. They fear it may undermine their own power. Jesus preferred the company of sinners and tax collectors who made no claim to any authority of their own.

- True authority is not a personal possession. It comes from God and is to be used always with an eye on God. Whatever authority we have we must use sensitively, so that God would be pleased.

May 31—June 6

Something to think and pray about each day this week:

A Here-and-Now Kingdom

What does Jesus mean when he states that his kingdom "is not from this world" (Jn 18:36)? Does he mean that his kingdom belongs to another world, so that we can ignore it for now? No! He means rather that his project for our world comes from God, not from human beings. And when Matthew uses the term "kingdom of heaven" (Mt 13:45), is he referring to a kingdom distant from ours? No! He is respecting Jewish sensitivity about God's holy name, but he tells us clearly that the kingdom is at hand.

Jesus ushers in a new world order in which divine values prevail right now. He tells us to pray that God's will be done here on earth in the present time. This is our task. God will look after the heaven of the future.

We think of Mary as mild; we would not expect to find her in a protest march! But her Magnificat is an impassioned comment about what God is doing right before our eyes: "He has scattered the proud. He has brought down the powerful, and lifted up the lowly; he has filled the hungry, and sent the rich away empty" (see Lk 1:46–55). She sees the kingdom already being made visible in human history.

Mary's spirituality is contemporary, outward looking, other centered. It focuses on serving those around us in justice and love. Her concern is to be in tune with the divine project in the here and now. This concern is to be ours also.

The Presence of God

"I stand at the door and knock," says the Lord.
What a wonderful privilege
that the Lord of all creation desires to come to me.
I welcome his presence.

Freedom

Lord, grant me the grace to be free from the excesses of this life.
Let me not get caught up with the desire for wealth.
Keep my heart and mind free to love and serve you.

Consciousness

"There is a time and place for everything," as the saying goes.
Lord, grant that I may always desire
to spend time in your presence, to hear your call.

The Word

God speaks to each one of us individually. I need to listen to what
he is saying to me. (Please turn to your scripture on the following
pages. Inspiration points are there should you need them. When you
are ready, return here to continue.)

Conversation

The gift of speech is a wonderful gift.
May I use this gift with kindness.
May I be slow to utter harsh words,
hurtful words, and words spoken in anger.

Conclusion

Glory be to the Father, and to the Son, and to the Holy Spirit,
as it was in the beginning, is now, and ever shall be,
world without end. Amen.

Sunday 31st May,
Trinity Sunday
Matthew 28:16−20

Now the eleven disciples went to Galilee, to the mountain to which Jesus had directed them. When they saw him, they worshipped him; but some doubted. And Jesus came and said to them, "All authority in heaven and on earth has been given to me. Go therefore and make disciples of all nations, baptizing them in the name of the Father and of the Son and of the Holy Spirit, and teaching them to obey everything that I have commanded you. And remember, I am with you always, to the end of the age."

- The Gospel of Matthew was written for Jewish Christians. As the story unfolded, outsiders were introduced, such as the wise men, the centurion, and the Canaanite woman. We, too, were outsiders once, but now are inside. We are baptized into community, sharing in the life of the Father, Son, and Spirit.

- The disciples were slow to believe in Jesus' resurrection. He shared authority with them, that they might continue what he had begun in bringing others into the faith community. He calls us to live our baptism and to move beyond exclusion of others to a community that is open to all.

Monday 1st June
Mark 12:1−12

Then Jesus began to speak to them in parables. "A man planted a vineyard, put a fence around it, dug a pit for the wine press, and built a watch-tower; then he leased it to tenants and went to another country. When the season came, he sent a slave to the tenants to collect from them his share of the produce of the vineyard. But they seized him, and beat him, and sent him away empty-handed. And again he sent another slave to them; this one they beat over the head and insulted. Then he sent another, and that one they killed. And so it was with many others; some they beat, and others they killed.

He had still one other, a beloved son. Finally he sent him to them, saying, 'They will respect my son.' But those tenants said to one another, 'This is the heir; come, let us kill him, and the inheritance will be ours.' So they seized him, killed him, and threw him out of the vineyard. What then will the owner of the vineyard do? He will come and destroy the tenants and give the vineyard to others. Have you not read this scripture: 'The stone that the builders rejected has become the cornerstone; this was the Lord's doing, and it is amazing in our eyes'?" When they realized that he had told this parable against them, they wanted to arrest him, but they feared the crowd. So they left him and went away.

- "Silence the prophet!" Many prophets were ill-treated or killed because they disturbed people. Jesus, the beloved Son, would suffer the same fate as many prophets.

- How do I see my prophetic role? Do I feel silenced by an unfriendly environment, or do I have the courage to be prophetic by my life, word, and example?

Tuesday 2nd June
Mark 12:13—17

Then they sent to Jesus some Pharisees and some Herodians to trap him in what he said. And they came and said to him, "Teacher, we know that you are sincere, and show deference to no one; for you do not regard people with partiality, but teach the way of God in accordance with truth. Is it lawful to pay taxes to the emperor, or not? Should we pay them, or should we not?" But knowing their hypocrisy, he said to them, "Why are you putting me to the test? Bring me a denarius and let me see it." And they brought one. Then he said to them, "Whose head is this, and whose title?" They answered, "The emperor's." Jesus said to them, "Give to the emperor the things that are the emperor's, and to God the things that are God's." And they were utterly amazed at him.

- "Yes" or "No" will not always suffice today. We are citizens of the state and members of the Church. State laws and programs may be at variance with basic Christian beliefs.

- We ask ourselves, what values guide our lives and decisions? Do we have the courage to stand by our convictions?

Wednesday 3rd June
Mark 12:18—27

Some Sadducees, who say there is no resurrection, came to Jesus and asked him a question, saying, "Teacher, Moses wrote for us that if a man's brother dies, leaving a wife but no child, the man shall marry the widow and raise up children for his brother. There were seven brothers; the first married and, when he died, left no children; and the second married her and died, leaving no children; and the third likewise; none of the seven left children. Last of all the woman herself died. In the resurrection whose wife will she be? For the seven had married her." Jesus said to them, "Is not this the reason you are wrong, that you know neither the scriptures nor the power of God? For when they rise from the dead, they neither marry nor are given in marriage, but are like angels in heaven. And as for the dead being raised, have you not read in the book of Moses, in the story about the bush, how God said to him, 'I am the God of Abraham, the God of Isaac, and the God of Jacob'? He is God not of the dead, but of the living; you are quite wrong."

- God, Jesus says, is a God of the living, not of the dead. To be fully with God after death is a different way of being. We go through death to a new life; we do not merely come back to the equivalent of earthly living. As we are transformed by Love, there is continuity, yet radical difference.

- The Sadducees were confined by the old Law, and their beliefs were a filter that blocked hearing something new. We, too, can ask the wrong questions, hear what we want to hear, and thus limit receiving the true message of Jesus.

Thursday 4th June
Mark 12:28—34

One of the scribes came near and heard them disputing with one another, and seeing that Jesus answered them well, he asked him, "Which commandment is the first of all?" Jesus answered, "The first is, 'Hear, O Israel: the Lord our God, the Lord is one; you shall love the Lord your God with all your heart, and with all your soul, and with all your mind, and with all your strength.' The second is this, 'You shall love your neighbour as yourself.' There is no other commandment greater than these." Then the scribe said to him, "You are right, Teacher; you have truly said that 'he is one, and besides him there is no other'; and 'to love him with all the heart, and with all the understanding, and with all the strength,' and 'to love one's neighbour as oneself,'—this is much more important than all whole burnt-offerings and sacrifices." When Jesus saw that he answered wisely, he said to him, "You are not far from the kingdom of God." After that no one dared to ask him any question.

- "Love God!" This seems easy. "Love your neighbour!" This is harder. "Love yourself!" This seems alien to the Gospel, but there is a healthy self-love that acknowledges God's creative love in ourselves.

- God sees all that is made, including me, and says it is very good. Can I accept this gift happily?

Friday 5th June
Mark 12:35—37

While Jesus was teaching in the temple, he said, "How can the scribes say that the Messiah is the son of David? David himself, by the Holy Spirit, declared, 'The Lord said to my Lord,

"Sit at my right hand, until I put your enemies under your feet."' David himself calls him Lord; so how can he be his son?" And the large crowd was listening to him with delight.

- Jesus provoked people to think about who he really was. God, who was revealed in mysterious ways in the past, is now being made known by the incarnate Word.

- Who is Jesus for me? How would I introduce him to someone else? All titles are inadequate for him. Above all, he is the Son of God. Spending time with him is a means to knowing him more fully. There is an ongoing invitation to form a deeper relationship with him.

Saturday 6th June
Mark 12:38–44

As Jesus taught in the temple, he said, "Beware of the scribes, who like to walk around in long robes, and to be greeted with respect in the market-places, and to have the best seats in the synagogues and places of honour at banquets! They devour widows' houses and for the sake of appearance say long prayers. They will receive the greater condemnation." He sat down opposite the treasury, and watched the crowd putting money into the treasury. Many rich people put in large sums. A poor widow came and put in two small copper coins, which are worth a penny. Then he called his disciples and said to them, "Truly I tell you, this poor widow has put in more than all those who are contributing to the treasury. For all of them have contributed out of their abundance; but she out of her poverty has put in everything she had, all she had to live on."

- The poor widow, who would have been despised as such, is in fact the model for a disciple. What the widow gave might seem insignificant to many from the viewpoint of quantity. She is praised for her total generosity in giving all she had, not just what was over and above.

- Lord, let me be as generous with others as you are with me.

June 7—13

Something to think and pray about each day this week:

A Vote of Confidence

The Jesus of the gospels was always surprising people. He constantly cut across expectations. He was never dull or bland. Someone recently expressed this well by saying that Jesus was "funny." She wasn't referring to his sense of humour, but to the ways he disconcerted her and made her revise her own ways of looking at things.

It is good for us to ask the Holy Spirit to help us to overcome our familiarity with the words and story of Jesus, and to open us up daily to this surprising, disturbing, and captivating person. The gospel is like fresh bread for each day. Its freshness is a gift.

At the heart of the mystery of Jesus, we find his unique relationship with God. He calls God "Father" or "Abba," meaning "Daddy." This relationship dominates his life. It is this experience of being totally loved by God that gives him the courage to set out on his public ministry. In preaching the kingdom of God, Jesus is inviting us to share in his special relationship with the Father. We are offered the extravagant gift of being children of God just as we are.

Jesus fully accepted God's lavish love. It gave divine meaning to his life. It transformed everything he did and all that happened to him. When we live out of God's unconditional vote of confidence in us, everything changes, and our capacity for greatness is liberated.

The Presence of God

I remind myself that, as I sit here now,
God is gazing on me with love and holding me in being.
I pause for a moment and think of this.

Freedom

I need to rise above the noise—
the noise that interrupts and separates,
the noise that isolates.
I need to listen to God again.

Consciousness

In God's loving presence, I unwind the past day,
starting from now and looking back, moment by moment.
I gather in all the goodness and light in gratitude.
I attend to the shadows and what they say to me,
seeking healing, courage, forgiveness.

The Word

I take my time to read the Word of God, slowly, a few times, allowing myself to dwell on anything that strikes me. (Please turn to your scripture on the following pages. Inspiration points are there should you need them. When you are ready, return here to continue.)

Conversation

Do I notice myself reacting as I pray with the Word of God?
Do I feel challenged, comforted, angry?
Imagining Jesus sitting or standing by me,
I speak out my feelings, as one trusted friend to another.

Conclusion

Glory be to the Father, and to the Son, and to the Holy Spirit,
as it was in the beginning, is now, and ever shall be,
world without end. Amen.

June 2015

Sunday 7th June,
Feast of the Body and Blood of Christ
Mark 14:22—26

While they were eating, he took a loaf of bread, and after blessing it he broke it, gave it to them, and said, "Take; this is my body." Then he took a cup, and after giving thanks he gave it to them, and all of them drank from it. He said to them, "This is my blood of the covenant, which is poured out for many. Truly I tell you, I will never again drink of the fruit of the vine until that day when I drink it new in the kingdom of God." When they had sung the hymn, they went out to the Mount of Olives.

- Jesus became bread broken for us. The cup of blessing is the blood of the new covenant that would be poured out for us. Jesus drew on simple, everyday signs to present a profound message. His self-giving is complete, as are bread when it is eaten and wine when it is drunk. Nothing is left.

- As Eucharistic people, we are to be taken, blessed, broken, and given to others as Jesus was. His continued presence among us gives us nourishment, and we in turn nourish others.

Monday 8th June
Matthew 5:1—9

When Jesus saw the crowds, he went up the mountain; and after he sat down, his disciples came to him. Then he began to speak, and taught them, saying: "Blessed are the poor in spirit, for theirs is the kingdom of heaven. Blessed are those who mourn, for they will be comforted. Blessed are the meek, for they will inherit the earth. Blessed are those who hunger and thirst for righteousness, for they will be filled. Blessed are the merciful, for they will receive mercy. Blessed are the pure in heart, for they will see God. Blessed are the peacemakers, for they will be called children of God."

- I allow these blessings to come home to me. I imagine Jesus carefully speaking them to me, aware of my poverty, sadness, and hunger.

- As I live with difficulties, I seek to hear Jesus speaking the Beatitudes to me as I encounter them.

Tuesday 9th June
Matthew 5:13

Jesus said, "You are the salt of the earth; but if salt has lost its taste, how can its saltiness be restored? It is no longer good for anything, but is thrown out and trampled underfoot."

- Riches, power, and control are valued highly in our world. But Jesus draws on little things to teach deeper values.

- Salt preserves food; in the hands of a skilled cook it adds flavour to food. But its work is hidden. As salt of the earth, we can be effective in bringing more taste to life for others.

Wednesday 10th June
Matthew 5:17—19

Jesus said to the crowds, "Do not think that I have come to abolish the law or the prophets; I have come not to abolish but to fulfil. For truly I tell you, until heaven and earth pass away, not one letter, not one stroke of a letter, will pass from the law until all is accomplished. Therefore, whoever breaks one of the least of these commandments, and teaches others to do the same, will be called least in the kingdom of heaven; but whoever does them and teaches them will be called great in the kingdom of heaven."

- The historical words of the prophets are endorsed by Jesus. The Word of God endures forever, and salvation is for all who heed the prophetic warnings.

- Jesus fulfils the Law and the prophets by living as God would wish. He crowns the Law by putting love above all. We may forget law, but we must never forget love, because God is love and wants love to dominate human living.

Thursday 11th June
Matthew 5:20—24

Jesus said to the crowds, "For I tell you, unless your righteousness exceeds that of the scribes and Pharisees, you will never enter the kingdom of heaven. You have heard that it was said to those of ancient times, 'You shall not murder'; and 'whoever murders shall be liable to judgement.' But I say to you that if you are angry with a brother or sister, you will be liable to judgement; and if you insult a brother or sister, you will be liable to the council; and if you say, 'You fool,' you will be liable to the hell of fire. So when you are offering your gift at the altar, if you remember that your brother or sister has something against you, leave your gift there before the altar and go; first be reconciled to your brother or sister, and then come and offer your gift."

- Unlike the Pharisees, we must "walk the walk" rather than just "talk the talk." Jesus warns us not to condemn others while expecting forgiveness for ourselves.

- Arrogance and old grudges are to be replaced by humility and love. Reconciliation must be a top priority in the family of God's people, or else the Christian community will be no different from the world at large.

Friday 12th June,
Feast of the Sacred Heart
John 19:31—37

Since it was the day of Preparation, the Jews did not want the bodies left on the cross during the sabbath, especially because that sabbath was a day of great solemnity. So they asked Pilate to have the legs of the crucified men broken and the bodies removed. Then the soldiers came and broke the legs of the first and of the other who had been crucified with him. But when they came to Jesus and saw that he was already dead, they did not break his legs. Instead, one of the soldiers pierced his side with a spear, and at once blood and water came out. (He who saw this has testified so that you also may believe. His testimony is true, and he knows that he tells the truth.) These things occurred so that the scripture might be fulfilled, "None of his bones shall be broken." And again another passage of scripture says, "They will look on the one whom they have pierced."

• We see pictures of hearts with a little spear through them, telling us of loving hearts. The hearts of Jesus and Mary were entwined in love and were faithful to the end.

• Such love brings us beyond the convenient and the mediocre to what is deeper and of lasting value. We are reminded that we are to be people for others in this way.

Saturday 13th June,
St. Anthony of Padua
Matthew 5:33—37

Jesus said to the crowds, "Again, you have heard that it was said to those of ancient times, 'You shall not swear falsely, but carry out the vows you have made to the Lord.' But I say to you, Do not swear at all, either by heaven, for it is the throne of God, or by the earth, for it is his footstool, or by Jerusalem, for it is the city of the great King. And do not swear by your head, for you cannot make one hair white or black. Let your word be 'Yes, Yes' or 'No, No'; anything more than this comes from the evil one."

• God's word is creative and fruitful and does not return empty (see Is 55:11). By giving us Jesus, God says in effect, "I give you my Word for it." Jesus is the way, the truth, and the life (see Jn 14:6). I ask that I may live out of God's truth.

- Would people learn the Gospel message by studying my life?

June 14—20

Something to think and pray about each day this week:

What Makes God Love Us?

It is good to be law-abiding and dependable. But it is bad to think that this makes God love us! Why so? Because Jesus shows us something totally different, and we need again and again to be shocked by God's upside-down ways of viewing things. Jesus reveals God's strange point of view by associating with the rejects and the despised of his society. The poor, the sick, the possessed, and the non-nationals are his table companions. So, too, are women, tax collectors, and prostitutes. Add in for good measure the "accursed crowd" who don't know the Law (see Jn 7:49), and you have a thoroughly disreputable bunch!

But these are in fact the associates of the Son of God. The message is that God's special compassion is for the poor, the despised, and the unwanted. God's heart is drawn first to those at the bottom of the human pyramid, so Jesus has his eye out for them first.

God seems to love people just as they are, despite their inadequacies and brokenness. We don't earn God's love because we don't have to! We are already totally loved. Even the most law-abiding and dependable do not merit divine love; we have only to abandon self-sufficiency and to respond gratefully. And by showing that same kind of love for our most unlovable neighbours, we can positively transform human society!

The Presence of God

For a few moments, I think of God's veiled presence in things:
in the elements, giving them existence;
in plants, giving them life; in animals, giving them sensation;
and finally, in me, giving me all this and more,
making me a temple, a dwelling place of the Spirit.

Freedom

God is not foreign to my freedom.
Instead the Spirit breathes life into my most intimate desires,
gently nudging me toward all that is good.
I ask for the grace to let myself be enfolded by the Spirit.

Consciousness

Knowing that God loves me unconditionally,
I can afford to be honest about how I am.
How has the last day been, and how do I feel now?
I share my feelings openly with the Lord.

The Word

I take my time to read the Word of God, slowly, a few times, allowing myself to dwell on anything that strikes me. (Please turn to your
scripture on the following pages. Inspiration points are there should
you need them. When you are ready, return here to continue.)

Conversation

How has God's Word moved me? Has it left me cold?
Has it consoled me or moved me to act in a new way?
I imagine Jesus standing or sitting beside me;
I turn and share my feelings with him.

Conclusion

Glory be to the Father, and to the Son, and to the Holy Spirit,
as it was in the beginning, is now, and ever shall be,
world without end. Amen

June 2015

Sunday 14th June,
Eleventh Sunday of Ordinary Time
Mark 4:26–29

Jesus said to the crowd, "The kingdom of God is as if someone would scatter seed on the ground, and would sleep and rise night and day, and the seed would sprout and grow, he does not know how. The earth produces of itself, first the stalk, then the head, then the full grain in the head. But when the grain is ripe, at once he goes in with his sickle, because the harvest has come."

- Our role in life is to sow seeds and not to be preoccupied with producing a harvest. The seed given to us is the Word of God that serves to bring about a kingdom of justice, love, and peace.

- We each have a contribution to make, small though it may seem. We have to begin somewhere, perhaps with a small initiative.

Monday 15th June
Matthew 5:38–42

Jesus said to the crowds, "You have heard that it was said, 'An eye for an eye and a tooth for a tooth.' But I say to you, Do not resist an evildoer. But if anyone strikes you on the right cheek, turn the other also; and if anyone wants to sue you and take your coat, give your cloak as well; and if anyone forces you to go one mile, go also the second mile. Give to everyone who begs from you, and do not refuse anyone who wants to borrow from you."

- For the Hebrews, the Law was an attempt to moderate vengeance: the punishment should fit the crime, not exceed it.

- But Jesus went far beyond this. He was transforming the Law. He tells his startled disciples: "Do not retaliate; do not resist; go beyond what is demanded." Great generosity of heart is needed for this, and Jesus gives the example.

Tuesday 16th June
Matthew 5:43—48

Jesus said to the crowds, "You have heard that it was said, 'You shall love your neighbour and hate your enemy.' But I say to you, Love your enemies and pray for those who persecute you, so that you may be children of your Father in heaven; for he makes his sun rise on the evil and on the good, and sends rain on the righteous and on the unrighteous. For if you love those who love you, what reward do you have? Do not even the tax-collectors do the same? And if you greet only your brothers and sisters, what more are you doing than others? Do not even the Gentiles do the same? Be perfect, therefore, as your heavenly Father is perfect."

• Jesus emphasises that the easy option is not the correct one. How simple to love and be happy with those who love you! But the kingdom of God is much bigger than that; you must love all.

• Lord, you call us out of our comfort zones. We are to be as God is. Our growth is measured by the breadth of our love. Help us to grow in love!

Wednesday 17th June
Matthew 6:1—4

Jesus said to the disciples, "Beware of practising your piety before others in order to be seen by them; for then you have no reward from your Father in heaven. So whenever you give alms, do not sound a trumpet before you, as the hypocrites do in the synagogues and in the streets, so that they may be praised by others. Truly I tell you, they have received their reward. But when you give alms, do not let your left hand know what your right hand is doing, so that your alms may be done in secret; and your Father who sees in secret will reward you."

• We are asked to carry out almsgiving, prayer, and fasting in secret. Yet we are helped by good example.

- Whatever is done with sincere love will last eternally. I ask for a heart that is free, that enables me to live with sincere love.

Thursday 18th June
Matthew 6:7—15

Jesus said, "When you are praying, do not heap up empty phrases as the Gentiles do; for they think that they will be heard because of their many words. Do not be like them, for your Father knows what you need before you ask him. Pray then in this way: Our Father in heaven, hallowed be your name. Your kingdom come. Your will be done, on earth as it is in heaven. Give us this day our daily bread. And forgive us our debts, as we also have forgiven our debtors. And do not bring us to the time of trial, but rescue us from the evil one. For if you forgive others their trespasses, your heavenly Father will also forgive you; but if you do not forgive others, neither will your Father forgive your trespasses."

- Listening to God and letting God work is the heart of prayer, though we can spend much time in wanting God to listen to us. Empty phrases, hollow words, and one-sided conversations do not give life.

- It is the action of God that is most important, not words or great ideas. God alone can transform us. Prayer is a call to conversion.

Friday 19th June
Matthew 6:19—23

Jesus said to his disciples, "Do not store up for yourselves treasures on earth, where moth and rust consume and where thieves break in and steal; but store up for yourselves treasures in heaven, where neither moth nor rust consumes and where thieves do not break in and steal. For where your treasure is, there your heart will be also. The eye is the lamp of the body. So, if your eye is healthy, your whole body will be full of light; but if your eye is unhealthy, your whole body will be full of darkness. If then the light in you is darkness, how great is the darkness!"

- Everybody desires security. If possessions are our god, then we try to find security behind closed gates or in safe-deposit boxes locked in vaults. What Jesus desires for us is far different. He wants to hold our hearts and be our treasure that is not threatened by moths, rust, or thieves.

- Where is your security? What is your treasure?

Saturday 20th June
Matthew 6:26—34

Jesus said to the disciples, "Look at the birds of the air; they neither sow nor reap nor gather into barns, and yet your heavenly Father feeds them. Are you not of more value than they? And can any of you by worrying add a single hour to your span of life? And why do you worry about clothing? Consider the lilies of the field, how they grow; they neither toil nor spin, yet I tell you, even Solomon in all his glory was not clothed like one of these. But if God so clothes the grass of the field, which is alive today and tomorrow is thrown into the oven, will he not much more clothe you—you of little faith? Therefore do not worry, saying, 'What will we eat?' or 'What will we drink?' or 'What will we wear?' For it is the Gentiles who strive for all these things; and indeed your heavenly Father knows that you need all these things. But strive first for the kingdom of God and his righteousness, and all these things will be given to you as well. So do not worry about tomorrow, for tomorrow will bring worries of its own. Today's trouble is enough for today."

- This passage is one of great beauty. Let me savour it for a few moments and find peace and joy in it. God is Beauty itself, so in meeting beauty, I can meet God.

- Jesus promises us that God is generous. God can be trusted to provide what we need as we "strive first for the kingdom of God."

June 21—27

Something to think and pray about each day this week:

Indiscriminate Loving

"God is love in the same way as an emerald is green." So says Simone Weil. What does this mean? It means that God is love through and through. There isn't something else hidden behind God's love. Nothing I do could make God love me more—or less! Jesus compares his Father to the sun, which simply shines, so that both the just and the unjust are warmed by it. Every time I see the sun, I can say, "God is a bit like that!" God is not discriminating in loving.

The task of the Son is to reveal the generous nature of divine loving and then to show people a new way of relating. "Be loving, as my Father and I are loving!" he says.

Jesus illustrates in word and deed this new way of relating. His parables jolted and disconcerted his hearers. What a shock that the good neighbour to the injured man was a Samaritan! And surely the good father should have disowned his wayward son? Surely again those who laboured all day should get more than the last-minute arrivals?

Jesus was a well-integrated personality. He could be gentle but also challenging and angry. So he clashes head-on with the religious leaders of the day and throws the money lenders out of the Temple. Wise love takes many forms: it is not timid and passive; it can be demanding as well as long-suffering.

The Presence of God

At any time of the day or night we can call on Jesus.
He is always waiting, listening for our call.
What a wonderful blessing.
No phone needed, no e-mails—just a whisper.

Freedom

Lord, grant me the grace to be free from the excesses of this life.
Let me not get caught up with the desire for wealth.
Keep my heart and mind free to love and serve you.

Consciousness

I exist in a web of relationships—links to nature, people, God.
I trace out these links, giving thanks for the life that flows through them.
Some links are twisted or broken; I may feel regret, anger, disappointment.
I pray for the gift of acceptance and forgiveness.

The Word

God speaks to each one of us individually. I need to listen to what he is saying to me. (Please turn to your scripture on the following pages. Inspiration points are there should you need them. When you are ready, return here to continue.)

Conversation

Remembering that I am still in God's presence,
I imagine Jesus himself standing or sitting beside me,
and I say whatever is on my mind, whatever is in my heart,
speaking as one friend to another.

Conclusion

Glory be to the Father, and to the Son, and to the Holy Spirit,
as it was in the beginning, is now, and ever shall be,
world without end. Amen.

Sunday 21st June,
Twelfth Sunday of Ordinary Time
Mark 4:35—41

On that day, when evening had come, he said to them, "Let us go across to the other side." And leaving the crowd behind, they took him with them in the boat, just as he was. Other boats were with him. A great gale arose, and the waves beat into the boat, so that the boat was already being swamped. But he was in the stern, asleep on the cushion; and they woke him up and said to him, "Teacher, do you not care that we are perishing?" He woke up and rebuked the wind, and said to the sea, "Peace! Be still!" Then the wind ceased, and there was a dead calm. He said to them, "Why are you afraid? Have you still no faith?" And they were filled with great awe and said to one another, "Who then is this, that even the wind and the sea obey him?"

- They were asking a question which they would ask again, "Who is this man?" Our involvement with Jesus and our engagement with him in our lives will often bring that question to the fore.

- In prayer, we grow in heart-knowledge of Jesus, not always being able to put words on our faith in him. Like the apostles, we know that he is a mystery—at once Son of God and son of the earth.

Monday 22nd June
Matthew 7:1—5

Jesus said to the crowds, "Do not judge, so that you may not be judged. For with the judgement you make you will be judged, and the measure you give will be the measure you get. Why do you see the speck in your neighbour's eye, but do not notice the log in your own eye? Or how can you say to your neighbour, 'Let me take the speck out of your eye,' while the log is in your own eye? You hypocrite, first take the log out of your own eye, and then you will see clearly to take the speck out of your neighbour's eye."

- We can be quite blind to our own faults but be very alert to those of others. Human bias tends to favour ourselves and be prejudiced regarding others. It is easier to propose that the problem is not in me but out there.

- The truth is more often that the other person is a challenge to me, since otherwise why would I need to be critical? It can be challenging to admit the truth about myself.

Tuesday 23rd June
Matthew 7:12—14

Jesus said, "In everything do to others as you would have them do to you; for this is the law and the prophets. Enter through the narrow gate; for the gate is wide and the road is easy that leads to destruction, and there are many who take it. For the gate is narrow and the road is hard that leads to life, and there are few who find it."

- The easy option is to avoid personal responsibilities and to go with the crowd. The choice between right and wrong can often be lonely and narrow. Lord, please show me the road that leads to you. May I follow it with joy, whether it is hard or easy.

- The gifts God gives to each of us must not be wasted or ignored but used in the service of others.

Tuesday 24th June,
Birth of St. John the Baptist
Luke 1:57—64

Now the time came for Elizabeth to give birth, and she bore a son. Her neighbours and relatives heard that the Lord had shown his great mercy to her, and they rejoiced with her. On the eighth day they came to circumcise the child, and they were going to name him Zechariah after his father. But his mother said, "No; he is to be called John." They said to her, "None of your relatives has this name." Then they began motioning to his father to find out what name he wanted to give him. He asked for a writing-tablet and wrote, "His name is John." And all of them were amazed. Immediately his mouth was opened and his tongue freed, and he began to speak, praising God.

- No doubt Elizabeth had wanted this birth and prayed for it for many years; instead she had her son in God's time.

- I imagine I am one of Elizabeth's relatives who comes to celebrate John's birth. I, too, wonder, "What will this child become?" Then I ask myself, "What am I becoming?"

Thursday 25th June
Matthew 7:21—29

Jesus said to his disciples, "Not everyone who says to me, 'Lord, Lord,' will enter the kingdom of heaven, but only one who does the will of my Father in heaven. On that day many will say to me, 'Lord, Lord, did we not prophesy in your name, and cast out demons in your name, and do many deeds of power in your name?' Then I will declare to them, 'I never knew you; go away from me, you evildoers.'

"Everyone then who hears these words of mine and acts on them will be like a wise man who built his house on rock. The rain fell, the floods came, and the winds blew and beat on that house, but it did not fall, because it had been founded on rock. And everyone who hears these words of mine and does not act on them will be like a foolish man who built his house on sand. The rain fell, and the floods came, and the winds blew and beat against that house, and it fell—and great was its fall!" Now when Jesus had finished saying these things, the crowds were astounded at his teaching, for he taught them as one having authority, and not as their scribes.

- Jesus hits hard at every form of pretence. He has no time for it. Does he see any traces of pretence in me? Do I tell small lies? I ask him to remove my deceptiveness.

- The humble people begin to discern the source of Jesus' authority, and see his teachings as a benchmark for their own beliefs and practices. Lord, let you be the rock that supports my faith and my actions, so that I fear neither wind nor flood.

Friday 26th June
Matthew 8:1—4

When Jesus had come down from the mountain, great crowds followed him; and there was a leper who came to him and knelt before him, saying, "Lord, if you choose, you can make me clean." He stretched out his hand and touched him, saying, "I do choose. Be made clean!" Immediately his leprosy was cleansed. Then Jesus said to him, "See that you say nothing to anyone; but go, show yourself to the priest, and offer the gift that Moses commanded, as a testimony to them."

- Throughout our lives, Jesus wants us with him, offering us the gift of love and calling, asking only love and the effort to love in return.

- "How can I repay the Lord for his goodness to me?" is a psalm we might pray as we grow in awareness of all that Jesus does for his people.

Saturday 27th June
Matthew 8:5—13

When he entered Capernaum, a centurion came to him, appealing to him and saying, "Lord, my servant is lying at home paralysed, in terrible distress." And he said to him, "I will come and cure him." The centurion answered, "Lord, I am not worthy to have you come under my roof; but only speak the word, and my servant will be healed. For I also am a man under authority, with soldiers under me; and I say to one, 'Go,' and he goes, and to another, 'Come,' and he comes, and to my slave, 'Do this,' and the slave does it." When Jesus heard him, he was amazed and said to those who followed him, "Truly I tell you, in no one in Israel have I found such faith. I tell you, many will come from east and west and will eat with Abraham and Isaac and Jacob in the kingdom of heaven, while the heirs of the kingdom will be thrown into the outer darkness, where there will be weeping and gnashing of teeth." And to the centurion Jesus said, "Go; let it be done for you according to your faith." And the servant was healed in that hour.

- Faith provided the link. The centurion's courageous request was inspired by the conviction that Jesus could cure in this way, that he had the authority to do so.

- "Lord, I am not worthy that you should enter under my roof, but only say the word and my soul shall be healed." The faith of the centurion meets with the power of Jesus to heal, and all is changed.

June 28—July 4

Something to think and pray about each day this week:

Suffering and Joy

In the culture of Jesus' time, crucifixion was seen as a disgraceful way to die. So it took time for the disciples to see in this dreadful event the supreme revelation of God's love for us. We must never trivialize or domesticate this enduring shock. The Cross remains to convert us to God's way of seeing the appalling damage caused by sin and evil. We learn how demanding reconciliation is. Amazing grace is revealed, but it is costly grace, too. It seemed to Jesus that only the Cross would break open our hearts, so it was worth it. That hope brought him joy.

We are asked to suffer, if necessary, in order to foster the values of the kingdom. As followers of Jesus, we, too, must be in solidarity with a wounded humanity. This may mean living simply for the sake of others, or working with the sick, or spending time with life's victims. For all of us it means enduring with patience the day-to-day difficulties of life.

Suffering is often unearned and always undesired; often we can't change it, but Jesus shows us how to bear it with love. Such love radiates and inspires others. You know such people, and perhaps you are such yourself without feeling in any way heroic. Martin Luther King Jr. remarked, "I have come to live with the conviction that unearned suffering is redemptive." We can add that, mysteriously, joy is possible even in suffering, perhaps because suffering brings us so close to God.

The Presence of God
God is with me, but more,
God is within me, giving me existence.
Let me dwell for a moment on God's life-giving presence
in my body, my mind, my heart,
and in the whole of my life.

Freedom
God is not foreign to my freedom.
Instead, the Spirit breathes life into my most intimate desires,
gently nudging me toward all that is good.
I ask for the grace to let myself be enfolded by the Spirit.

Consciousness
How am I really feeling? Lighthearted? Heavy hearted?
I may be very much at peace, happy to be here.
Equally, I may be frustrated, worried, or angry.
I acknowledge how I really am. It is the real me that the Lord loves.

The Word
I read the Word of God slowly, a few times over, and I listen to what
God is saying to me. (Please turn to your scripture on the following
pages. Inspiration points are there should you need them. When you
are ready, return here to continue.)

Conversation
How has God's Word moved me? Has it left me cold?
Has it consoled me or moved me to act in a new way?
I imagine Jesus standing or sitting beside me;
I turn and share my feelings with him.

Conclusion
Glory be to the Father, and to the Son, and to the Holy Spirit,
as it was in the beginning, is now, and ever shall be,
world without end. Amen.

June 2015

Sunday 28th June,
Thirteenth Sunday of Ordinary Time
Mark 5:21—34

When Jesus had crossed again in the boat to the other side, a great crowd gathered round him; and he was by the lake. Then one of the leaders of the synagogue named Jairus came and, when he saw him, fell at his feet and begged him repeatedly, "My little daughter is at the point of death. Come and lay your hands on her, so that she may be made well, and live." So he went with him.

And a large crowd followed him and pressed in on him. Now there was a woman who had been suffering from haemorrhages for twelve years. She had endured much under many physicians, and had spent all that she had; and she was no better, but rather grew worse. She had heard about Jesus, and came up behind him in the crowd and touched his cloak, for she said, "If I but touch his clothes, I will be made well." Immediately her haemorrhage stopped; and she felt in her body that she was healed of her disease. Immediately aware that power had gone forth from him, Jesus turned about in the crowd and said, "Who touched my clothes?" And his disciples said to him, "You see the crowd pressing in on you; how can you say, 'Who touched me?'" He looked all round to see who had done it. But the woman, knowing what had happened to her, came in fear and trembling, fell down before him, and told him the whole truth. He said to her, "Daughter, your faith has made you well; go in peace, and be healed of your disease."

- I reflect on the two contrasting approaches to Jesus—the strong pleading of Jairus against the tentative approach of the woman. She is hesitant because she had been ritually impure for years.

- Jesus is fully attentive to both of them. He commends the woman's faith. I note, too, his thoughtfulness for the starving child. What can I learn from all this?

Monday 29th June,
Ss. Peter & Paul, Apostles
Matthew 16:13—17

Now when Jesus came into the district of Caesarea Philippi, he asked his disciples, "Who do people say that the Son of Man is?" And they said, "Some say John the Baptist, but others Elijah, and still others Jeremiah or one of the prophets." He said to them, "But who do you say that I am?" Simon Peter answered, "You are the Messiah, the Son of the living God." And Jesus answered him, "Blessed are you, Simon son of Jonah! For flesh and blood has not revealed this to you, but my Father in heaven."

- Jesus changed Simon's name to Peter, giving him a new assignment, as was true of the change of Saul's name to Paul in his mission to the Gentiles.

- Jesus saw the potential in Peter to become the rock, the solid foundation of the building for the fragile faith community. He was given the keys of the household with the authority and responsibility of making decisions. God can work through frail people to bring his kingdom about.

Tuesday 30th June
Matthew 8:23—27

And when Jesus got into the boat, his disciples followed him. A gale arose on the lake, so great that the boat was being swamped by the waves; but he was asleep. And they went and woke him up, saying, "Lord, save us! We are perishing!" And he said to them, "Why are you afraid, you of little faith?" Then he got up and rebuked the winds and the sea; and there was a dead calm. They were amazed, saying, "What sort of man is this, that even the winds and the sea obey him?"

- Note the contrasts here. There is the terror of the disciples and the composure of Jesus who is asleep! There is the chaos of the storm and the "dead calm" which follows after the intervention of Jesus.

- Jesus shows complete trust in the protection of God, whereas the disciples are seen to be "of little faith." What about me?

Wednesday 1st July
Matthew 8:28—34

When he came to the other side, to the country of the Gadarenes, two demoniacs coming out of the tombs met him. They were so fierce that no one could pass that way. Suddenly they shouted, "What have you to do with us, Son of God? Have you come here to torment us before the time?" Now a large herd of swine was feeding at some distance from them. The demons begged him, "If you cast us out, send us into the herd of swine." And he said to them, "Go!" So they came out and entered the swine; and suddenly, the whole herd rushed down the steep bank into the lake and perished in the water. The swineherds ran off, and on going into the town, they told the whole story about what had happened to the demoniacs. Then the whole town came out to meet Jesus; and when they saw him, they begged him to leave their neighbourhood.

- This is in Gentile territory, where Jews would not normally go. Sometimes when they went "to the other side," the disciples did not even leave the boat, through fear or intolerance. Deeply entrenched traditions can be a barrier to welcoming the stranger.

- Jesus is always the man of the other side, the stranger, the one nobody wants to know. He moves from one people to another, without distinction. He has come for all peoples.

Thursday 2nd July
Matthew 9:1—8

And after getting into a boat he crossed the water and came to his own town. And just then some people were carrying a paralysed man lying on a bed. When Jesus saw their faith, he said to the paralytic, "Take heart, son; your sins are forgiven." Then some of the scribes said to themselves, "This man is blaspheming." But Jesus, perceiving their thoughts, said, "Why do you think evil in your hearts? For which is easier, to say, 'Your sins are forgiven,' or to say, 'Stand up and walk'? But so that you may know that the Son of Man has authority on earth to forgive sins"—he then said to the paralytic—"Stand up, take your bed and go to your home." And he stood up and went to his home. When the crowds saw it, they were filled with awe, and they glorified God, who had given such authority to human beings.

- Jesus is touched by the trouble which his friends took for the paralysed man. It is their faith and concern that moves him to heal the man both spiritually and physically.

- Likewise, my prayer of faith for others moves Jesus to meet their needs and gives me a share in the healing mission of Christ and of all Christians.

Friday 3rd July,
St. Thomas, Apostle
John 20:24—29

Thomas (who was called the Twin), one of the twelve, was not with them when Jesus came. So the other disciples told him, "We have seen the Lord." But he said to them, "Unless I see the mark of the nails in his hands, and put my finger in the mark of the nails and my hand in his side, I will not believe." A week later his disciples were again in the house, and Thomas was with them. Although the doors were shut, Jesus came and stood among them and said, "Peace be with you." Then he said to Thomas, "Put your finger here and see my hands. Reach out your hand and put it in my side. Do not doubt but believe." Thomas answered him, "My Lord and my God!" Jesus said to him, "Have you believed because you have seen me? Blessed are those who have not seen and yet have come to believe."

- People sometimes worry when they question the Church's teaching, but it is healthy to examine what we believe, in order to come to an adult understanding of our faith.

- Believers are to be thinkers, and doubting can be an honest step in our struggle to believe.

Saturday 4th July
Matthew 9:14—17

Then the disciples of John came to him, saying, "Why do we and the Pharisees fast often, but your disciples do not fast?" And Jesus said to them, "The wedding-guests cannot mourn as long as the bridegroom is with them, can they? The days will come when the bridegroom is taken away from them, and then they will fast. No one sews a piece of unshrunk cloth on an old cloak, for the patch pulls away from the cloak, and a worse tear is made. Neither is new wine put into old wineskins; otherwise, the skins burst, and the wine is spilled, and the skins are destroyed; but new wine is put into fresh wineskins, and so both are preserved."

- For Jesus, old cloaks or old wineskins are not appropriate. His coming marks a fresh beginning, a new era in our relationship with God.

- Jesus fits no formula. He does not abolish old ways but fulfils them beyond human imagining.

July 5—11

Something to think and pray about each day this week:

Recognizing and Accepting Anger

If I have been badly hurt, I will be angry. This can cause me fear because I know I may not be able to control my anger. I may also feel guilty because I may have been taught that I should not become angry or even feel angry. But what am I supposed to do with these feelings if others expect me always to be polite, gentle, and mild? People do not like to listen to my anger, perhaps because they cannot cope well with their own anger, much less with someone else's.

Anger and revengeful feelings are natural reactions to hurt. I want the persons who wronged me to know what my pain feels like. I want to give them a dose of their own medicine so that they understand what they did. This is a primitive and normal response when you are wronged. It would help so much if my family and friends could accept that my anger is natural and appropriate. Without that, I turn the anger onto myself, so that it burns me inside and leads to depression. Or I try to get the burning coals of anger out of my system by aggressive behaviour.

Anger and the desire for revenge are normal. In his passion, Jesus experienced anger and surely also a desire for revenge. We watch how he coped with them, and we learn. The advice "Be angry but do not sin" (Eph 4:26) gets the balance right.

The Presence of God

To be present is to arrive as one is and open up to the other.
At this instant, as I arrive here, God is present waiting for me.
God always arrives before me, desiring to connect with me
even more than my most intimate friend.
I take a moment and greet my loving God.

Freedom

Everything has the potential to draw forth from me a fuller love
and life.
Yet my desires are often fixed, caught, on illusions of fulfillment.
I ask that God, through my freedom, may orchestrate
my desires in a vibrant, loving melody rich in harmony.

Consciousness

Knowing that God loves me unconditionally,
I can afford to be honest about how I am.
How has the last day been, and how do I feel now?
I share my feelings openly with the Lord.

The Word

I take my time to read the Word of God, slowly, a few times, allowing myself to dwell on anything that strikes me. (Please turn to your
scripture on the following pages. Inspiration points are there should
you need them. When you are ready, return here to continue.)

Conversation

What feelings are rising in me
as I pray and reflect on God's Word?
I imagine Jesus himself sitting or standing beside me,
and I open my heart to him.

Conclusion

Glory be to the Father, and to the Son, and to the Holy Spirit,
as it was in the beginning, is now, and ever shall be,
world without end. Amen.

July 2015

Sunday 5th July,
Fourteenth Sunday of Ordinary Time
Mark 6:1—6

Jesus left that place and came to his home town, and his disciples followed him. On the sabbath he began to teach in the synagogue, and many who heard him were astounded. They said, "Where did this man get all this? What is this wisdom that has been given to him? What deeds of power are being done by his hands! Is not this the carpenter, the son of Mary and brother of James and Joses and Judas and Simon, and are not his sisters here with us?" And they took offence at him. Then Jesus said to them, "Prophets are not without honour, except in their home town, and among their own kin, and in their own house." And he could do no deed of power there, except that he laid his hands on a few sick people and cured them. And he was amazed at their unbelief. Then he went about among the villages teaching.

• Why do his fellow townspeople take offence at Jesus? Why do they resent this ordinary building worker they all knew so well? Do I tend to pull people down to my own low level, or do I help them to feel as great as God has made them?

• For Jesus, this event is a learning experience. He is shocked at his hostile reception. While he is truly God, he is truly man, too. He does not know everything but grows in wisdom, as we do. God is patient with me as I grow through making mistakes.

Monday 6th July
Matthew 9:18—26

While Jesus was saying these things to them, suddenly a leader of the synagogue came in and knelt before him, saying, "My daughter has just died; but come and lay your hand on her, and she will live." And Jesus got up and followed him, with his disciples. Then suddenly a woman who had been suffering from haemorrhages for twelve years came up behind him and touched the fringe of his cloak, for she said to herself, "If I only touch his cloak, I will be made well." Jesus turned, and seeing her he said, "Take heart, daughter; your faith has made you well." And instantly the woman was made well. When Jesus came to the leader's house and saw the flute-players and the crowd making a commotion, he said, "Go away; for the girl is not dead but sleeping." And they laughed at him. But when the crowd had been put outside, he went in and took her by the hand, and the girl got up. And the report of this spread throughout that district.

- This event challenges the strength of my own faith in the power of Christ to work effectively in my life, too, if I but turn to him.

- Is my own faith weakened by the same scepticism and cynicism as expressed by the flute players and the crowd? Lord, "I believe; help my unbelief" (Mk 9:24).

Tuesday 7th July
Matthew 9:35—38

Then Jesus went about all the cities and villages, teaching in their synagogues, and proclaiming the good news of the kingdom, and curing every disease and every sickness. When he saw the crowds, he had compassion for them, because they were harassed and helpless, like sheep without a shepherd. Then he said to his disciples, "The harvest is plentiful, but the labourers are few; therefore ask the Lord of the harvest to send out labourers into his harvest."

- To what extent am I like Jesus in my attitude toward others, especially the poor and the needy? Or am I dismissive and judgemental toward others, as are the Pharisees in today's gospel?

- Lord, please give me something of your genuine humanity and compassion in all my relations with others.

Wednesday 8th July
Matthew 10:1—7

Then Jesus summoned his twelve disciples and gave them authority over unclean spirits, to cast them out, and to cure every disease and every sickness. These are the names of the twelve apostles: first, Simon, also known as Peter, and his brother Andrew; James son of Zebedee, and his brother John; Philip and Bartholomew; Thomas and Matthew the tax-collector; James son of Alphaeus, and Thaddaeus; Simon the Cananaean, and Judas Iscariot, the one who betrayed him. These twelve Jesus sent out with the following instructions: "Go nowhere among the Gentiles, and enter no town of the Samaritans, but go rather to the lost sheep of the house of Israel. As you go, proclaim the good news, 'The kingdom of heaven has come near.'"

- The Lord also calls me by name to play my part in spreading the Good News of God's infinite love and mercy in my own time and world.

- Lord, may I always hear your personal call to me and respond to it generously and courageously in my daily life.

Thursday 9th July
Matthew 10:7—14

Jesus said to the Twelve, "As you go, proclaim the good news, 'The kingdom of heaven has come near.' Cure the sick, raise the dead, cleanse the lepers, cast out demons. You received without payment; give without payment. Take no gold, or silver, or copper in your belts, no bag for your journey, or two tunics, or sandals, or a staff; for labourers deserve their food. Whatever town or village you enter, find out who in it is worthy, and stay there until you leave. As you enter the house, greet it. If the house is worthy, let your peace come upon it; but if it is not worthy, let your peace return to you. If anyone will not welcome you or listen to your words, shake off the dust from your feet as you leave that house or town."

- We are to be open-minded and open-hearted followers of Christ. We are to be people for whom this relationship is a priority in life, and nothing else should sour it or come before it.

- All love, all friendships, all we are, all we have, and all we do are in the love of Christ, and to him all can be given.

Friday 10th July
Matthew 10:16–20

Jesus said to the Twelve, "See, I am sending you out like sheep into the midst of wolves; so be wise as serpents and innocent as doves. Beware of them, for they will hand you over to councils and flog you in their synagogues; and you will be dragged before governors and kings because of me, as a testimony to them and the Gentiles. When they hand you over, do not worry about how you are to speak or what you are to say; for what you are to say will be given to you at that time; for it is not you who speak, but the Spirit of your Father speaking through you."

- Jesus teaches the Twelve how to persevere in times of persecution. He warns them that they will be met with hostility and hatred because of him.

- The ultimate reassurance and promise of the Lord is that the one who endures to the end will be saved.

Saturday 11th July
Matthew 10:26–31

Jesus said to the Twelve, "So have no fear of them; for nothing is covered up that will not be uncovered, and nothing secret that will not become known. What I say to you in the dark, tell in the light; and what you hear whispered, proclaim from the housetops. Do not fear those who kill the body but cannot kill the soul; rather fear him who can destroy both soul and body in hell. Are not two sparrows sold for a penny? Yet not one of them will fall to the ground unperceived by your Father. And even the hairs of your head are all counted. So do not be afraid; you are of more value than many sparrows."

- We read here of the sovereignty of God over all creation. His loving regard extends even to the hairs of our head. He is aware of a sparrow alighting on the ground.

- How much more of his attention do I enjoy, given that I am the apple of his eye, created in his own image and likeness? So whatever happens, I am not to be afraid. All will be well for me.

July 12—18

Something to think and pray about each day this week:

Wanting to Forgive

If I absolutely refuse even to *want* to forgive, I cannot pray the Our Father. It makes no sense. But if I have problems with forgiving, then I can pray it. In effect I am saying: "Lord, I have great problems with what you call me to. Please help me. You are better at forgiving than I am, so please forgive me fully, no matter how I hurt you. I accept that you want me to keep on trying to forgive, and I will try."

So the divine call to forgive is addressed to me as I am, in my actual situation. I am called to do what I can, no more, no less. But I know that the love of Christ is always inviting me beyond where I am.

On that difficult journey toward loving our enemy, we have a friend in Our Lord, not another enemy throwing even more burdens on us. Because he is our friend, he is not going to be shocked at our feelings of anger or revenge. He will understand these, because he shares our anger and horror at what has been done to us. He will walk with us as we move slowly toward freedom, where we are no longer dominated by what has happened to us.

Loving an enemy does not exclude anger at their wrongdoing. It does not minimise or justify it. And it does not exclude punishment, which may be good not only for the wrongdoer but also for society at large.

The Presence of God

What is present to me is what has a hold on my becoming.
I reflect on the presence of God always there in love,
amidst the many things that have a hold on me.
I pause and pray that I may let God
affect my becoming in this precise moment.

Freedom

"There are very few people
who realize what God would make of them
if they abandoned themselves into his hands,
and let themselves be formed by his grace" (St. Ignatius).
I ask for the grace to trust myself totally to God's love.

Consciousness

In the presence of my loving Creator,
I look honestly at my feelings over the last day—
the highs, the lows, and the level ground.
Can I see where the Lord has been present?

The Word

God speaks to each one of us individually. I need to listen to what
he is saying to me. (Please turn to your scripture on the following
pages. Inspiration points are there should you need them. When you
are ready, return here to continue.)

Conversation

What is stirring in me as I pray?
Am I consoled, troubled, left cold?
I imagine Jesus himself standing or sitting at my side,
and I share my feelings with him.

Conclusion

Glory be to the Father, and to the Son, and to the Holy Spirit,
as it was in the beginning, is now, and ever shall be,
world without end. Amen.

July 2015

Sunday 12th July,
Fifteenth Sunday of Ordinary Time
Mark 6:7—13

Jesus called the twelve and began to send them out two by two, and gave them authority over the unclean spirits. He ordered them to take nothing for their journey except a staff; no bread, no bag, no money in their belts; but to wear sandals and not to put on two tunics. He said to them, "Wherever you enter a house, stay there until you leave the place. If any place will not welcome you and they refuse to hear you, as you leave, shake off the dust that is on your feet as a testimony against them." So they went out and proclaimed that all should repent. They cast out many demons, and anointed with oil many who were sick and cured them.

- Jesus does not ask of the apostles any more than he does himself: he already has left family and home and has become a wandering preacher. He lives on the margins of society; he battles against evil, and invites people into a deep relationship with God.

- Jesus opposes all forms of domination, and wants us to do likewise. So he stands by the poor and the outcast; he liberates those who are possessed by demons or dominated by sickness. He wants us all to be free to live out our lives to the full.

Monday 13th July
Matthew 10:34—39, 11:1

Jesus said to the Twelve, "Do not think that I have come to bring peace to the earth; I have not come to bring peace, but a sword. For I have come to set a man against his father, and a daughter against her mother, and a daughter-in-law against her mother-in-law; and one's foes will be members of one's own household. Whoever loves father or mother more than me is not worthy of me; and whoever loves son or daughter more than me is not worthy of me; and whoever does not take up the cross and follow me is not worthy of me. Those who find their life will lose it, and those who lose their life for my sake will find it." . . . Now when Jesus had finished instructing his twelve disciples, he went on from there to teach and proclaim his message in their cities.

- Giving "a cup of cold water to one of these little ones" has eternal significance. This truth highlights the dignity of each and every human being, no matter how lowly or insignificant they are.

- Lord, help me to see your face in my neighbour, and especially the poor and the needy, and to respond accordingly. When did I last buy a beggar a cup of coffee?

Tuesday 14th July
Matthew 11:20—24

Then Jesus began to reproach the cities in which most of his deeds of power had been done, because they did not repent. "Woe to you, Chorazin! Woe to you, Bethsaida! For if the deeds of power done in you had been done in Tyre and Sidon, they would have repented long ago in sackcloth and ashes. But I tell you, on the day of judgement it will be more tolerable for Tyre and Sidon than for you. And you, Capernaum, will you be exalted to heaven? No, you will be brought down to Hades. For if the deeds of power done in you had been done in Sodom, it would have remained until this day. But I tell you that on the day of judgement it will be more tolerable for the land of Sodom than for you."

- Jesus lived in Capernaum for some time. He preached in the synagogue there. And yet his miracles were not enough to convince its citizens that he was from God.

- May my faith in the Lord Jesus and in his gospel enable me always to marvel at his wonderful deeds and to give him unending praise and thanks.

Wednesday 15th July
Matthew 11:25–27

At that time Jesus said, "I thank you, Father, Lord of heaven and earth, because you have hidden these things from the wise and the intelligent and have revealed them to infants; yes, Father, for such was your gracious will. All things have been handed over to me by my Father; and no one knows the Son except the Father, and no one knows the Father except the Son and anyone to whom the Son chooses to reveal him."

- The Son has privileged access to the Father. It is not an exclusive or closed relationship, however, because Jesus invites others to participate in it. We in Sacred Space are among those "to whom the Son chooses to reveal him."

- Lord Jesus, help each of us to experience that we, too, are truly beloved sons and daughters of our heavenly Father.

Thursday 16th July
Matthew 11:28–30

Jesus said, "Come to me, all you that are weary and are carrying heavy burdens, and I will give you rest. Take my yoke upon you, and learn from me; for I am gentle and humble in heart, and you will find rest for your souls. For my yoke is easy, and my burden is light."

- Those who burden the weary are the religious leaders, with their emphasis on the Law. Jesus is not proposing a lax interpretation of the Law. But he interprets the Law in the context of love because of God's great and total love for us.

- Do I find "rest for my soul" in this network of love?

Friday 17th July
Matthew 12:1–8

At that time Jesus went through the cornfields on the sabbath; his disciples were hungry, and they began to pluck heads of grain and to eat. When the Pharisees saw it, they said to him, "Look, your disciples are doing what is not lawful to do on the sabbath." He said to them, "Have you not read what David did when he and his companions were hungry? He entered the house of God and ate the bread of the Presence, which it was not lawful for him or his companions to eat, but only for the priests. Or have you not read in the law that on the sabbath the priests in the temple break the sabbath and yet are guiltless? I tell you, something greater than the temple is here. But if you had known what this means, 'I desire mercy and not sacrifice,' you would not have condemned the guiltless. For the Son of Man is lord of the sabbath."

- For Jesus, the practice of mercy and compassion, and especially toward the "guiltless" and the needy, is far more important than Temple sacrifice and empty ritual.

- Lord, release me from slavery to law, and help me to experience "the freedom of the glory of the children of God" (Rom 8:21).

Saturday 18th July
Matthew 12:14—21

But the Pharisees went out and conspired against him, how to destroy him. When Jesus became aware of this, he departed. Many crowds followed him, and he cured all of them, and he ordered them not to make him known. This was to fulfil what had been spoken through the prophet Isaiah: "Here is my servant, whom I have chosen, my beloved, with whom my soul is well pleased. I will put my Spirit upon him, and he will proclaim justice to the Gentiles. He will not wrangle or cry aloud, nor will anyone hear his voice in the streets. He will not break a bruised reed or quench a smouldering wick until he brings justice to victory. And in his name the Gentiles will hope."

- By referring to the great prophet Isaiah, Matthew identifies Jesus with the Suffering Servant of the Book of Isaiah. This servant is filled with God's spirit.

- In spite of the aggression of his opponents, Jesus mirrors the Suffering Servant, who is full of gentleness and compassion. "The LORD is merciful and gracious, slow to anger and abounding in steadfast love" (Ps 103:8). Am I a bit like him?

July 19—25

Something to think and pray about each day this week:

Are We Freed?

When did you last hear a homily on "freedom"? I have never heard one, yet the conviction that we have been radically freed by Jesus is central to Christianity. Luke celebrates God's visitation of his people, which frees us from fear and saves us from the hands of our foes (see Lk 1:71). Because "Christ has set us free," St. Paul asserts, "you were called to freedom, brothers and sisters" (Gal 5:1, 13).

Could it be that Jesus has in fact set us free, but that we can't take this in? Twice in the Acts of the Apostles prison doors are miraculously opened so the apostles can come out to preach the Good News. Is this perhaps an image of Jesus' work of salvation? After he has already opened the prison gates for us, are we still sitting inside, waiting for something else to happen? And does this imagined imprisonment keep us from putting this divine energy where it belongs—at the service of the world?

Am I anxious about my final status before God? A teacher of highly gifted music students found that anxiety about their final marks inhibited the creative self-expression hidden in them. To liberate them, he announced that every one of them would get high marks. Suddenly they began to play at their best!

Are we like them, gifted with freedom and talent, but needing reassurance that God loves to see us at our creative best, doing great works (see Jn 14:12)?

The Presence of God
Jesus waits silent and unseen to come into my heart.
I will respond to his call.
He comes with his infinite power and love.
May I be filled with joy in his presence.

Freedom
"A thick and shapeless tree-trunk would never believe
that it could become a statue, admired as a miracle of sculpture,
and would never submit itself to the chisel of the sculptor,
who sees by her genius what she can make of it" (St. Ignatius).
I ask for the grace to let myself be shaped by my loving Creator.

Consciousness
Knowing that God loves me unconditionally,
I look honestly over the last day, its events and my feelings.
Do I have something to be grateful for? Then I give thanks.
Is there something I am sorry for? Then I ask forgiveness.

The Word
I read the Word of God slowly, a few times over, and I listen to what
God is saying to me. (Please turn to your scripture on the following
pages. Inspiration points are there should you need them. When you
are ready, return here to continue.)

Conversation
Do I notice myself reacting as I pray with the Word of God?
Do I feel challenged, comforted, angry?
Imagining Jesus sitting or standing by me,
I speak out my feelings, as one trusted friend to another.

Conclusion
Glory be to the Father, and to the Son, and to the Holy Spirit,
as it was in the beginning, is now, and ever shall be,
world without end. Amen.

July 2015

Sunday 19th July,
Sixteenth Sunday of Ordinary Time
Mark 6:30—34

The apostles gathered around Jesus, and told him all that they had done and taught. He said to them, "Come away to a deserted place all by yourselves and rest a while." For many were coming and going, and they had no leisure even to eat. And they went away in the boat to a deserted place by themselves. Now many saw them going and recognized them, and they hurried there on foot from all the towns and arrived ahead of them. As he went ashore, he saw a great crowd; and he had compassion for them, because they were like sheep without a shepherd; and he began to teach them many things.

- Jesus cares about me and invites me, too, to come away and rest a while. If I can go to a "deserted place" occasionally, it will allow my soul to catch up. Otherwise, as T. S. Eliot says, I have the experience of God's action in my life, but miss its meaning because I don't give time to reflection.

- I may be too busy or too poor "to get away from it all." But each day *Sacred Space* provides me with an oasis of calm and refreshment. I will never regret the time I give to this daily encounter with God.

Monday 20th July
Matthew 12:38—42

Then some of the scribes and Pharisees said to him, "Teacher, we wish to see a sign from you." But he answered them, "An evil and adulterous generation asks for a sign, but no sign will be given to it except the sign of the prophet Jonah. For just as Jonah was for three days and three nights in the belly of the sea monster, so for three days and three nights the Son of Man will be in the heart of the earth. The people of Nineveh will rise up at the judgement with this generation and condemn it, because they repented at the proclamation of Jonah, and see, something greater than Jonah is here! The queen of the South will rise up at the judgement with this generation and condemn it, because she came from the ends of the earth to listen to the wisdom of Solomon, and see, something greater than Solomon is here!"

- Most of us are fascinated by spectacular events. This is why the scribes want "a sign" from Jesus to prove that he possessed exceptional powers. But Jesus is not interested in superficial curiosity about himself. He is not a magician! Rather, he is God-among-them, mysterious and blessed.

- Does my faith depend on dramatic things happening in answer to my prayer? Or do I simply and humbly place my faith and hope in the person of Jesus Christ and unite my prayer with his? Can I simply say, "Your will be done" (Mt 6:10)?

Tuesday 21st July
Matthew 12:46–50

While he was still speaking to the crowds, his mother and his brothers were standing outside, wanting to speak to him. Someone told him, "Look, your mother and your brothers are standing outside, wanting to speak to you." But to the one who had told him this, Jesus replied, "Who is my mother, and who are my brothers?" And pointing to his disciples, he said, "Here are my mother and my brothers! For whoever does the will of my Father in heaven is my brother and sister and mother."

- I imagine myself in the crowd outside the door. I like listening to Jesus and watching him. Somehow he gives meaning to my life, and opens up worlds I could never have dreamed of.

- In my daily prayer, I come to him like a beggar . . . with a desire to be nourished and enriched.

240 ·

Wednesday 22nd July
Matthew 13:3—9

J esus told them many things in parables, saying: "Listen! A sower went out to sow. And as he sowed, some seeds fell on the path, and the birds came and ate them up. Other seeds fell on rocky ground, where they did not have much soil, and they sprang up quickly, since they had no depth of soil. But when the sun rose, they were scorched; and since they had no root, they withered away. Other seeds fell among thorns, and the thorns grew up and choked them. Other seeds fell on good soil and brought forth grain, some a hundredfold, some sixty, some thirty. Let anyone with ears listen!"

- Such large crowds gathered to see and hear Jesus, he had to preach from a boat. They were hungry for spiritual nourishment and for leadership.

- Lord Jesus, I pray for the Church and for all believers today. Make of us a community of disciples, all looking to you.

Thursday 23rd July
Matthew 13:10—17

T hen the disciples came and asked Jesus, "Why do you speak to them in parables?" He answered, "To you it has been given to know the secrets of the kingdom of heaven, but to them it has not been given. For to those who have, more will be given, and they will have an abundance; but from those who have nothing, even what they have will be taken away. The reason I speak to them in parables is that 'seeing they do not perceive, and hearing they do not listen, nor do they understand.' With them indeed is fulfilled the prophecy of Isaiah that says: 'You will indeed listen, but never understand, and you will indeed look, but never perceive. For this people's heart has grown dull, and their ears are hard of hearing, and they have shut their eyes; so that they might not look with their eyes, and listen with their ears, and understand with their heart and turn—and I would heal them.' But blessed are your eyes, for they see, and your ears, for they hear. Truly I tell you, many prophets and righteous people longed to see what you see, but did not see it, and to hear what you hear, but did not hear it."

- Some people find faith easy; others find it impossible. But it would be wrong to think that a good God deliberately shuts anyone out from belief. Instead, Jesus is emphasising by contrast how blessed the disciples are.

- I thank him that I do see and hear and that I know the secrets of God. I ask to cultivate this gift by becoming more intimate with God in my prayer.

Friday 24th July
Matthew 13:18—23

Jesus said to his disciples, "Hear then the parable of the sower. When anyone hears the word of the kingdom and does not understand it, the evil one comes and snatches away what is sown in the heart; this is what was sown on the path. As for what was sown on rocky ground, this is the one who hears the word and immediately receives it with joy; yet such a person has no root, but endures only for a while, and when trouble or persecution arises on account of the word, that person immediately falls away. As for what was sown among thorns, this is the one who hears the word, but the cares of the world and the lure of wealth choke the word, and it yields nothing. But as for what was sown on good soil, this is the one who hears the word and understands it, who indeed bears fruit and yields, in one case a hundredfold, in another sixty, and in another thirty."

- The Word of God is sown in my heart day after day through *Sacred Space*. How would I describe my heart? Is it part hard, part rocky, part thorny? I ask the Lord to till the soil of my heart so that it becomes fresh and fertile.

- If I were challenged in court to explain my faith, what would I say? Would I talk about what I know about God, or rather that

I try to live according to the command of love? Would there be much evidence available to support my statements?

Saturday 25th July,
St. James, Apostle
Matthew 20:20−23

Then the mother of the sons of Zebedee came to him with her sons, and kneeling before him, she asked a favour of him. And he said to her, "What do you want?" She said to him, "Declare that these two sons of mine will sit, one at your right hand and one at your left, in your kingdom." But Jesus answered, "You do not know what you are asking. Are you able to drink the cup that I am about to drink?" They said to him, "We are able." He said to them, "You will indeed drink my cup, but to sit at my right hand and at my left, this is not mine to grant, but it is for those for whom it has been prepared by my Father."

- Jesus responds to an ambitious mother by explaining that the ways and values of this world are not those of God. This gospel challenges me regarding my own pride.

- Does selfish ambition ever get in the way of my service of God and neighbour? Do I ever lord it over others? Can I be a tyrant on occasion?

July 26—August 1

Something to think and pray about each day this week:

The Joy of Freedom

We belong to God's own family. How then, St. Paul asks, can we act as if we were still slaves? We can move beyond lives of quiet desperation; we can stop feeling burdened, hopeless, dull, and passive. Our liberation was Jesus' agenda: "The Spirit . . . has sent me to proclaim release to the captives . . . to let the oppressed go free" (Lk 4:18). "If the Son makes you free, you will be free indeed" (Jn 8:36). The liberation of humankind is his great achievement. "The Spirit of life in Christ Jesus has set you free" (Rom 8:2).

Our freedom is God's primary gift to us. In fact it makes us like God. We need not be afraid to claim it and exercise it. Even when we misuse our free will, God does not take it away, but works to undo the damage we cause. We learn from Jesus how to use our freedom well. He makes us a free people, a chosen race, sons and daughters of God. How should such people live? Not as slaves or sheep, surely, but as people who had been imprisoned but have just been let out into the open air and the sunlight that the free enjoy.

Of course, I have to struggle to grow in freedom. It doesn't happen all at once. But I can make a fresh start every day. I pray: "God, thank you for my freedom. Let me live it out well today. Give me joy, energy, enthusiasm, and commitment for all that is worthwhile."

The Presence of God

As I sit here, the beating of my heart,
the ebb and flow of my breathing, the movements of my mind
are all signs of God's ongoing creation of me.
I pause for a moment, and become aware
of this presence of God within me.

Freedom

I ask for the grace
to let go of my own concerns
and be open to what God is asking of me,
to let myself be guided and formed by my loving Creator.

Consciousness

How do I find myself today?
Where am I with God? With others?
Do I have something to be grateful for? Then I give thanks.
Is there something I am sorry for? Then I ask forgiveness.

The Word

I take my time to read the Word of God, slowly, a few times, allowing myself to dwell on anything that strikes me. (Please turn to your scripture on the following pages. Inspiration points are there should you need them. When you are ready, return here to continue.)

Conversation

Remembering that I am still in God's presence,
I imagine Jesus himself standing or sitting beside me,
and I say whatever is on my mind, whatever is in my heart,
speaking as one friend to another.

Conclusion

Glory be to the Father, and to the Son, and to the Holy Spirit,
as it was in the beginning, is now, and ever shall be,
world without end. Amen.

Sunday 26th July,
Seventeenth Sunday of Ordinary Time
John 6:1—13

After this Jesus went to the other side of the Sea of Galilee, also called the Sea of Tiberias. A large crowd kept following him, because they saw the signs that he was doing for the sick. Jesus went up the mountain and sat down there with his disciples. Now the Passover, the festival of the Jews, was near. When he looked up and saw a large crowd coming towards him, Jesus said to Philip, "Where are we to buy bread for these people to eat?" He said this to test him, for he himself knew what he was going to do. Philip answered him, "Six months' wages would not buy enough bread for each of them to get a little." One of his disciples, Andrew, Simon Peter's brother, said to him, "There is a boy here who has five barley loaves and two fish. But what are they among so many people?" Jesus said, "Make the people sit down." Now there was a great deal of grass in the place; so they sat down, about five thousand in all. Then Jesus took the loaves, and when he had given thanks, he distributed them to those who were seated; so also the fish, as much as they wanted. When they were satisfied, he told his disciples, "Gather up the fragments left over, so that nothing may be lost." So they gathered them up, and from the fragments of the five barley loaves, left by those who had eaten, they filled twelve baskets.

- I enter in imagination into this amazing scene. I share Philip's puzzlement; I watch the little boy as he gives up the lunch his mother made for him. I gaze at Jesus as he prays, then as he breaks the bread and the fish. It takes so long to feed everyone, but he is smiling as he works.

- Jesus fills my empty and grubby hands, too, and I look into his eyes and thank him.

Monday 27th July
Matthew 13:31–35

He put before them another parable: "The kingdom of heaven is like a mustard seed that someone took and sowed in his field; it is the smallest of all the seeds, but when it has grown it is the greatest of shrubs and becomes a tree, so that the birds of the air come and make nests in its branches." He told them another parable: "The kingdom of heaven is like yeast that a woman took and mixed in with three measures of flour until all of it was leavened." Jesus told the crowds all these things in parables; without a parable he told them nothing. This was to fulfil what had been spoken through the prophet: "I will open my mouth to speak in parables; I will proclaim what has been hidden from the foundation of the world."

- Jesus was a wandering preacher from an out-of-the-way village. He had nowhere to lay his head. Yet he initiates a network of loving relationships that reaches across time and space.

- While the Christian community has many failings, I thank God for all it achieves.

Tuesday 28th July
Matthew 13:36–43

His disciples approached Jesus, saying, "Explain to us the parable of the weeds of the field." He answered, "The one who sows the good seed is the Son of Man; the field is the world, and the good seed are the children of the kingdom; the weeds are the children of the evil one, and the enemy who sowed them is the devil; the harvest is the end of the age, and the reapers are angels. Just as the weeds are collected and burned up with fire, so will it be at the end of the age. The Son of Man will send his angels, and they will collect out of his kingdom all causes of sin and all evildoers, and they will throw them into the furnace of fire, where there will be weeping and gnashing of teeth. Then the righteous will shine like the sun in the kingdom of their Father. Let anyone with ears listen!"

- I sit with the disciples as Jesus explains the parable. He sows good seed in an evil world. The disciples are told not to pass judgement on bad people, but to leave judgement to God.

- Am I judgemental? Do I condemn the faults of others? If I do, do I think I am faultless?

Wednesday 29th July
Matthew 13:44—46

Jesus said to the disciples, "The kingdom of heaven is like treasure hidden in a field, which someone found and hid; then in his joy he goes and sells all that he has and buys that field. Again, the kingdom of heaven is like a merchant in search of fine pearls; on finding one pearl of great value, he went and sold all that he had and bought it."

- "Selling all I have" means letting go of the things that have an inordinate share of my time and attention: hobbies, work, popularity, ambition, sex, and so on. All these things must make room for the most precious treasure that gives meaning to my life, namely, working to realize the kingdom of God at the center of my life.

- Lord, help me to order rightly my priorities, that I might not miss this pearl of great value.

Thursday 30th July
Matthew 13:47—51

Jesus said, "Again, the kingdom of heaven is like a net that was thrown into the sea and caught fish of every kind; when it was full, they drew it ashore, sat down, and put the good into baskets but threw out the bad. So it will be at the end of the age. The angels will come out and separate the evil from the righteous and throw them into the furnace of fire, where there will be weeping and gnashing of teeth. Have you understood all this?" They answered, "Yes."

- Jesus speaks in parables, a form of storytelling, to help his words come to life for his followers in everyday language. Many of the disciples were fishermen who spent their lives casting out their nets to draw in the fish. They could understand the method of separating the "good" from the "bad."

- Father, as we weave our way through life, help us to discern what is pleasing to you and how we can reach for the heavens in our daily communion with our brothers and sisters.

Friday 31st July,
St. Ignatius Loyola
Matthew 13:54—58

Jesus came to his home town and began to teach the people in their synagogue, so that they were astounded and said, "Where did this man get this wisdom and these deeds of power? Is not this the carpenter's son? Is not his mother called Mary? And are not his brothers James and Joseph and Simon and Judas? And are not all his sisters with us? Where then did this man get all this?" And they took offence at him. But Jesus said to them, "Prophets are not without honour except in their own country and in their own house." And he did not do many deeds of power there, because of their unbelief.

- How deeply human is this gospel reading. Human nature has not changed since Jesus' time! Jealousy rears its ugly head. Can't you hear them say, "Who does this guy think he is? What would he know—isn't he only a carpenter's son? Take no notice of him, and maybe he will move on to someplace else!"

- Jesus, how many times have we closed our ears to your gentle whispering, your attempts at reaching our hearts? Forgive us our judgemental attitude and our slowness in recognizing you in one another.

Saturday 1st August
Matthew 14:1—12

At that time Herod the ruler heard reports about Jesus; and he said to his servants, "This is John the Baptist; he has been raised from the dead, and for this reason these powers are at work in him." For Herod had arrested John, bound him, and put him in prison on account of Herodias, his brother Philip's wife, because John had been telling him, "It is not lawful for you to have her." Though Herod wanted to put him to death, he feared the crowd, because they regarded him as a prophet. But when Herod's birthday came, the daughter of Herodias danced before the company, and she pleased Herod so much that he promised on oath to grant her whatever she might ask. Prompted by her mother, she said, "Give me the head of John the Baptist here on a platter." The king was grieved, yet out of regard for his oaths and for the guests, he commanded it to be given; he sent and had John beheaded in the prison. The head was brought on a platter and given to the girl, who brought it to her mother. His disciples came and took the body and buried it; then they went and told Jesus.

- Herod did not like what John had to say. But do any of us like someone else who names our sin? The power that Herod held, coupled with the jealousy of his wife Herodias, led to the death of one of Jesus' most faithful followers.

- Lord, how often do we influence others to behave badly toward another person? How often does the word of scandal trip lightly off our tongues and so degrade the dignity of another? Teach us, Lord, how to behave justly and generously in our dealings with those we meet on life's journey.

August 2—8

Something to think and pray about each day this week:

The Lover Gives All

An older Jesuit was restless and upset on his deathbed. His friends tried to comfort him, assuring him that God is all-merciful and forgiving. Nothing helped. Eventually he whispered, "It's not God I'm afraid of; it's Ignatius!"

Prior to Vatican II, St. Ignatius was often caricatured as a hard military man who insisted on rules and demanded blind obedience of his followers. But contemporary research reveals him as a deeply loving man. Before his conversion at the ripe age of thirty, he loved his feudal lord and also a mysterious but important lady, about whom he would daydream endlessly. When the Christ of the New Testament was opened up to him, he fell in love again, and this love transformed his remaining thirty-five years. He fell in love, too, with all God's people, and his life's goal was simply expressed: "to help others." Even to help one person brought him joy, and he devoted much of his time in one-to-one spiritual conversation. His was a ministry of consolation.

"What ought I do for Christ?" was his abiding question. As one of the great mystics of the Church, St. Ignatius saw God as the great Lover who gives everything to us. Filled with love and gratitude, he made himself over to God's service. He believed that God deals directly with us, and that we can thus "find God in all things." It was said that "no one went away from him sad." Our dying Jesuit had nothing to fear from him!

The Presence of God

I pause for a moment
and reflect on God's life-giving presence
in every part of my body, in everything around me,
in the whole of my life.

Freedom

I ask for the grace to believe
in what I could be and do
if I only allowed God, my loving Creator,
to continue to create me, guide me, and shape me.

Consciousness

In God's loving presence, I unwind the past day,
starting from now and looking back, moment by moment.
I gather in all the goodness and light in gratitude.
I attend to the shadows and what they say to me,
seeking healing, courage, forgiveness.

The Word

God speaks to each one of us individually. I need to listen to what
he is saying to me. (Please turn to your scripture on the following
pages. Inspiration points are there should you need them. When you
are ready, return here to continue.)

Conversation

How has God's Word moved me? Has it left me cold?
Has it consoled me or moved me to act in a new way?
I imagine Jesus standing or sitting beside me;
I turn and share my feelings with him.

Conclusion

Glory be to the Father, and to the Son, and to the Holy Spirit,
as it was in the beginning, is now, and ever shall be,
world without end. Amen.

August 2015

Sunday 2nd August,
Eighteenth Sunday of Ordinary Time
John 6:26—34

Jesus said to the crowd, "Very truly, I tell you, you are looking for me, not because you saw signs, but because you ate your fill of the loaves. Do not work for the food that perishes, but for the food that endures for eternal life, which the Son of Man will give you. For it is on him that God the Father has set his seal." Then they said to him, "What must we do to perform the works of God?" Jesus answered them, "This is the work of God, that you believe in him whom he has sent." So they said to him, "What sign are you going to give us then, so that we may see it and believe you? What work are you performing? Our ancestors ate the manna in the wilderness; as it is written, 'He gave them bread from heaven to eat.'" Then Jesus said to them, "Very truly, I tell you, it was not Moses who gave you the bread from heaven, but it is my Father who gives you the true bread from heaven. For the bread of God is that which comes down from heaven and gives life to the world." They said to him, "Sir, give us this bread always."

- Jesus speaks bluntly with the people he had fed the previous day. He knows they came looking for him because they had eaten their fill of bread. Why do I look for Jesus? Is it out of love or for what I can get?

- The truth can be uncomfortable and make us defensive and even cynical. Or it can make us stop, look, reflect, and change. Lord, give me the humility to follow the truth always, because it alone "will make me free" (Jn 8:32).

Monday 3rd August
Matthew 14:13—21

Now when Jesus heard of the death of John the Baptist, he withdrew from there in a boat to a deserted place by himself. But when the crowds heard it, they followed him on foot from the towns.

When he went ashore, he saw a great crowd; and he had compassion for them and cured their sick. When it was evening, the disciples came to him and said, "This is a deserted place, and the hour is now late; send the crowds away so that they may go into the villages and buy food for themselves." Jesus said to them, "They need not go away; you give them something to eat." They replied, "We have nothing here but five loaves and two fish." And he said, "Bring them here to me." Then he ordered the crowds to sit down on the grass. Taking the five loaves and the two fish, he looked up to heaven, and blessed and broke the loaves, and gave them to the disciples, and the disciples gave them to the crowds. And all ate and were filled; and they took up what was left over of the broken pieces, twelve baskets full. And those who ate were about five thousand men, besides women and children.

- Here Jesus challenges the disciples to "feed" the people themselves. Is this a hint of how Jesus shares *himself* in the Eucharist? It hints that we in our own turn are to be given for others, like bread which he can take, bless, break, and share with those around us.

- Father, help us to share our giftedness with one another. Help us to share what we have with the poor. Free us from the desire to hold on to what we have. Every good thing is a gift from you.

Tuesday 4th August
Matthew 14:25—33

Early in the morning he came walking towards them on the lake. But when the disciples saw him walking on the lake, they were terrified, saying, "It is a ghost!" And they cried out in fear. But immediately Jesus spoke to them and said, "Take heart, it is I; do not be afraid." Peter answered him, "Lord, if it is you, command me to come to you on the water." He said, "Come." So Peter got out of the boat, started walking on the water, and came towards Jesus. But when he noticed the strong wind, he became frightened, and beginning to sink, he cried out, "Lord, save me!" Jesus immediately reached out his hand and caught him, saying to him, "You of little faith, why did you doubt?" When they got into the boat, the wind ceased. And those in the boat worshipped him, saying, "Truly you are the Son of God."

- We may notice that Peter failed, but we will see, too, that he always responded energetically and fully, risking everything. His faltering seems to have begun when he took his eyes off Jesus and realized that he couldn't rely just on himself.

- Jesus made his way to the boat where the disciples were having some trouble. Intent on their own efforts, they did not realize he was there. I do what I can, as a disciple, but try not to forget that the one I follow is very near.

Wednesday 5th August
Matthew 15:21—28

Jesus left that place and went away to the district of Tyre and Sidon. Just then a Canaanite woman from that region came out and started shouting, "Have mercy on me, Lord, Son of David; my daughter is tormented by a demon." But he did not answer her at all. And his disciples came and urged him, saying, "Send her away, for she keeps shouting after us." He answered, "I was sent only to the lost sheep of the house of Israel." But she came and knelt before him, saying, "Lord, help me." He answered, "It is not fair to take the children's food and throw it to the dogs." She said, "Yes, Lord, yet even the dogs eat the crumbs that fall from their masters' table." Then Jesus answered her, "Woman, great is your faith! Let it be done for you as you wish." And her daughter was healed instantly.

- The Canaanite woman acknowledges Jesus as Son of David, a messianic title. She kneels before him and calls him "Lord."

- She refuses to take offence at a seemingly rude insult. She knows the power and the mercy of this man. She believes in him. Her request is granted.

Thursday 6th August,
Transfiguration of the Lord
Luke 9:28—30, 32—36

Jesus took with him Peter and John and James, and went up on the mountain to pray. And while he was praying, the appearance of his face changed, and his clothes became dazzling white. Suddenly they saw two men, Moses and Elijah, talking to him. . . . Now Peter and his companions were weighed down with sleep; but since they had stayed awake, they saw his glory and the two men who stood with him. Just as they were leaving him, Peter said to Jesus, "Master, it is good for us to be here; let us make three dwellings, one for you, one for Moses, and one for Elijah"—not knowing what he said. While he was saying this, a cloud came and overshadowed them; and they were terrified as they entered the cloud. Then from the cloud came a voice that said, "This is my Son, my Chosen; listen to him!" When the voice had spoken, Jesus was found alone.

- Peter, John, and James were heavy with sleep, but on waking they saw his glory! They slept again in Gethsemane.

- Jesus, how often have our eyes been closed in sleep as we walk with you through life? How often are our ears closed, too, to the Word you speak to us through our daily conversations? May your Word become awake, alive, and active in us each day as we travel the road together with you.

Friday 7th August
Matthew 16:24—26

Then Jesus told his disciples, "If any want to become my followers, let them deny themselves and take up their cross and follow me. For those who want to save their life will lose it, and those who lose their life for my sake will find it. For what will it profit them if they gain the whole world but forfeit their life? Or what will they give in return for their life?"

- One of the key ideas in the gospel is that we take up the cross of doing what is right and being willing to bear it. Taking up your own cross includes accepting and living with pain, suffering of any sort, and the griefs of life we can do nothing about.

- Jesus bore a cross to the end of his convictions with love.

Saturday 8th August
Matthew 17:14—20

When they came to the crowd, a man came to Jesus, knelt before him, and said, "Lord, have mercy on my son, for he is an epileptic and he suffers terribly; he often falls into the fire and often into the water. And I brought him to your disciples, but they could not cure him." Jesus answered, "You faithless and perverse generation, how much longer must I be with you? How much longer must I put up with you? Bring him here to me." And Jesus rebuked the demon, and it came out of him, and the boy was cured instantly. Then the disciples came to Jesus privately and said, "Why could we not cast it out?" He said to them, "Because of your little faith. For truly I tell you, if you have faith the size of a mustard seed, you will say to this mountain, 'Move from here to there,' and it will move; and nothing will be impossible for you."

- Notice Jesus' impatience in this situation. In it, we can find resonance with our own human impatience and also find the strength to persevere.

- Doubt can be an important part of belief in God. It is honest. If there are no moments of doubt, the space for us to grow in trust and faith is reduced.

August 9—15

Something to think and pray about each day this week:

No Sacred Space?

A recent report claims that in today's world we have no sacred space, due to the overuse of digital technology. Online dependency is growing, even among young children. A parent describes how she took away her child's iPad one night, and the child had "an absolute meltdown." First thing in the morning, the child searched for it and used it all day. But the child may be only imitating its parents who feel "left out" if they are not responding to the endless calls made to them.

To free ourselves from Internet-use disorder, we need discipline. Its positive purpose would be to safeguard a sacred space in our lives. Our Sacred Space does just that! St. Paul insists that God is generous (see 2 Cor 9:8), so we will never regret quality time given to prayer and reflection on the things of God. To stay alive and grow deep down, we need to preserve a silent, empty, open space which only the Word of God can fill.

Jesus was very aware of this. As he says, "One does not live by bread alone, but by every word that comes from the mouth of God" (Mt 4:4, from Dt 8:3). In our practice of Sacred Space, the voice of the Good Spirit speaks to us. In the cave of our hearts the Lord waits—for what? God "waits to be gracious to us" (Is 30:18). It is thus that divine love is kindled in us, which enriches us and radiates to others.

The Presence of God

"The world is charged with the grandeur of God" (Gerard Manley Hopkins).
I dwell for a moment on the presence of God
around me, in every part of my body,
and deep within my being.

Freedom

"In these days, God taught me
as a schoolteacher teaches a pupil" (St. Ignatius).
I remind myself that there are things God has to teach me yet,
and I ask for the grace to hear them and let them change me.

Consciousness

Help me, Lord, to be more conscious of your presence.
Teach me to recognize your presence in others.
Fill my heart with gratitude for the times your love
has been shown to me through the care of others.

The Word

I read the Word of God slowly, a few times over, and I listen to what God is saying to me. (Please turn to your scripture on the following pages. Inspirations points are there should you need them. When you are ready, return here to continue.)

Conversation

What feelings are rising in me
as I pray and reflect on God's Word?
I imagine Jesus himself sitting or standing beside me,
and I open my heart to him.

Conclusion

Glory be to the Father, and to the Son, and to the Holy Spirit,
as it was in the beginning, is now, and ever shall be,
world without end. Amen.

Sunday 9th August,
Nineteenth Sunday of Ordinary Time
John 6:47—51

Jesus said to the crowd, "Very truly, I tell you, whoever believes has eternal life. I am the bread of life. Your ancestors ate the manna in the wilderness, and they died. This is the bread that comes down from heaven, so that one may eat of it and not die. I am the living bread that came down from heaven. Whoever eats of this bread will live for ever; and the bread that I will give for the life of the world is my flesh."

- Faith is an ongoing gift. Jesus says plainly that it is a gift of the Father which enables us to come to him and to believe in him. And whoever has that gift has—present tense—eternal life. Does this stir my heart with joy?

- Jesus, let me give my heart to you; this heart-to-heart relationship is what faith is really about, not just head-knowledge.

Monday 10th August,
St. Lawrence, Martyr
John 12:24—26

Jesus said, "Very truly, I tell you, unless a grain of wheat falls into the earth and dies, it remains just a single grain; but if it dies, it bears much fruit. Those who love their life lose it, and those who hate their life in this world will keep it for eternal life. Whoever serves me must follow me, and where I am, there will my servant be also. Whoever serves me, the Father will honour."

- God can use us to affect the lives of many people for good. But for this we need to be following Jesus, not following our own whims and preferences. We are to surrender our lives and ask the question, "Lord, what do you want me to do with my life today?"

260

- Lord, grace me with the gift of letting go of all that I cling to. May I not block your Spirit moving in me. Work through me so that, like Mary, I may carry you to all those whose lives I touch.

Tuesday 11th August
Matthew 18:12—14

Jesus said to the disciples, "What do you think? If a shepherd has a hundred sheep, and one of them has gone astray, does he not leave the ninety-nine on the mountains and go in search of the one that went astray? And if he finds it, truly I tell you, he rejoices over it more than over the ninety-nine that never went astray. So it is not the will of your Father in heaven that one of these little ones should be lost."

- "How great is your name, Lord, above all the earth!" Jesus, over and over again you seek ways to tell us of your great love for us.

- You are a searching God—you look for us when we are lost. Yet time and time again we pay no attention to you.

Wednesday 12th August
Matthew 18:15—17

Jesus said, "If another member of the church sins against you, go and point out the fault when the two of you are alone. If the member listens to you, you have regained that one. But if you are not listened to, take one or two others along with you, so that every word may be confirmed by the evidence of two or three witnesses. If the member refuses to listen to them, tell it to the church; and if the offender refuses to listen even to the church, let such a one be to you as a Gentile and a tax-collector."

- How do we take the first step to heal a broken relationship, if the hurt done to us is very painful? Where can we find the courage to speak face-to-face with the one who has caused such hurt?

August 2015

- We may need to seek the help and prayer of our friends so that we will find the right words and the right way to settle our differences.

Thursday 13th August
Matthew 18:21—22

Then Peter came and said to him, "Lord, if another member of the church sins against me, how often should I forgive? As many as seven times?" Jesus said to him, "Not seven times, but, I tell you, seventy-seven times."

- Forgiveness is tough. I ask Jesus now in my prayer: "Why should I forgive?" Let me listen to his reply: "Because you have been forgiven by God."

- We who have been forgiven so much by God do not have the right to withhold forgiveness from someone else, no matter how tough it may be.

Friday 14th August
Matthew 19:3—11

Some Pharisees came to him, and to test him they asked, "Is it lawful for a man to divorce his wife for any cause?" He answered, "Have you not read that the one who made them at the beginning 'made them male and female,' and said, 'For this reason a man shall leave his father and mother and be joined to his wife, and the two shall become one flesh'? So they are no longer two, but one flesh. Therefore what God has joined together, let no one separate." They said to him, "Why then did Moses command us to give a certificate of dismissal and to divorce her?" He said to them, "It was because you were so hard-hearted that Moses allowed you to divorce your wives, but at the beginning it was not so. And I say to you, whoever divorces his wife, except for unchastity, and marries another commits adultery." His disciples said to him, "If such is the case of a man with his wife, it is better not to marry." But he said to them, "Not every-one can accept this teaching, but only those to whom it is given."

- The divorce debate was there at the time of Jesus and is still with us. His teaching is clear and his standards are high. He says that a married man and woman are "one flesh." Marriage in the plan of God is meant to be for life.

- Being the merciful man he is, Jesus knows that not everyone can, or will, accept his teaching. I ask God to bless the marriages I know of and indeed every marriage.

Saturday 15th August,
Assumption of the Virgin Mary
Luke 1:46—56

And Mary said, "My soul magnifies the Lord, and my spirit rejoices in God my Saviour, for he has looked with favour on the lowliness of his servant. Surely, from now on all generations will call me blessed; for the Mighty One has done great things for me, and holy is his name. His mercy is for those who fear him from generation to generation. He has shown strength with his arm; he has scattered the proud in the thoughts of their hearts. He has brought down the powerful from their thrones, and lifted up the lowly; he has filled the hungry with good things, and sent the rich away empty. He has helped his servant Israel, in remembrance of his mercy, accord-ing to the promise he made to our ancestors, to Abraham and to his descendants forever." And Mary remained with Elizabeth about three months and then returned to her home.

- When the two mothers-to-be meet, John, while in the womb of Elizabeth, recognizes Jesus in the womb of Mary and leaps for joy. Inspired by the Holy Spirit, Elizabeth declares Mary to be the most blessed of women.

- Mary's response is to sing God's praises in words that echo those of Hannah in 1 Samuel 2:1–10. We can ponder, like Mary, on the richness of this passage.

August 16—22

Something to think and pray about each day this week:

The Sounds of Silence

The monks of old fled from the noise and distraction of the world into the desert. If we did likewise today, our temptation would be to bring our mobile devices in our backpacks! But like the good monks, we, too, are meant to be seeking God, and people are beginning to search out how to do that. The movement called The New Monasticism tries to replant ancient values in our lives today. It proposes that our hearts can be our monasteries in the middle of busy lives. We can be still and quiet and can cultivate a place of silence in the cave of our hearts, which we share only with God.

The experience of Elijah of old still raises an echo in us and tugs at our hearts. He was told to stand on the mountain, for the Lord was about to pass by. There came the roar of a mighty wind, but the Lord was not in the wind, nor in the earthquake which followed, nor again in the fire. Then we are told: "After the fire came a sound of sheer silence." Elijah heard this mysterious silence and went out to meet God (1 Kgs 19:11–13). They spoke together, after which conversation Elijah knew what he was to do.

Such experiences can be ours whenever we choose to leave the busy world behind and go down into the cave of our hearts, the secret place where, Jesus says, we "will meet our God who dwells there" (see Mt 6:6).

The Presence of God

As I sit here, God is present,
breathing life into me and into everything around me.
For a few moments, I sit silently
and become aware of God's loving presence.

Freedom

If God were trying to tell me something, would I know?
If God were reassuring me or challenging me, would I notice?
I ask for the grace to be free of my own preoccupations
and open to what God may be saying to me.

Consciousness

How am I really feeling? Lighthearted? Heavy hearted?
I may be very much at peace, happy to be here.
Equally, I may be frustrated, worried, or angry.
I acknowledge how I really am. It is the real me that the Lord loves.

The Word

I take my time to read the Word of God, slowly, a few times, allowing myself to dwell on anything that strikes me. (Please turn to your scripture on the following pages. Inspiration points are there should you need them. When you are ready, return here to continue.)

Conversation

What is stirring in me as I pray?
Am I consoled, troubled, left cold?
I imagine Jesus himself standing or sitting at my side,
and I share my feelings with him.

Conclusion

Glory be to the Father, and to the Son, and to the Holy Spirit,
as it was in the beginning, is now, and ever shall be,
world without end. Amen.

Sunday 16th August,
Twentieth Sunday of Ordinary Time
John 6:51—58

Jesus said to the people, "I am the living bread that came down from heaven. Whoever eats of this bread will live for ever; and the bread that I will give for the life of the world is my flesh." The Jews then disputed among themselves, saying, "How can this man give us his flesh to eat?" So Jesus said to them, "Very truly, I tell you, unless you eat the flesh of the Son of Man and drink his blood, you have no life in you. Those who eat my flesh and drink my blood have eternal life, and I will raise them up on the last day; for my flesh is true food and my blood is true drink. Those who eat my flesh and drink my blood abide in me, and I in them. Just as the living Father sent me, and I live because of the Father, so whoever eats me will live because of me. This is the bread that came down from heaven, not like that which your ancestors ate, and they died. But the one who eats this bread will live for ever."

- This is one of the most amazing passages in all of scripture. For the Hebrews, flesh and blood meant the full person, so Jesus chooses this dramatic way to reveal the extraordinary intimacy of his relationship with us.

- Bread nourishes us, so Jesus uses that term to describe himself. But "living" bread is an effort to reveal more deeply how profoundly he nourishes us. He offers us a relationship in which we can "abide" in security. We need that life-giving relationship more than ever today.

Monday 17th August
Matthew 19:16—22

Then someone came to Jesus and said, "Teacher, what good deed must I do to have eternal life?" And he said to him, "Why do you ask me about what is good? There is only one who is good. If you wish to enter into life, keep the commandments." He said to him, "Which ones?" And Jesus said, "You shall not murder; You shall not commit adultery; You shall not steal; You shall not bear false witness; Honour your father and mother; also, You shall love your neighbour as yourself." The young man said to him, "I have kept all these; what do I still lack?" Jesus said to him, "If you wish to be perfect, go, sell your possessions, and give the money to the poor, and you will have treasure in heaven; then come, follow me." When the young man heard this word, he went away grieving, for he had many possessions.

- Sometimes when we ask a question of God, we do not like the answer! When Jesus challenges this good young man to let go of the material things that he treasures, he walks away from Jesus, grieving.

- Does my heart ever ache because I know God is asking something which I am not ready to give to him?

Tuesday 18th August
Matthew 19:23—26

Jesus said to his disciples, "Truly I tell you, it will be hard for a rich person to enter the kingdom of heaven. Again I tell you, it is easier for a camel to go through the eye of a needle than for someone who is rich to enter the kingdom of God." When the disciples heard this, they were greatly astounded and said, "Then who can be saved?" But Jesus looked at them and said, "For mortals it is impossible, but for God all things are possible."

- To enter through a narrow gate, a camel must kneel in order for its load to be taken off. We, too, must surrender all that burdens us and weighs us down. No sacrifice that we make to draw closer to God will go unrewarded.

- Our prayer today, Lord, is that we will not be afraid that you will ask anything of us that we cannot do. Help us to surrender totally to you, trusting that you, and you alone, are all we need.

Wednesday 19th August
Matthew 20:1—16

Jesus said to his disciples, "For the kingdom of heaven is like a landowner who went out early in the morning to hire labourers for his vineyard. After agreeing with the labourers for the usual daily wage, he sent them into his vineyard. When he went out about nine o'clock, he saw others standing idle in the market-place; and he said to them, 'You also go into the vineyard, and I will pay you whatever is right.' So they went. When he went out again about noon and about three o'clock, he did the same. And about five o'clock he went out and found others standing around; and he said to them, 'Why are you standing here idle all day?' They said to him, 'Because no one has hired us.' He said to them, 'You also go into the vineyard.' When evening came, the owner of the vineyard said to his manager, 'Call the labourers and give them their pay, beginning with the last and then going to the first.' When those hired about five o'clock came, each of them received the usual daily wage. Now when the first came, they thought they would receive more; but each of them also received the usual daily wage. And when they received it, they grumbled against the landowner, saying, 'These last worked only one hour, and you have made them equal to us who have borne the burden of the day and the scorching heat.' But he replied to one of them, 'Friend, I am doing you no wrong; did you not agree with me for the usual daily wage? Take what belongs to you and go; I choose to give to this last the same as I give to you. Am I not allowed to do what I choose with what belongs to me? Or are you envious because I am generous?' So the last will be first, and the first will be last."

- How different are God's ways from our ways! He uses dramatic images to turn upside down our ideas of self-importance. Else-where he says: "Sit at the bottom table, not at the top" and "The first shall be last and the last, first." There is no place for competitiveness in the kingdom of God.

- Forgive us, Lord, for our jealous attitudes. Help us to be grateful for what we have and not to begrudge others any good fortune that comes their way. Help us to be generous in our treatment of others and never think of ourselves as more deserving.

Thursday 20th August
Matthew 22:1—2, 8—14

Once more Jesus spoke to them in parables, saying: "The kingdom of heaven may be compared to a king who gave a wedding banquet for his son. . . . Then he said to his slaves, 'The wedding is ready. . . . Go therefore into the main streets, and invite everyone you find to the wedding banquet.' Those slaves went out into the streets and gathered all whom they found, both good and bad; so the wedding hall was filled with guests. But when the king came in to see the guests, he noticed a man there who was not wearing a wedding robe, and he said to him, 'Friend, how did you get in here without a wedding robe?' And he was speechless. Then the king said to the attendants, 'Bind him hand and foot, and throw him into the outer darkness, where there will be weeping and gnashing of teeth.' For many are called, but few are chosen."

- The grace and mercy of God are free for all who will accept them with a grateful heart. The wedding invitation is extended to everyone, and God provides our wedding garments for us.

- He offers us the garments of baptism, reconciliation, Eucharist. He offers to take us into his keeping, forgive us our wrongdoings, feed us with his body and blood.

Friday 21st August
Matthew 22:34—40

When the Pharisees heard that Jesus had silenced the Sadducees, they gathered together, and one of them, a lawyer, asked him a question to test him. "Teacher, which commandment in the law is the greatest?" He said to him, "'You shall love the Lord your God with all your heart, and with all your soul, and with all your mind.' This is the greatest and first commandment. And a second is like it: 'You shall love your neighbour as yourself.' On these two commandments hang all the law and the prophets."

- If we love God, then we will see him in others and treat them justly and honourably. We will not hurt our neighbours but do our utmost to live in peace with them. Imagine how wonderful the world would be if we all did this!

- Jesus, we are far from loving our neighbour as you ask us to do. Because we do not appreciate ourselves rightly, we do not appreciate others rightly either. Make us aware of the dignity which you give us, and then we shall see more easily the dignity hidden in our neighbour.

Saturday 22nd August
Matthew 23:1—12

Then Jesus said to the crowds and to his disciples, "The scribes and the Pharisees sit on Moses' seat; therefore, do whatever they teach you and follow it; but do not do as they do, for they do not practise what they teach. They tie up heavy burdens, hard to bear, and lay them on the shoulders of others; but they themselves are unwilling to lift a finger to move them. They do all their deeds to be seen by others; for they make their phylacteries broad and their fringes long. They love to have the place of honour at banquets and the best seats in the synagogues, and to be greeted with respect in the market-places, and to have people call them rabbi. But you are not to be called rabbi, for you have one teacher, and you are all students. And call no one your father on earth, for you have one Father—the one in heaven. Nor are you to be called instructors, for you have one instructor, the Messiah. The greatest among you will be your servant. All who exalt themselves will be humbled, and all who humble themselves will be exalted."

- Pray for religious leaders all over the world, that they may never be distracted by human honour or forget who it is they serve.

- I think of what it would be like for me to start again, to assume the lowest place, to really take to heart what Jesus says about humility. I begin my prayer by asking God for the help I need, humbly and sincerely.

August 23—29

Something to think and pray about each day this week:

Meeting God in the World

Fr. Pedro Arrupe, Superior General of the Jesuits after Vatican II, travelled extensively. In Latin America, he was invited to celebrate Mass in a large slum located in a hollow which filled with mud when it rained. There was no church, just a canopy over the little altar. The guitarist played the following hymn:

> To love is to give yourself.
> It is to forget yourself, by seeking what can make others happy.
> How beautiful it is to live for love.

These people, who had nothing, were ready to give *themselves* to make others happy! During the Mass, the absolute silence of the consecration contrasted with the heartfelt shout of the Our Father. These people knew they were meeting Jesus, their hope and consolation.

At the end, a big man said to Fr. Pedro, "Come to my house. I have something to honour you with." His host made him sit on a rickety chair, from which Pedro could see the setting sun, and said, "See, *señor*, how beautiful it is!" They sat silent, watching the sun disappear. The man added: "I did not know how to thank you for all that you have done for us. I have nothing to give you, but I thought you would like to see this sunset. It pleased you, didn't it? Good evening." Then he brought him down the hill, shook hands, and so they parted.

The Presence of God

As I sit here with these words in front of me, God is here.
He is around me, in my sensations, in my thoughts, and deep within me.
I pause for a moment, and become aware
of God's life-giving presence.

Freedom

I need to rise above the noise—
the noise that interrupts and separates,
the noise that isolates.
I need to listen to God again.

Consciousness

Knowing that God loves me unconditionally,
I can afford to be honest about how I am.
How has the last day been, and how do I feel now?
I share my feelings openly with the Lord.

The Word

God speaks to each one of us individually. I need to listen to what he is saying to me. (Please turn to your scripture on the following pages. Inspiration points are there should you need them. When you are ready, return here to continue.)

Conversation

Do I notice myself reacting as I pray with the Word of God?
Do I feel challenged, comforted, angry?
Imagining Jesus sitting or standing by me,
I speak out my feelings, as one trusted friend to another.

Conclusion

Glory be to the Father, and to the Son, and to the Holy Spirit,
as it was in the beginning, is now, and ever shall be,
world without end. Amen.

August 2015

Sunday 23rd August,
Twenty-First Sunday of Ordinary Time
John 6:60—69

When many of Jesus' disciples heard it, they said, "This teaching is difficult; who can accept it?" But Jesus, being aware that his disciples were complaining about it, said to them, "Does this offend you? Then what if you were to see the Son of Man ascending to where he was before? It is the spirit that gives life; the flesh is useless. The words that I have spoken to you are spirit and life. But among you there are some who do not believe." For Jesus knew from the first who were the ones that did not believe, and who was the one that would betray him. And he said, "For this reason I have told you that no one can come to me unless it is granted by the Father." Because of Jesus' teaching many of his disciples turned back and no longer went about with him. So Jesus asked the twelve, "Do you also wish to go away?" Simon Peter answered him, "Lord, to whom can we go? You have the words of eternal life. We have come to believe and know that you are the Holy One of God."

- The teaching about the real presence of Jesus in the Eucharist is difficult. Believing in it is an act of faith, itself a gift of the Father. Like any gift we receive, it is useless unless we use it. We renew our faith each time we kneel in Jesus' presence and adore him.

- Jesus did not try to explain away what he had said, even when "many of his disciples no longer went about with him." He knows that he is nothing less than the longed-for divine presence in our world. Lord, deepen my commitment to you and to your Word.

Monday 24th August,
St. Bartholomew, Apostle
John 1:45—51

Philip found Nathanael and said to him, "We have found him about whom Moses in the law and also the prophets wrote, Jesus son of Joseph from Nazareth." Nathanael said to him, "Can anything good come out of Nazareth?" Philip said to him, "Come and see." When Jesus saw Nathanael coming towards him, he said of him, "Here is truly an Israelite in whom there is no deceit!" Nathanael asked him, "Where did you come to know me?" Jesus answered, "I saw you under the fig tree before Philip called you." Nathanael replied, "Rabbi, you are the Son of God! You are the King of Israel!" Jesus answered, "Do you believe because I told you that I saw you under the fig tree? You will see greater things than these." And he said to him, "Very truly, I tell you, you will see heaven opened and the angels of God ascending and descending upon the Son of Man."

- There is a wonderful humanity in this reading. Nathanael was a good and honest man, but he was still subject to inherited prejudices. Do we, like him, limit the places, persons, and events in which God may choose to meet us?

- Jesus knows me fully as he knew Nathanael. What would he say of me—am I a person without deceit? Nathanael in turn comes to know Jesus. What title would I give Jesus if I met him? How convinced am I of his divine connections?

Tuesday 25th August
Matthew 23:23—24

Jesus said, "Woe to you, scribes and Pharisees, hypocrites! For you tithe mint, dill, and cumin, and have neglected the weightier matters of the law: justice and mercy and faith. It is these you ought to have practised without neglecting the others. You blind guides! You strain out a gnat but swallow a camel!"

- Jesus reprimands the scribes and Pharisees: they are self-satisfied and think that they are above the Law. They look good from the outside but have neglected the deeper things.

- Jesus, you challenge us to change our ways of life, to change from the inside out! This is a hard challenge. We need to change in so many ways. Help us first of all to want to change, even if we cannot see the ways in which we should.

Wednesday 26th August
Matthew 23:27–28

Jesus said to the people, "Woe to you, scribes and Pharisees, hypocrites! For you are like whitewashed tombs, which on the outside look beautiful, but inside they are full of the bones of the dead and of all kinds of filth. So you also on the outside look righteous to others, but inside you are full of hypocrisy and lawlessness."

- Again, Jesus challenges the scribes and Pharisees to think again about how they live from day to day. He challenges them to look at what is going on in their inner selves, the part of themselves they hide from one another and, indeed, from themselves.

- They are living on the surface of life, but it has no real meaning. They cannot see how their way of life has its impact on others.

Thursday 27th August
Matthew 24:42–44

Jesus said to his disciples, "Keep awake therefore, for you do not know on what day your Lord is coming. But understand this: if the owner of the house had known in what part of the night the thief was coming, he would have stayed awake and would not have let his house be broken into. Therefore you also must be ready, for the Son of Man is coming at an unexpected hour."

- Jesus speaks of being alert to the coming of the kingdom. We do not know the day the Lord is coming. Our watchfulness must be constant. We must waken from slumber and live out our lives before God, so that when the Lord does come we will be ready.

- Keep guard over us, Jesus, so that we may always be aware of your hand on the tiller of our lives, directing us and steering us on the right path through life. Help us to be awake to the whisperings and promptings of your Holy Spirit in our hearts.

Friday 28th August
Matthew 25:1—13

Jesus said to his disciples, "Then the kingdom of heaven will be like this. Ten bridesmaids took their lamps and went to meet the bridegroom. Five of them were foolish, and five were wise. When the foolish took their lamps, they took no oil with them; but the wise took flasks of oil with their lamps. As the bridegroom was delayed, all of them became drowsy and slept. But at midnight there was a shout, 'Look! Here is the bridegroom! Come out to meet him.' Then all those bridesmaids got up and trimmed their lamps. The foolish said to the wise, 'Give us some of your oil, for our lamps are going out.' But the wise replied, 'No! there will not be enough for you and for us; you had better go to the dealers and buy some for yourselves.' And while they went to buy it, the bridegroom came, and those who were ready went with him into the wedding banquet; and the door was shut. Later the other bridesmaids came also, saying, 'Lord, lord, open to us.' But he replied, 'Truly I tell you, I do not know you.' Keep awake therefore, for you know neither the day nor the hour."

- The foolish virgins did have some oil, so they had made some preparation, but foolishly not enough! So their lamps were going out. The wise virgins felt that they could not share their oil with them, because they might not have enough for themselves.

- If the Lord were to come today, would he find me watching? Would he even know me?

Saturday 29th August
Matthew 25:14—28

Jesus told his disciples this parable, "For it is as if a man, going on a journey, summoned his slaves and entrusted his property to them; to one he gave five talents, to another two, to another one, to each according to his ability. Then he went away. The one who had received the five talents went off at once and traded with them, and made five more talents. In the same way, the one who had the two talents made two more talents. But the one who had received the one talent went off and dug a hole in the ground and hid his master's money. After a long time the master of those slaves came and settled accounts with them. Then the one who had received the five talents came forward, bringing five more talents, saying, 'Master, you handed over to me five talents; see, I have made five more talents.' His master said to him, 'Well done, good and trustworthy slave; you have been trustworthy in a few things, I will put you in charge of many things; enter into the joy of your master.' And the one with the two talents also came forward, saying, 'Master, you handed over to me two talents; see, I have made two more talents.' His master said to him, 'Well done, good and trustworthy slave; you have been trustworthy in a few things, I will put you in charge of many things; enter into the joy of your master.' Then the one who had received the one talent also came forward, saying, 'Master, I knew that you were a harsh man, reaping where you did not sow, and gathering where you did not scatter seed; so I was afraid, and I went and hid your talent in the ground. Here you have what is yours.' But his master replied, 'You wicked and lazy slave! You knew, did you, that I reap where I did not sow, and gather where I did not scatter? Then you ought to have invested my money with the bankers, and on my return I would have received what was my own with interest. So take the talent from him, and give it to the one with the ten talents.'"

- This is the parable of wasted opportunities! Do not be afraid to use your talents: stop comparing your gifts with others; share what you have received. To bury your giftedness leads only to sorrow and regret—the gnashing of teeth.

- The parable can remind us of the beautiful hymn attributed to St. Teresa of Avila: "Christ has no body now but yours. No hands, no feet on earth but yours. Yours are the eyes through which he looks compassion on this world, yours are the feet with which he walks to do good."

August 2015

August 30—September 5

Something to think and pray about each day this week:

Good Decisions Emerge from Deep Prayer

In the story of Martha and Mary (Lk 10:38–42), Jesus highlights two dimensions that must be balanced in the life of a Christian. We can recognize this balance in Pope Benedict XVI. For years, he was endlessly available to the needs of the Church. Then, as his health declined, he felt called to give priority to the contemplative dimension of life. I say "he felt called"—he was open to hearing in his heart the quiet invitation of God. His decision to step down was born out of deep prayer and inner freedom.

How well do I balance in my life the Martha and the Mary? Do I ever "feel called" by God? Am I quiet enough within to notice what God may be asking of me? Or do I never even imagine that I am sufficiently important for God to ask me anything? Do I rush into decisions and ignore "the still small voice" which Elijah heard on the mountain? St. Ignatius, although a busy administrator, advised against making any decision without first consulting God, "as a wise and loving Father."

Openness to major change also requires Benedict's inner freedom. "To live is to change, and to be perfect is to have changed often," says Cardinal Newman. Am I truly alive and open to "new things" (Is 48:6) that have the touch of God about them? And finally, am I strong enough, as Benedict was, to go against the expectations of those around me in responding to God's call?

The Presence of God
I pause for a moment, aware that God is here.
I think of how everything around me,
the air I breathe, and my whole body
is tingling with the presence of God.

Freedom
I will ask God's help
to be free from my own preoccupations,
to be open to God in this time of prayer,
to come to love and serve him more.

Consciousness
In the presence of my loving Creator,
I look honestly at my feelings over the last day—
the highs, the lows, and the level ground.
Can I see where the Lord has been present?

The Word
I read the Word of God slowly, a few times over, and I listen to what
God is saying to me. (Please turn to your scripture on the following
pages. Inspiration points are there should you need them. When you
are ready, return here to continue.)

Conversation
Remembering that I am still in God's presence,
I imagine Jesus himself standing or sitting beside me,
and I say whatever is on my mind, whatever is in my heart,
speaking as one friend to another.

Conclusion
Glory be to the Father, and to the Son, and to the Holy Spirit,
as it was in the beginning, is now, and ever shall be,
world without end. Amen.

August 2015

Sunday 30th August,
Twenty-Second Sunday of Ordinary Time
Mark 7:1—8

Now when the Pharisees and some of the scribes who had come from Jerusalem gathered around Jesus, they noticed that some of his disciples were eating with defiled hands, that is, without washing them. (For the Pharisees, and all the Jews, do not eat unless they thoroughly wash their hands, thus observing the tradition of the elders; and they do not eat anything from the market unless they wash it; and there are also many other traditions that they observe, the washing of cups, pots, and bronze kettles.) So the Pharisees and the scribes asked him, "Why do your disciples not live according to the tradition of the elders, but eat with defiled hands?" He said to them, "Isaiah prophesied rightly about you hypocrites, as it is written, 'This people honours me with their lips, but their hearts are far from me; in vain do they worship me, teaching human precepts as doctrines.' You abandon the commandment of God and hold to human tradition."

- This is shocking stuff! Jesus wipes aside mere adherence to the externals rituals of the Law. The Pharisees' version of religion warped human life and stunted personal growth. Jesus protested against hypocrisy that abandoned the commandments of God in order to cling to "human traditions."

- Lord, legalism is a travesty of true religion. You invite me to look to the inside—to the heart of the matter. Free me from putting law before love.

Monday 31st August
Luke 4:16—22

When he came to Nazareth, where he had been brought up, he went to the synagogue on the sabbath day, as was his custom. He stood up to read, and the scroll of the prophet Isaiah was given to him. He unrolled the scroll and found the place where it was written:

"The Spirit of the Lord is upon me, because he has anointed me to bring good news to the poor. He has sent me to proclaim release to the captives and recovery of sight to the blind, to let the oppressed go free, to proclaim the year of the Lord's favour." And he rolled up the scroll, gave it back to the attendant, and sat down. The eyes of all in the synagogue were fixed on him. Then he began to say to them, "Today this scripture has been fulfilled in your hearing." All spoke well of him and were amazed at the gracious words that came from his mouth.

- Jesus invites us to share in the Spirit that so fully energizes him. His mission is to awaken hope in the promises of God. His life program is to bring freedom to us who are oppressed by sin and evil. He desires to touch our broken hearts with his healing grace.

- Lord, lift me out of my apathy and my sense of emptiness. Capture my heart with your invigorating companionship and presence. Send me to others with a message of hope.

Tuesday 1st September
Luke 4:31—37

He went down to Capernaum, a city in Galilee, and was teaching them on the sabbath. They were astounded at his teaching, because he spoke with authority. In the synagogue there was a man who had the spirit of an unclean demon, and he cried out with a loud voice, "Let us alone! What have you to do with us, Jesus of Nazareth? Have you come to destroy us? I know who you are, the Holy One of God." But Jesus rebuked him, saying, "Be silent, and come out of him!" When the demon had thrown him down before them, he came out of him without having done him any harm. They were all amazed and kept saying to one another, "What kind of utterance is this? For with authority and power he commands the unclean spirits, and out they come!" And a report about him began to reach every place in the region.

- Demons? Is this just an old story, or are my own demons alive and well? Am I resistant to God's help in fighting them? I ask: "What have you to do with me, Jesus of Nazareth?"

- Lord, may I acknowledge my demons and let you invade my poverty with the authority of your powerful compassion and healing.

Wednesday 2nd September
Luke 4:38–42

Now Simon's mother-in-law was suffering from a high fever, and they asked Jesus about her. Then he stood over her and rebuked the fever, and it left her. Immediately she got up and began to serve them. As the sun was setting, all those who had any who were sick with various kinds of diseases brought them to Jesus; and he laid his hands on each of them and cured them. Demons also came out of many, shouting, "You are the Son of God!" But he rebuked them and would not allow them to speak, because they knew that he was the Messiah. At daybreak he departed and went into a deserted place.

- To whom can a family go to in their troubles? How many will take their troubles to the Lord in prayer?

- Lord, let me then be an ambassador of prayer for those who cannot pray.

Thursday 3rd September
Luke 5:1–6

Once while Jesus was standing beside the lake of Gennesaret, and the crowd was pressing in on him to hear the word of God, he saw two boats there at the shore of the lake. . . . He got into one of the boats, the one belonging to Simon, and asked him to put out a little way from the shore. Then he sat down and taught the crowds from the boat. When Jesus had finished speaking, he said to Simon, "Put out into the deep water and let down your nets for a catch."

Simon answered, "Master, we have worked all night long but have caught nothing. Yet if you say so, I will let down the nets." When they had done this, they caught so many fish that their nets were beginning to break.

- God uses the ordinary experiences of life to draw people to him. The gate of heaven is always open to everyone. Why then should I ever become despondent about people—perhaps in my own family circle—who do not practise their religion?

- Are we not living through an exciting time? The churches must shed their skins, become humble, and grow in grace. They must break free to celebrate the God of new beginnings. Lord, at your word we will let out the nets into the deep waters of our lives.

Friday 4th September
Luke 5:33—38

Then the Pharisees and the scribes said to Jesus, "John's disciples, like the disciples of the Pharisees, frequently fast and pray, but your disciples eat and drink." Jesus said to them, "You cannot make wedding-guests fast while the bridegroom is with them, can you? The days will come when the bridegroom will be taken away from them, and then they will fast in those days." He also told them a parable: "No one tears a piece from a new garment and sews it on an old garment; otherwise the new will be torn, and the piece from the new will not match the old. And no one puts new wine into old wineskins; otherwise the new wine will burst the skins and will be spilled, and the skins will be destroyed. But new wine must be put into fresh wineskins."

- Each dawn announces the birth of a new day—a day of gift, a day for sharing bread, a day to receive the bread of life from the Lord. All is made new by God who meets us where we are. God shares in the good things that happen to us. From him comes everything that is good in life.

- Jesus is always with us, if only we can see.

Saturday 5th September
Luke 6:1—5

One sabbath while Jesus was going through the cornfields, his disciples plucked some heads of grain, rubbed them in their hands, and ate them. But some of the Pharisees said, "Why are you doing what is not lawful on the sabbath?" Jesus answered, "Have you not read what David did when he and his companions were hungry? He entered the house of God and took and ate the bread of the Presence, which it is not lawful for any but the priests to eat, and gave some to his companions?" Then he said to them, "The Son of Man is lord of the sabbath."

- Sunday. Blessed Sunday. Is it a day of rest for me? Sunday can be a gift, a privileged moment to find inner calm. It is a time to shed the stress of work and let cares fall away. It is a time to walk leisurely with my God in his world of nature. It is a time to recapture reverence for the holy world gifted to us. It is a time for speaking the names of each member of the family with love and gratitude.

- Is Sunday my day for meeting the Lord of the Sabbath? Is it the day of Resurrection, when I celebrate the joy that the Lord Jesus is with me forever?

September 6—12

Something to think and pray about each day this week:

Mary, Undoer of Knots

This is a strange-sounding title for Our Lady! But human imagination goes beyond the rational, and this humble devotion has a fascinating history.

A German nobleman in the early seventeenth century discovered that his wife was about to divorce him. Distraught, he brought to a local Jesuit the wedding ribbon which had joined the arms of bride and groom in their wedding ceremony. The Jesuit prayerfully untied its knots before an image of Our Lady of the Snows. The ribbon became dazzlingly white, and this was taken as confirmation that the prayer to save the marriage was heard. The divorce was averted!

The website describing a novena to "Mary, Undoer of Knots" (www.theholyrosary.org/maryundoerknots) explains that among the "knots" Mary can be asked to untie are the problems and struggles for which we do not see any solution. They include family discord, lack of understanding between parents and children, disrespect, violence, deep hurts between husband and wife, the absence of peace and joy at home. There are also the knots of anguish and despair of separated couples, of the dissolution of the family, the knots of an addicted son or daughter, of those sick or separated from home or God. Included finally are the knots of alcoholism, depression, unemployment, fear, solitude, and the problems arising from abortion. Pope Francis has encouraged the whole Christian community to pray this powerful novena.

The Presence of God

For a few moments, I think of God's veiled presence in things:
in the elements, giving them existence;
in plants, giving them life; in animals, giving them sensation;
and finally, in me, giving me all this and more,
making me a temple, a dwelling-place of the Spirit.

Freedom

God is not foreign to my freedom.
Instead, the Spirit breathes life into my most intimate desires,
gently nudging me toward all that is good.
I ask for the grace to let myself be enfolded by the Spirit.

Consciousness

Knowing that God loves me unconditionally,
I look honestly over the last day, its events and my feelings.
Do I have something to be grateful for? Then I give thanks.
Is there something I am sorry for? Then I ask forgiveness.

The Word

I take my time to read the Word of God, slowly, a few times, allowing myself to dwell on anything that strikes me. (Please turn to your scripture on the following pages. Inspiration points are there should you need them. When you are ready, return here to continue.)

Conversation

How has God's Word moved me? Has it left me cold?
Has it consoled me or moved me to act in a new way?
I imagine Jesus standing or sitting beside me;
I turn and share my feelings with him.

Conclusion

Glory be to the Father, and to the Son, and to the Holy Spirit,
as it was in the beginning, is now, and ever shall be,
world without end. Amen.

September 2015

Sunday 6th September,
Twenty-Third Sunday of Ordinary Time
Mark 7:31—35

Then he returned from the region of Tyre, and went by way of Sidon towards the Sea of Galilee, in the region of the Decapolis. They brought to him a deaf man who had an impediment in his speech; and they begged him to lay his hand on him. He took him aside in private, away from the crowd, and put his fingers into his ears, and he spat and touched his tongue. Then looking up to heaven, he sighed and said to him, "Ephphatha," that is, "Be opened." And immediately his ears were opened, his tongue was released, and he spoke plainly.

- This man is doubly afflicted—as a foreigner he suffers isolation, and he is also excluded by his physical impairment. Jesus' action initiates a new age. He comes close enough to touch us, one by one. He indeed does all things well.

- Lord, I hear your words to me, "Be open!" Unblock my ears, that I may listen to your Word. Open the door of my heart, that I may grow in sensitivity to the suffering of others. Liberate my tongue, that I may speak in gratitude of your loving kindness.

Monday 7th September
Luke 6:6—11

On another sabbath Jesus entered the synagogue and taught, and there was a man there whose right hand was withered. The scribes and the Pharisees watched him to see whether he would cure on the sabbath, so that they might find an accusation against him. Even though he knew what they were thinking, he said to the man who had the withered hand, "Come and stand here." He got up and stood there. Then Jesus said to them, "I ask you, is it lawful to do good or to do harm on the sabbath, to save life or to destroy it?" After looking around at all of them, he said to him, "Stretch out your hand." He did so, and his hand was restored. But they were filled with fury and discussed with one another what they might do to Jesus.

- Lord, our Church suffers today from those who use their position and power to dominate others. Transform by your spirit all those in need of healing.

- Reveal to me the ways you call me to stretch out my hand to empower those around me.

Tuesday 8th September, Birthday of the Blessed Virgin Mary
Matthew 1:18—23

Now the birth of Jesus the Messiah took place in this way. When his mother Mary had been engaged to Joseph, but before they lived together, she was found to be with child from the Holy Spirit. Her husband Joseph, being a righteous man and unwilling to expose her to public disgrace, planned to dismiss her quietly. But just when he had resolved to do this, an angel of the Lord appeared to him in a dream and said, "Joseph, son of David, do not be afraid to take Mary as your wife, for the child conceived in her is from the Holy Spirit. She will bear a son, and you are to name him Jesus, for he will save his people from their sins." All this took place to fulfil what had been spoken by the Lord through the prophet: "Look, the virgin shall conceive and bear a son, and they shall name him Emmanuel," which means, "God is with us."

- Consider how "God is with us" is the reality of your life today.

- In thanksgiving, offer this prayer of St. Ignatius:

  Take, O Lord, and receive my entire liberty,
  my memory, my understanding and my whole will.
  All that I am and all that I possess you have given me.
  I surrender it all to you to be disposed of according to
  your will.

Give me only your love and your grace;
with these I will be rich enough,
and will desire nothing more.

Wednesday 9th September
Luke 6:20–23

Then Jesus looked up at his disciples and said: "Blessed are you who are poor, for yours is the kingdom of God. Blessed are you who are hungry now, for you will be filled. Blessed are you who weep now, for you will laugh. Blessed are you when people hate you, and when they exclude you, revile you, and defame you on account of the Son of Man. Rejoice on that day and leap for joy, for surely your reward is great in heaven; for that is what their ancestors did to the prophets."

- God's mercy means doing justice for the poorest and the most humiliated. We, too, see poor and powerless people today. Are we, his followers, defenders of the poor?

- What meaningful action will I do today to bring a smile to the lips of someone who is poor or broken? Christian living is neither an armchair occupation nor a spectator sport.

Thursday 10th September
Luke 6:27, 32–36

Jesus said, "But I say to you that listen . . . if you love those who love you, what credit is that to you? For even sinners love those who love them. If you do good to those who do good to you, what credit is that to you? For even sinners do the same. If you lend to those from whom you hope to receive, what credit is that to you? Even sinners lend to sinners, to receive as much again. But love your enemies, do good, and lend, expecting nothing in return. Your reward will be great, and you will be children of the Most High; for he is kind to the ungrateful and the wicked. Be merciful, just as your Father is merciful."

- It is grace that makes the Christian message different. Jesus calls on us bluntly not to treat others as they deserve but as the Father treats them—with compassion, mercy, and forgiveness.

- A prayer for those who have done us mischief is liberating. It frees us from the prison of hatred and revenge. Lord, set my heart free. Take away the last vestiges of bitterness in me.

Friday 11th September
Luke 6:39–42

He also told them a parable: "Can a blind person guide a blind person? Will not both fall into a pit? A disciple is not above the teacher, but everyone who is fully qualified will be like the teacher. Why do you see the speck in your neighbour's eye, but do not notice the log in your own eye? Or how can you say to your neighbour, 'Friend, let me take out the speck in your eye,' when you yourself do not see the log in your own eye? You hypocrite, first take the log out of your own eye, and then you will see clearly to take the speck out of your neighbour's eye."

- Do I make a practice of thinking the best of other people? Do I challenge my habit of making quick judgements about others? Jesus uses humour to invite us not to take ourselves too seriously.

- God sees each of us from the inside. God sees us with a generous and compassionate gaze. God does not despise or condemn us for our shortcomings and failings. Lord, today make me gaze at annoying people as kindly as you do.

Saturday 12th September
Luke 6:43–45

Jesus said to the people, "No good tree bears bad fruit, nor again does a bad tree bear good fruit; for each tree is known by its own fruit. Figs are not gathered from thorns, nor are grapes picked from a bramble bush. The good person out of the good treasure of the heart produces good, and the evil person out of evil treasure produces evil; for it is out of the abundance of the heart that the mouth speaks."

- For Jesus' audience, fig trees symbolised fertility, peace, and prosperity. Grapes symbolised joy. Brambles and thorns served only as firewood.

- Fruit, like character, takes time to ripen and mature. Jesus connects soundness of heart with good fruit.

September 13—19

Something to think and pray about each day this week:

Meeting God Within

When people succeed in coming home to themselves and glimpsing their own inner beauty, something amazing happens: they are blessed with a real compassion for who they themselves are, in all their vulnerability. This compassion, in turn, carves out a space where they can welcome God into their hearts. It is as if they must first become aware of the marvel of themselves, and only then are they ready to get in touch with the wonder of God. Their new relationship with themselves ushers in a nourishing friendship with the One who has always been calling them.

This journey inward does not take place overnight. Although the heart is only fifteen inches from the head, it can take us years to arrive at our emotional core. I used to imagine that God didn't particularly like the world because it wasn't spiritual enough. Only later it dawned on me that God had created the world in love, and had passionately left clues to this fact everywhere. The persons and events of my daily life were already signs of God. Had I paid compassionate attention to my longings and my joys, I would have heard in them the symphony of God's own infinite joy. God was intimately involved in my life, but I was sadly ignorant of the riches inside me. To find God, I did not have to leave the world, but to come home to it—and to myself—and God would be there, waiting for me.

The Presence of God
Jesus waits silent and unseen to come into my heart.
I will respond to his call.
He comes with his infinite power and love.
May I be filled with joy in his presence.

Freedom
Everything has the potential to draw forth from me a fuller love and life.
Yet my desires are often fixed, caught on illusions of fulfillment.
I ask that God, through my freedom, may orchestrate
my desires in a vibrant, loving melody rich in harmony.

Consciousness
How do I find myself today?
Where am I with God? With others?
Do I have something to be grateful for? Then I give thanks.
Is there something I am sorry for? Then I ask forgiveness.

The Word
God speaks to each one of us individually. I need to listen to what he is saying to me. (Please turn to your scripture on the following pages. Inspiration points are there should you need them. When you are ready, return here to continue.)

Conversation
What feelings are rising in me
as I pray and reflect on God's Word?
I imagine Jesus himself sitting or standing beside me,
and open my heart to him.

Conclusion
Glory be to the Father, and to the Son, and to the Holy Spirit,
as it was in the beginning, is now, and ever shall be,
world without end. Amen.

September 2015

Sunday 13th September,
Twenty-Fourth Sunday of Ordinary Time
Mark 8:27—35

Jesus went on with his disciples to the villages of Caesarea Philippi; and on the way he asked his disciples, "Who do people say that I am?" And they answered him, "John the Baptist; and others, Elijah; and still others, one of the prophets." He asked them, "But who do you say that I am?" Peter answered him, "You are the Messiah." And he sternly ordered them not to tell anyone about him.

Then he began to teach them that the Son of Man must undergo great suffering, and be rejected by the elders, the chief priests, and the scribes, and be killed, and after three days rise again. He said all this quite openly. And Peter took him aside and began to rebuke him. But turning and looking at his disciples, he rebuked Peter and said, "Get behind me, Satan! For you are setting your mind not on divine things but on human things." He called the crowd with his disciples, and said to them, "If any want to become my followers, let them deny themselves and take up their cross and follow me. For those who want to save their life will lose it, and those who lose their life for my sake, and for the sake of the gospel, will save it."

- This crucial moment draws the first half of Mark's Gospel to a close. Jesus is not a triumphant Messiah but a suffering one. On a surface level, Peter gets Jesus' identity right. But he is reprimanded for his earthbound vision: he seeks to bend Jesus' words and ways to his own all-too-human thinking. He learns that compromise has no place in Jesus' life.

- Lord, your question to the disciples echoes down the centuries, and I hear it addressed now to me. Strengthen the bonds between us. Keep me close behind you, as I pick up the crosses and burdens that come from being your disciple.

Monday 14th September,
Triumph of the Holy Cross
John 3:14—17

Jesus said, "And just as Moses lifted up the serpent in the wilderness, so must the Son of Man be lifted up, that whoever believes in him may have eternal life. For God so loved the world that he gave his only Son, so that everyone who believes in him may not perish but may have eternal life. Indeed, God did not send the Son into the world to condemn the world, but in order that the world might be saved through him."

- In John's Gospel, the cross reveals the vast breadth and width of God's love. It reverses all human values. Once a symbol of shame, it becomes the symbol of glory.

- The love revealed is not exclusive for just a few. Rather, it is a redemptive love that embraces the whole world. Equally, it is a personal love for each and every individual whom God sustains in existence.

Tuesday 15th September
Luke 7:11—15

Soon afterwards he went to a town called Nain, and his disciples and a large crowd went with him. As he approached the gate of the town, a man who had died was being carried out. He was his mother's only son, and she was a widow; and with her was a large crowd from the town. When the Lord saw her, he had compassion for her and said to her, "Do not weep." Then he came forward and touched the bier, and the bearers stood still. And he said, "Young man, I say to you, rise!" The dead man sat up and began to speak, and Jesus gave him to his mother.

- Death, as Jesus speaks of it and lives it, is that moment in which total defeat is transformed by total victory. The world bids us farewell; but God welcomes us home. We are already children of the Father, whose love is stronger than death. Life is eternal because his love is everlasting.

- Our life is a gradual learning to let go and say an unqualified "Yes." We can let God in a little more each day by becoming more free, more emptied. "For all that has been, Thanks. For all that shall be, Yes" (Dag Hammerskjold).

Wednesday 16th September
Luke 7:31—35

Jesus said to the people, "To what then will I compare the people of this generation, and what are they like? They are like children sitting in the market-place and calling to one another, 'We played the flute for you, and you did not dance; we wailed, and you did not weep.' For John the Baptist has come eating no bread and drinking no wine, and you say, 'He has a demon'; the Son of Man has come eating and drinking, and you say, 'Look, a glutton and a drunkard, a friend of tax-collectors and sinners!' Nevertheless, wisdom is vindicated by all her children."

- God wants us to rejoice in the good things of life. We should celebrate friendship, marriage, family, births, achievements, and games. God will ask us at the end: "Did you enjoy my creation?" God will hope for the answer, "Yes!"

- But there is also another side to life. We are to follow Jesus in the breaking of bread and in drinking of the cup of his passion. I am reluctant, Lord, to take up your Cross daily. I shun pain, hurt, and loss. Teach me to find you in suffering.

Thursday 17th September,
St. Robert Bellarmine
Luke 7:36—50

One of the Pharisees asked Jesus to eat with him, and he went into the Pharisee's house and took his place at the table. And a woman in the city, who was a sinner, having learned that he was eating in the Pharisee's house, brought an alabaster jar of ointment. She stood behind him at his feet, weeping, and began to bathe his feet with her tears and to dry them with her hair. Then she continued kissing his feet and anointing them with the ointment. Now when the Pharisee who had invited him saw it, he said to himself, "If this man were a prophet, he would have known who and what kind of woman this is who is touching him—that she is a sinner." Jesus spoke up and said to him, "Simon, I have something to say to you." "Teacher," he replied, "speak." "A certain creditor had two debtors; one owed five hundred denarii, and the other fifty. When they could not pay, he cancelled the debts for both of them. Now which of them will love him more?" Simon answered, "I suppose the one for whom he cancelled the greater debt." And Jesus said to him, "You have judged rightly." Then turning towards the woman, he said to Simon, "Do you see this woman? I entered your house; you gave me no water for my feet, but she has bathed my feet with her tears and dried them with her hair. You gave me no kiss, but from the time I came in she has not stopped kissing my feet. You did not anoint my head with oil, but she has anointed my feet with ointment. Therefore, I tell you, her sins, which were many, have been forgiven; hence she has shown great love. But the one to whom little is forgiven, loves little." Then he said to her, "Your sins are forgiven." But those who were at the table with him began to say among themselves, "Who is this who even forgives sins?" And he said to the woman, "Your faith has saved you; go in peace."

- Simon's image is of a God who doesn't mix with sinners. He despises this woman, who has no name but "sinner." Yet she recognizes her need of Jesus and encounters his compassionate gaze, his total forgiveness, and his peace. Tears of gratitude flow from her converted heart. Simon, however, who feels no need of forgiveness, misses the point completely.

- Lord, when I am narrow-minded, remind me that expansive forgiveness is your constant response to the darkness of my soul. May your compassionate gaze illuminate the closed-off places within me that need your unconditional and forgiving love.

Friday 18th September
Luke 8:1—3

Soon afterwards he went on through cities and villages, proclaiming and bringing the good news of the kingdom of God. The twelve were with him, as well as some women who had been cured of evil spirits and infirmities: Mary, called Magdalene, from whom seven demons had gone out, and Joanna, the wife of Herod's steward Chuza, and Susanna, and many others, who provided for them out of their resources.

- Each of the women in this reading met Jesus from a place of weakness or brokenness and became strong because of it.

- Before her martyrdom in the gas chambers of Auschwitz in 1942, Edith Stein (St. Teresa Benedicta of the Cross) had these last words: "If you want to follow the Savior with purity of heart, your heart must be free of every earthly desire. Jesus, the crucified, wants your life in order to give you his." Her terrible times shaped her greatness. May we take courage from such a life.

Saturday 19th September
Luke 8:4—8

When a great crowd gathered and people from town after town came to Jesus, he said in a parable: "A sower went out to sow his seed; and as he sowed, some fell on the path and was trampled on, and the birds of the air ate it up. Some fell on the rock; and as it grew up, it withered for lack of moisture. Some fell among thorns, and the thorns grew with it and choked it. Some fell into good soil, and when it grew, it produced a hundredfold." As he said this, he called out, "Let anyone with ears to hear listen!"

- The very parable is thrown out like a seed; to flourish or perish in the heart of the hearer. Jesus knows his word might not be given the attention or consideration it merits.

- It is easy to be become preoccupied with the leaking vessel, the withered seed. They are part of the picture—but only a part. Jesus describes a rich ecology in which there is also success and growth. With God, I attend to the growth and life that is in me and ask that it spill over into such barren patches as there are.

September 2015

September 20—26

Something to think and pray about each day this week:

Babylon

In the scriptures, Babylon is a godless construction which tries to reach to the skies and displace God. Today the term can stand for a widespread culture that is seductive and glamorous but unreal and unsatisfying. It is black and white rather than abundant in colour. Instead of fostering healthy imagination, it limits and prepackages it. Thus, advertisements tell us what to eat and drink, what to do and wear. Babylon impoverishes us. It cuts us off from many enriching dimensions of human life. It imprisons the spark that is within us, the soul that is invisible, free, and immortal.

The churches are not safe from this culture. In the United States today, there are twenty-two million ex-Catholics. Their overriding reason for leaving their Church is that their spiritual needs were not being met. They were looking for sustaining spiritual nourishment, but they felt that they were being fed on junk food. Our task is to rediscover the riches of faith, for God has bigger hopes for us than Babylon could ever entertain. God offers us an undreamt-of gift, conveyed to us by his Son. We need divine food, because we are made for greatness. We live in an open-ended world where we can risk becoming who we really are, persons who can love without limits. We need, then, to cultivate our Christian imagination carefully. *Sacred Space* does this; here we meet God in human form and see how to become like him.

The Presence of God
"I stand at the door and knock," says the Lord.
What a wonderful privilege
that the Lord of all creation desires to come to me.
I welcome his presence.

Freedom
Lord, grant me the grace to be free from the excesses of this life.
Let me not get caught up with the desire for wealth.
Keep my heart and mind free to love and serve you.

Consciousness
"There is a time and place for everything," as the saying goes.
Lord, grant that I may always desire
to spend time in your presence, to hear your call.

The Word
God speaks to each one of us individually. I need to listen to what
he is saying to me. (Please turn to your scripture on the following
pages. Inspiration points are there should you need them. When you
are ready, return here to continue.)

Conversation
The gift of speech is a wonderful gift.
May I use this gift with kindness.
May I be slow to utter harsh words,
hurtful words, and words spoken in anger.

Conclusion
Glory be to the Father, and to the Son, and to the Holy Spirit,
as it was in the beginning, is now, and ever shall be,
world without end. Amen.

Sunday 20th September,
Twenty-Fifth Sunday of Ordinary Time
Mark 9:30—35

They went on from there and passed through Galilee. He did not want anyone to know it; for he was teaching his disciples, saying to them, "The Son of Man is to be betrayed into human hands, and they will kill him, and three days after being killed, he will rise again." But they did not understand what he was saying and were afraid to ask him. Then they came to Capernaum; and when he was in the house he asked them, "What were you arguing about on the way?" But they were silent, for on the way they had argued with one another about who was the greatest. He sat down, called the twelve, and said to them, "Whoever wants to be first must be last of all and servant of all."

- The gospel reveals the disciples as slow and dense: they do not understand the implications of following Jesus. Fear deters them from asking the core questions. Instead, they are preoccupied with false ambition, self-seeking, and rivalry.

- Lord, your message is clear. Ambition that pleases God is shown by humble service of others. Greatness is found not in lording it over other people, but in being the servant of the most insignificant people—the poor, the weak, the despised.

Monday 21st September,
St. Matthew, Apostle and Evangelist
Matthew 9:9—13

As Jesus was walking along, he saw a man called Matthew sitting at the tax booth; and he said to him, "Follow me." And he got up and followed him. And as he sat at dinner in the house, many tax-collectors and sinners came and were sitting with him and his disciples. When the Pharisees saw this, they said to his disciples, "Why does your teacher eat with tax-collectors and sinners?" But when he heard this, he said, "Those who are well have no need of a physician, but those who are sick. Go and learn what this means, 'I desire mercy, not sacrifice.' For I have come to call not the righteous but sinners."

- Lord, your call to Matthew comes right in the midst of the ordinariness of his life. He does not hesitate or delay in order to balance the books but gets up and follows you.

- As I move through this day, keep me alert to the many ways your grace seeks entry into my life. May I respond generously and without delay to your calls.

Tuesday 22nd September
Luke 8:19—21

Then his mother and his brothers came to him, but they could not reach him because of the crowd. And he was told, "Your mother and your brothers are standing outside, wanting to see you." But he said to them, "My mother and my brothers are those who hear the word of God and do it."

- Our bond with Jesus expands and enriches our family ties. Grace-inspired kinship goes beyond even the closeness of flesh and blood.

- Christian couples are bonded in Christ in a privileged way so that Christian families are the heartbeat of the Christian community.

Wednesday 23rd September
Luke 9:1—6

Jesus called the twelve together and gave them power and authority over all demons and to cure diseases, and he sent them out to proclaim the kingdom of God and to heal. He said to them, "Take nothing for your journey, no staff, nor bag, nor bread, nor money— not even an extra tunic. Whatever house you enter, stay there, and leave from there. Wherever they do not welcome you, as you are leaving that town shake the dust off your feet as a testimony against them." They departed and went through the villages, bringing the good news and curing diseases everywhere.

- Jesus weds power and authority with compassionate love and humble service. I pray for the Church, that its ministers may do the same.

- His promise is that he will be always with us if we allow him to use us in our weakness. He entrusts us with his gifts and healing power. The final word "everywhere" suggests that the grace we carry extends beyond all human boundaries. "Every act of love, every mute uplifting of the heart, draws the whole world nearer to God."

Thursday 24th September
Luke 9:7—9

Now Herod the ruler heard about all that had taken place, and he was perplexed, because it was said by some that John had been raised from the dead, by some that Elijah had appeared, and by others that one of the ancient prophets had arisen. Herod said, "John I beheaded; but who is this about whom I hear such things?" And he tried to see him.

- "Who is this Jesus?" When he looked at Jesus, Herod "tried" but was unable to see who he really was. When I look at Jesus, am I—like Herod—"perplexed"?

- Jesus, you are the gracious gift of the Father, dwelling among us. You bring us into God's friendship. Thus you touch us at the deepest core of our being.

Friday 25th September
Luke 9:18—22

Once when Jesus was praying alone, with only the disciples near him, he asked them, "Who do the crowds say that I am?" They answered, "John the Baptist; but others, Elijah; and still others, that one of the ancient prophets has arisen." He said to them, "But who do you say that I am?" Peter answered, "The Messiah of God." He sternly ordered and commanded them not to tell anyone, saying, "The Son of Man must undergo great suffering, and be rejected by the elders, chief priests, and scribes, and be killed, and on the third day be raised."

- To find God in suffering is hard. When Jesus says that he must undergo great suffering, he means that he sees this as being part of God's design. Christian tradition speaks of the "dynamic of the Cross." It means that unavoidable suffering, when patiently endured, brings good to the world because it reveals great love.

- Let me trust that this is so on the evidence of what we dare to call *Good* Friday. There great love overcomes human malice, and so we are saved.

Saturday 26th September
Luke 9:43—45

And all were astounded at the greatness of God. While everyone was amazed at all that he was doing, he said to his disciples, "Let these words sink into your ears: The Son of Man is going to be betrayed into human hands." But they did not understand this saying; its meaning was concealed from them, so that they could not perceive it. And they were afraid to ask him about this saying.

- The disciples were not prepared for the Passion of Jesus. Are we prepared for the Passion that so many people endure today and every day? We need a new way of seeing.

- When we are broken by trouble, Jesus is walking most closely by our side. He gives us the courage to take one more step.

September 2015

September 27—October 3

Something to think and pray about each day this week:

Touching the Flesh of Christ

The ecclesial community is a place to grow our faith. Pope Francis asked that Christians should not lose confidence in the Church, despite its obvious failings. It makes mistakes and clearly needs institutional reform, and this is a major task for the Holy Spirit. But it will be chiefly reformed by dedicating itself to its central mission. This means that it must move "to the periphery" and proclaim the Good News to all people from the standpoint of solidarity with the poor.

In an address to families, Pope Benedict XVI stressed that Christian charity is best understood in terms of "self-gift." Only in self-giving, he would say, do we find ourselves. Only by opening up to a partner, to children, and to family needs—which may be painful—do we discover the breadth of our humanity. But while family is the birthplace of our ability to give of ourselves, it does not represent the limit of where we express this love. We must open up to the ecclesial community and to the world. We cannot turn our backs on our struggling sisters and brothers. In the words of Pope Francis, we are to "touch the flesh of Christ" by caring for the needy.

The Church is meant to be a servant of all in need. This is a humble role. As Vatican II says, whatever promotes human dignity among the people of the world becomes the agenda of the Church. Injustice anywhere must stir the Christian heart to an appropriate response.

The Presence of God
I remind myself that, as I sit here now,
God is gazing on me with love and holding me in being.
I pause for a moment and think of this.

Freedom
Lord, grant me the grace to be free from the excesses of this life.
Let me not get caught up with the desire for wealth.
Keep my heart and mind free to love and serve you.

Consciousness
How am I really feeling? Lighthearted? Heavy hearted?
I may be very much at peace, happy to be here.
Equally, I may be frustrated, worried, or angry.
I acknowledge how I really am. It is the real me that the Lord loves.

The Word
I take my time to read the Word of God, slowly, a few times, allowing myself to dwell on anything that strikes me. (Please turn to your
scripture on the following pages. Inspiration points are there should
you need them. When you are ready, return here to continue.)

Conversation
Do I notice myself reacting as I pray with the Word of God?
Do I feel challenged, comforted, angry?
Imagining Jesus sitting or standing by me,
I speak out my feelings, as one trusted friend to another.

Conclusion
Glory be to the Father, and to the Son, and to the Holy Spirit,
as it was in the beginning, is now, and ever shall be,
world without end. Amen.

Sunday 27th September,
Twenty-Sixth Sunday of Ordinary Time
Mark 9:38—41

John said to Jesus, "Teacher, we saw someone casting out demons in your name, and we tried to stop him, because he was not following us." But Jesus said, "Do not stop him; for no one who does a deed of power in my name will be able soon afterwards to speak evil of me. Whoever is not against us is for us. For truly I tell you, whoever gives you a cup of water to drink because you bear the name of Christ will by no means lose the reward."

- Discipleship is not some personal privilege to be jealously guarded. We have no monopoly on Jesus. Appreciation of the good deeds done by others is essential. In his kingdom, power seeking and rivalry have no place; they are an obstacle and a cause of scandal.

- Lord, self-renunciation and attention to the needs of our brothers and sisters are the hallmark of belonging to you. You call me to be a stepping stone for others, not a stumbling block.

Monday 28th September
Luke 9:46—50

An argument arose among them as to which one of them was the greatest. But Jesus, aware of their inner thoughts, took a little child and put it by his side, and said to them, "Whoever welcomes this child in my name welcomes me, and whoever welcomes me welcomes the one who sent me; for the least among all of you is the greatest." John answered, "Master, we saw someone casting out demons in your name, and we tried to stop him, because he does not follow with us." But Jesus said to him, "Do not stop him; for whoever is not against you is for you."

- To do a kind act, no matter how small or insignificant, in Christ's name, is to do it to him and for him. Do I believe these words deeply enough so as to put them into practice?

- Jesus was always inclusive in his ministry and in his relations with others. Likewise, anyone who is on the side of goodness and love, truth and justice, is on God's side.

Tuesday 29th September,
Ss. Michael, Gabriel, and Raphael
John 1:47—51

When Jesus saw Nathanael coming towards him, he said of him, "Here is truly an Israelite in whom there is no deceit!" Nathanael asked him, "Where did you come to know me?" Jesus answered, "I saw you under the fig tree before Philip called you." Nathanael replied, "Rabbi, you are the Son of God! You are the King of Israel!" Jesus answered, "Do you believe because I told you that I saw you under the fig tree? You will see greater things than these." And he said to him, "Very truly, I tell you, you will see heaven opened and the angels of God ascending and descending upon the Son of Man."

- What a beautiful tribute Jesus gives to Nathanael! Here is a man without guile—sincere, faithful, and upright before God. Our deepest identity lies in our relationship with God.

- Lord, I come toward you this day. You know my heart. Is it without deceit?

Wednesday 30th September
Luke 9:57—62

As they were going along the road, someone said to him, "I will follow you wherever you go." And Jesus said to him, "Foxes have holes, and birds of the air have nests; but the Son of Man has nowhere to lay his head." To another he said, "Follow me." But he said, "Lord, first let me go and bury my father." But Jesus said to him, "Let the dead bury their own dead; but as for you, go and proclaim the kingdom of God." Another said, "I will follow you, Lord; but let me first say farewell to those at my home." Jesus said to him, "No one who puts a hand to the plough and looks back is fit for the kingdom of God."

- Jesus knows that I can have good intentions. But he reminds me that when I follow him there must be no conditions laid down. I must be prepared to share in his sorrows and joys of his ministry.

- Jesus, deepen my understanding of what it means to make a permanent commitment to you. Lead my enthusiasm to new places of determination, new understandings, new orientations, so that I may abide in you as I look forward to eternal life.

Thursday 1st October
Luke 10:1—7

After this the Lord appointed seventy others and sent them on ahead of him in pairs to every town and place where he himself intended to go. He said to them, "The harvest is plentiful, but the labourers are few; therefore ask the Lord of the harvest to send out labourers into his harvest. Go on your way. See, I am sending you out like lambs into the midst of wolves. Carry no purse, no bag, no sandals; and greet no one on the road. Whatever house you enter, first say, 'Peace to this house!' And if anyone is there who shares in peace, your peace will rest on that person; but if not, it will return to you. Remain in the same house, eating and drinking whatever they provide, for the labourer deserves to be paid."

- Lord, peace means tranquillity of spirit. It is a great gift to give to others. But before I share it, I must be possessed by it myself.

- Christian peace comes from knowing that you love me endlessly, that you are always with me and watching out for me. You are my Shepherd, and you will lead me along the right path.

Friday 2nd October
Luke 10:13—16

Jesus said, "Woe to you, Chorazin! Woe to you, Bethsaida! For if the deeds of power done in you had been done in Tyre and Sidon, they would have repented long ago, sitting in sackcloth and ashes. But at the judgement it will be more tolerable for Tyre and Sidon than for you. And you, Capernaum, will you be exalted to heaven? No, you will be brought down to Hades. Whoever listens to you listens to me, and whoever rejects you rejects me, and whoever rejects me rejects the one who sent me."

- Jesus laments the fact that people reject the Good News despite all he does for them. The truth can be painful at times and challenging to hear.

- When we speak our truths and live our lives according to the teaching of Christ, then we have chosen the better part and it cannot be taken away from us.

Saturday 3rd October
Luke 10:21—24

Jesus rejoiced in the Holy Spirit and said, "I thank you, Father, Lord of heaven and earth, because you have hidden these things from the wise and the intelligent and have revealed them to infants; yes, Father, for such was your gracious will. All things have been handed over to me by my Father; and no one knows who the Son is except the Father, or who the Father is except the Son and anyone to whom the Son chooses to reveal him." Then turning to the disciples, Jesus said to them privately, "Blessed are the eyes that see what you see! For I tell you that many prophets and kings desired to see what you see, but did not see it, and to hear what you hear, but did not hear it."

- What a privilege to be blessed with the eyes and ears of faith so as to see God's plan for humanity fully revealed in Christ Jesus!

- Am I humbly grateful for this great gift of faith in my life? How do I express that gratitude?

October 4—10

Something to think and pray about each day this week:

Humility and Compassion

Truly humble people have deep compassion. They may be saddened when others are unresponsive, but they do not lose their serenity through making harsh judgements. Instead, they step into the shoes of ungrateful people, trying to love in their place. They plead that God's love may shine forth upon bad as well as good, upon the indifferent as well as the committed. They do not rely upon their own resources, and their trust in God is so overwhelming that God cannot but respond to their prayers. They are kind enough to see that the badness of most people is due to the little love they may have received in their lives. They give their hearts and heads and hands to God so that God may work through them.

They are not burdened. They have responded to the gravitational pull of God, and so their yoke is easy and their burden is light. Love has given them wings. They have renounced their attempts to run their own lives, and, in surrendering themselves to God, they experience a joy that lifts them. They have become so attuned to God that they have also gratefully tuned into the wavelength of service.

The Presence of God
In the silence of my innermost being,
in the fragments of my yearned-for wholeness,
can I hear the whispers of God's presence?
Can I remember when I felt God's nearness,
when we walked together and I let myself be embraced by God's love?

Freedom
I ask for the grace
to let go of my own concerns
and be open to what God is asking of me,
to let myself be guided and formed by my loving Creator.

Consciousness
I exist in a web of relationships—links to nature, people, God.
I trace out these links, giving thanks for the life that flows through them.
Some links are twisted or broken; I may feel regret, anger, disappointment.
I pray for the gift of acceptance and forgiveness.

The Word
The Word of God comes to us through the scriptures. May the Holy Spirit enlighten my mind and my heart to respond to the Gospel teachings. (Please turn to your scripture on the following pages. Inspiration points are there should you need them. When you are ready, return here to continue.)

Conversation
Remembering that I am still in God's presence,
I imagine Jesus himself standing or sitting beside me,
and I say whatever is on my mind, whatever is in my heart,
speaking as one friend to another.

Conclusion
Glory be to the Father, and to the Son, and to the Holy Spirit,

October 2015

as it was in the beginning, is now, and ever shall be, world without end. Amen.

Sunday 4th October,
Twenty-Seventh Sunday of Ordinary Time
Mark 10:2—16

Some Pharisees came, and to test Jesus they asked, "Is it lawful for a man to divorce his wife?" He answered them, "What did Moses command you?" They said, "Moses allowed a man to write a certificate of dismissal and to divorce her." But Jesus said to them, "Because of your hardness of heart he wrote this commandment for you. But from the beginning of creation, 'God made them male and female.' 'For this reason a man shall leave his father and mother and be joined to his wife, and the two shall become one flesh.' So they are no longer two, but one flesh. Therefore what God has joined together, let no one separate." Then in the house the disciples asked him again about this matter. He said to them, "Whoever divorces his wife and marries another commits adultery against her; and if she divorces her husband and marries another, she commits adultery."

People were bringing little children to him in order that he might touch them; and the disciples spoke sternly to them. But when Jesus saw this, he was indignant and said to them, "Let the little children come to me; do not stop them; for it is to such as these that the kingdom of God belongs. Truly I tell you, whoever does not receive the kingdom of God as a little child will never enter it." And he took them up in his arms, laid his hands on them, and blessed them.

- God's plan for marriage was that of a man and woman to "become one flesh." This teaching calls each one of us to live out our own vocation in life as fully as possible, allowing that because of human weakness the ideal is not always totally achievable.

- The "little children" represent those who are among the most weak and vulnerable in society, without power or status. They act spontaneously by "receiving." Am I receptive to the kingdom, since it comes to me as free gift from God's bountiful hands?

Monday 5th October
Luke 10:25—37

Just then a lawyer stood up to test Jesus. "Teacher," he said, "what must I do to inherit eternal life?" He said to him, "What is written in the law? What do you read there?" He answered, "You shall love the Lord your God with all your heart, and with all your soul, and with all your strength, and with all your mind; and your neighbour as yourself." And he said to him, "You have given the right answer; do this, and you will live." But wanting to justify himself, he asked Jesus, "And who is my neighbour?" Jesus replied, "A man was going down from Jerusalem to Jericho, and fell into the hands of robbers, who stripped him, beat him, and went away, leaving him half dead. Now by chance a priest was going down that road; and when he saw him, he passed by on the other side. So likewise a Levite, when he came to the place and saw him, passed by on the other side. But a Samaritan while travelling came near him; and when he saw him, he was moved with pity. He went to him and bandaged his wounds, having poured oil and wine on them. Then he put him on his own animal, brought him to an inn, and took care of him. The next day he took out two denarii, gave them to the innkeeper, and said, 'Take care of him; and when I come back, I will repay you whatever more you spend.' Which of these three, do you think, was a neighbour to the man who fell into the hands of the robbers?" He said, "The one who showed him mercy." Jesus said to him, "Go and do likewise."

- When I am in trouble, Lord, you bandage my wounds and pour in oil and wine. You carry me on your shoulders when I cannot walk.

- God, forgive me when I fail to respond to the needs of others and pass by on the other side. Often selfishness or fear gets in the way of my standing for justice. Make me a good Samaritan in my time and place, please.

Tuesday 6th October
Luke 10:38—42

Now as they went on their way, Jesus entered a certain village, where a woman named Martha welcomed him into her home. She had a sister named Mary, who sat at the Lord's feet and listened to what he was saying. But Martha was distracted by her many tasks; so she came to him and asked, "Lord, do you not care that my sister has left me to do all the work by myself? Tell her then to help me." But the Lord answered her, "Martha, Martha, you are worried and distracted by many things; there is need of only one thing. Mary has chosen the better part, which will not be taken away from her."

- This is not the only time that Jesus calls his disciples away from their work to "rest awhile" with him. Good news indeed. For him discipleship is top priority. Work is, of course, necessary. But keeping busy can become a preoccupation in itself and can shield us from meeting the Lord. "I have no time to pray!"

- Lord, if we do not meet, I shall never come to know you. But knowing you is what life is about.

Wednesday 7th October
Luke 11:1—4

Jesus was praying in a certain place, and after he had finished, one of his disciples said to him, "Lord, teach us to pray, as John taught his disciples." He said to them, "When you pray, say: Father, hallowed be your name. Your kingdom come. Give us each day our daily bread. And forgive us our sins, for we ourselves forgive everyone indebted to us. And do not bring us to the time of trial."

- The disciples are impressed by the fact that Jesus prays. Then they want to get in on the mysterious relationship he has with his Father. So he teaches them how to have a conversation with God.

- God may seem silent to us, but he speaks to us in scripture, especially in the words and actions of Jesus.

Thursday 8th October
Luke 11:9—10

Jesus said, "I say to you, Ask, and it will be given to you; search, and you will find; knock, and the door will be opened for you. For everyone who asks receives, and everyone who searches finds, and for everyone who knocks, the door will be opened."

- Jesus sees his Father as a God who is always ready to give me what is best for me. Do I believe that God is like this? He is also telling me that persistent prayer is rewarded because the act of prayer is the work of the Holy Spirit and a gift from God.

- Lord, I thank you. You escort me through these difficult times of great need and uncertainty. Please increase my understanding of your loving ways.

Friday 9th October
Luke 11:15—23

Some of the crowd said of Jesus, "He casts out demons by Beelzebul, the ruler of the demons." Others, to test him, kept demanding from him a sign from heaven. But he knew what they were thinking and said to them, "Every kingdom divided against itself becomes a desert, and house falls on house. If Satan also is divided against himself, how will his kingdom stand?—for you say that I cast out the demons by Beelzebul. Now if I cast out the demons by Beelzebul, by whom do your exorcists cast them out? Therefore they will be your judges. But if it is by the finger of God that I cast out the demons, then the kingdom of God has come to you. When a strong man, fully armed, guards his castle, his property is safe. But when one stronger than he attacks him and overpowers him, he takes away his armour in which he trusted and divides his plunder.

Whoever is not with me is against me, and whoever does not gather with me scatters."

- What are my demons? Can I name even one of them? Whatever makes me unfree can be called a demon. Demons possess us, whereas angels liberate us for love and service.

- When I feel driven to work too hard, or to spend too much money on myself, I am in danger of being possessed by either urge. Lord, liberate me, please!

Saturday 10th October
Luke 11:27–28

While Jesus was saying this, a woman in the crowd raised her voice and said to him, "Blessed is the womb that bore you and the breasts that nursed you!" But he said, "Blessed rather are those who hear the word of God and obey it!"

- Jesus must have been delighted to hear this praise of his mother. But he uses the occasion to reveal another dimension of blessedness, that of the hearers of the Word of God. The Sacred Space community is deeply blessed by God!

- Jesus, I thank you for enfolding me in your blessing. The angel said to Mary that she was blessed, and I am also. Who am I, then? I am the blessed of God. Open my ears and remain with me always so that I may live out God's Word in my life.

October 11—17

Something to think and pray about each day this week:

Imagination and Hope

We used to imagine that, despite the diversity within particular societies and across the world, we could somehow all achieve safe middle-class ambitions like basic financial security, a wholesome family life, an education for excellence, a fulfilling job with a handsome wage, good health and white teeth, a house in the suburbs, freedom to worship, protection from terrorism, and an environment ready to do our bidding. Now we know that life is not so straightforward.

We are not here only to make money, though we need that, too. We are not here just to enjoy good health, though we all know what an incredible difference that makes. We are not here solely to live morally good lives, admirable though moral living is. We are here for a project so audacious that something within us finds it hard to believe: we are here to transform ourselves and our world. If we cannot believe this, it is because we have downsized our beliefs. It is our greatness rather than our littleness that intimidates us most of all.

But hope can heal us, for hope unsettles us with the passionate unrest that aims for the greatest things possible. Hope propels us toward great things, and it is imagination that gives us the entrance ticket into the hope-filled world of possibility. God is beyond all that we can ask for or imagine. We can hope in God, for God is the true fulfilment of everything for which we long and desire. God promises us that the best is yet to come.

The Presence of God
God is with me, but more,
God is within me, giving me existence.
Let me dwell for a moment on God's life-giving presence
in my body, my mind, my heart,
and in the whole of my life.

Freedom
I ask for the grace to believe
in what I could be and do
if I only allowed God, my loving Creator,
to continue to create me, guide me, and shape me.

Consciousness
Knowing that God loves me unconditionally,
I can afford to be honest about how I am.
How has the last day been, and how do I feel now?
I share my feelings openly with the Lord.

The Word
I read the Word of God slowly, a few times over, and I listen to what
God is saying to me. (Please turn to your scripture on the following
pages. Inspiration points are there should you need them. When you
are ready, return here to continue.)

Conversation
How has God's Word moved me? Has it left me cold?
Has it consoled me or moved me to act in a new way?
I imagine Jesus standing or sitting beside me;
I turn and share my feelings with him.

Conclusion
Glory be to the Father, and to the Son, and to the Holy Spirit,
as it was in the beginning, is now, and ever shall be,
world without end. Amen.

October 2015

Sunday 11th October,
Twenty-Eighth Sunday of Ordinary Time
Mark 10:17—27

As Jesus was setting out on a journey, a man ran up and knelt before him, and asked him, "Good Teacher, what must I do to inherit eternal life?" Jesus said to him, "Why do you call me good? No one is good but God alone. You know the commandments: 'You shall not murder; You shall not commit adultery; You shall not steal; You shall not bear false witness; You shall not defraud; Honour your father and mother.'" He said to him, "Teacher, I have kept all these since my youth." Jesus, looking at him, loved him and said, "You lack one thing; go, sell what you own, and give the money to the poor, and you will have treasure in heaven; then come, follow me." When he heard this, he was shocked and went away grieving, for he had many possessions. Then Jesus looked around and said to his disciples, "How hard it will be for those who have wealth to enter the kingdom of God!" And the disciples were perplexed at these words. But Jesus said to them again, "Children, how hard it is to enter the kingdom of God! It is easier for a camel to go through the eye of a needle than for someone who is rich to enter the kingdom of God." They were greatly astounded and said to one another, "Then who can be saved?" Jesus looked at them and said, "For mortals it is impossible, but not for God; for God all things are possible."

- The man's riches are not the problem as such, but his attitude toward them. It is as if he is possessed by his own possessions and not in charge of them. Wealth and material things can subtly control us.

- Do material things or worldly considerations get in the way of my relations with God and with others? Am I missing out on the real treasures in life—health, faith, friendship, love. . . ?

Monday 12th October
Luke 11:29—32

When the crowds were increasing, Jesus began to say, "This generation is an evil generation; it asks for a sign, but no sign will be given to it except the sign of Jonah. For just as Jonah became a sign to the people of Nineveh, so the Son of Man will be to this generation. The queen of the South will rise at the judgement with the people of this generation and condemn them, because she came from the ends of the earth to listen to the wisdom of Solomon, and see, something greater than Solomon is here! The people of Nineveh will rise up at the judgement with this generation and condemn it, because they repented at the proclamation of Jonah, and see, something greater than Jonah is here!"

• Jesus stands before me as a sign. Like Jonah, he is swallowed up by death, but rises from the dead and challenges me to walk in newness of life.

• Lord, stay with me in my times of blindness and usher me back into your saving presence.

Tuesday 13th October
Luke 11:37—41

While Jesus was speaking, a Pharisee invited him to dine with him; so he went in and took his place at the table. The Pharisee was amazed to see that he did not first wash before dinner. Then the Lord said to him, "Now you Pharisees clean the outside of the cup and of the dish, but inside you are full of greed and wickedness. You fools! Did not the one who made the outside make the inside also? So give for alms those things that are within; and see, everything will be clean for you."

• Have you ever been surprised when others do not ritually "toe the line"? Does this make me dismiss them? Jesus once again places love and inner goodness above the commands of law.

- What inner alms have I to share with others? Do I believe that even my little prayers for the world are blessed by God?

Wednesday 14th October
Luke 11:42—46

Jesus said, "But woe to you Pharisees! For you tithe mint and rue and herbs of all kinds, and neglect justice and the love of God; it is these you ought to have practised, without neglecting the others. Woe to you Pharisees! For you love to have the seat of honour in the synagogues and to be greeted with respect in the market-places. Woe to you! For you are like unmarked graves, and people walk over them without realizing it." One of the lawyers answered him, "Teacher, when you say these things, you insult us too." And he said, "Woe also to you lawyers! For you load people with burdens hard to bear, and you yourselves do not lift a finger to ease them."

- The people are overburdened with laws. Jesus feels for them and comes out strongly in their defence. Am I sensitive to what may be going on in a poor person's heart? Do I ever neglect justice and the love of God?

- Lord, make me aware of my needless preoccupations, and infuse my heart with your spirit of love and justice. Take my poor heart and make it like your own.

Thursday 15th October
Luke 11:47—51

Jesus said to the lawyers, "Woe to you! For you build the tombs of the prophets whom your ancestors killed. So you are witnesses and approve of the deeds of your ancestors; for they killed them, and you build their tombs. Therefore also the Wisdom of God said, 'I will send them prophets and apostles, some of whom they will kill and persecute,' so that this generation may be charged with the blood of all the prophets shed since the foundation of the world, from the blood of Abel to the blood of Zechariah, who perished between the altar and the sanctuary. Yes, I tell you, it will be charged against this generation."

- The lawyers whom Jesus faces use the Law as a weapon to attack others and to save themselves. This prevents others from entering the kingdom of God.

- Am I trapped by laws of my own making? Do I spend my time worrying about my status before God instead of living out a life of love?

Friday 16th October
Luke 12:1, 4—7

Meanwhile, when the crowd gathered by the thousands, so that they trampled on one another, Jesus began to speak first to his disciples, ". . . I tell you, my friends, do not fear those who kill the body, and after that can do nothing more. But I will warn you whom to fear: fear him who, after he has killed, has authority to cast into hell. Yes, I tell you, fear him! Are not five sparrows sold for two pennies? Yet not one of them is forgotten in God's sight. But even the hairs of your head are all counted. Do not be afraid; you are of more value than many sparrows."

- Jesus speaks encouraging words to his followers in the face of opposition—the reassurance of God's faithful love, care, and support.

- God cares for the smallest and most vulnerable of his creatures. How much more is God present for all who believe and trust in him?

Saturday 17th October
Luke 12:8—12

Jesus said to the disciples, "And I tell you, everyone who acknowledges me before others, the Son of Man also will acknowledge before the angels of God; but whoever denies me before others will be denied before the angels of God. And everyone who speaks a word against the Son of Man will be forgiven; but whoever blasphemes against the Holy Spirit will not be forgiven. When they bring you before the synagogues, the rulers, and the authorities, do not worry about how you are to defend yourselves or what you are to say; for the Holy Spirit will teach you at that very hour what you ought to say."

- Fear alienates and disables people. It can be employed as an instrument of manipulation, and it can lead to disintegration. Jesus is saying that the follower of Christ has nothing to fear. Disciples will be enabled by the Holy Spirit to speak out in the right way.

- As I pray with you, Lord, I thank you for your forgiveness when I have been disabled by fear. Your love can eliminate my fear. Over and over you tell me not to be afraid. Plant in me your spirit of courage.

October 18—24

Something to think and pray about each day this week:

Solitude and Mystery

Seven times I acted as a tourist guide on a tooth-shaped rock off the southwest coast of Ireland. Called *Sceilg Michael,* St. Michael's Rock, it towers eight hundred feet above the sea, is thirteen miles from the mainland, and can be accessed by boat only on calm days. From about the sixth to the twelfth century, it was the home of a small colony of monks, perhaps no more than twelve at a time. Their austere Rule has not survived. Removed from nearly all the secondary issues which preoccupy us, they spent their days in reciting the Divine Office, in personal prayer, and in eking out a frugal existence from a small garden and a turbulent sea. Surely also they found God in contemplating the waves and the birds, the moon and the stars. A few names survive, seven or eight over six centuries. The few graves are unnamed. What these anonymous men underwent in order to pray for all humankind—including ourselves—is beyond our imaginings.

It was exhilarating to live in so improbable a place. Solitude brought me into a sense of wonder at the beauty of nature by day and night. I found myself very alive there, and grateful, even when conditions were impossible. I experienced no great revelation. I met my old self, with its old feelings and follies. Surely the monks did, too. Yet we both met Mystery there—they under one form, and I under another—and I often crave to return.

The Presence of God

To be present is to arrive as one is and open up to the other.
At this instant, as I arrive here, God is present, waiting for me.
God always arrives before me, desiring to connect with me
even more than my most intimate friend.
I take a moment and greet my loving God.

Freedom

"In these days, God taught me
as a schoolteacher teaches a pupil" (St. Ignatius).
I remind myself that there are things God has to teach me yet,
and I ask for the grace to hear them and let them change me.

Consciousness

In the presence of my loving Creator,
I look honestly at my feelings over the last day—
the highs, the lows, and the level ground.
Can I see where the Lord has been present?

The Word

I take my time to read the Word of God, slowly, a few times, allowing myself to dwell on anything that strikes me. (Please turn to your
scripture on the following pages. Inspiration points are there should
you need them. When you are ready, return here to continue.)

Conversation

What feelings are rising in me
as I pray and reflect on God's Word?
I imagine Jesus himself sitting or standing beside me,
and I open my heart to him.

Conclusion

Glory be to the Father, and to the Son, and to the Holy Spirit,
as it was in the beginning, is now, and ever shall be,
world without end. Amen.

October 2015

Sunday 18th October,
Twenty-Ninth Sunday of Ordinary Time
Mark 10:42−45

Jesus called them and said to them, "You know that among the Gentiles those whom they recognize as their rulers lord it over them, and their great ones are tyrants over them. But it is not so among you; but whoever wishes to become great among you must be your servant, and whoever wishes to be first among you must be slave of all. For the Son of Man came not to be served but to serve, and to give his life a ransom for many."

• Christian leadership is not like human authority, nor is it based upon power and lording it over others. Quite the contrary; it is genuine when expressed in service. Jesus came not to be served but to serve.

• What about me? How am I of service to others?

Monday 19th October
Luke 12:13−21

Someone in the crowd said to Jesus, "Teacher, tell my brother to divide the family inheritance with me." But he said to him, "Friend, who set me to be a judge or arbitrator over you?" And he said to them, "Take care! Be on your guard against all kinds of greed; for one's life does not consist in the abundance of possessions." Then he told them a parable: "The land of a rich man produced abundantly. And he thought to himself, 'What should I do, for I have no place to store my crops?' Then he said, 'I will do this: I will pull down my barns and build larger ones, and there I will store all my grain and my goods. And I will say to my soul, Soul, you have ample goods laid up for many years; relax, eat, drink, be merry.' But God said to him, 'You fool! This very night your life is being demanded of you. And the things you have prepared, whose will they be?' So it is with those who store up treasures for themselves but are not rich towards God."

- The parable emphasises the stark contrast between a way of having and a way of being. When we have more than we need, we must give what we can to the poor. Otherwise we are "fools" because we miss the point of life.

- God enables us to amass possessions, but then we are to share them.

Tuesday 20th October
Luke 12:35—38

Jesus said to his disciples, "Be dressed for action and have your lamps lit; be like those who are waiting for their master to return from the wedding banquet, so that they may open the door for him as soon as he comes and knocks. Blessed are those slaves whom the master finds alert when he comes; truly I tell you, he will fasten his belt and have them sit down to eat, and he will come and serve them. If he comes during the middle of the night, or near dawn, and finds them so, blessed are those slaves."

- Is this only about the end time, or is Jesus knocking at my door on a daily basis? Am I being challenged to recognize him in the guise of a stranger, a person who is ill, or one who needs an encouraging word or a gentle touch? Do I treasure these opportunities as an encounter with Christ?

- Lord, make me vigilant so that I may recognize your face in my daily encounters. As C. S. Lewis says, there are no ordinary mortals in this world. Everyone is an extraordinary immortal, destined for eternal joy. Let me be reverent to them all.

Wednesday 21st October
Luke 12:39—46

Jesus said to the people, "But know this: if the owner of the house had known at what hour the thief was coming, he would not have let his house be broken into. You also must be ready, for the Son of

Man is coming at an unexpected hour." Peter said, "Lord, are you telling this parable for us or for everyone?" And the Lord said, "Who then is the faithful and prudent manager whom his master will put in charge of his slaves, to give them their allowance of food at the proper time? Blessed is that slave whom his master will find at work when he arrives. Truly I tell you, he will put that one in charge of all his possessions. But if that slave says to himself, 'My master is delayed in coming,' and if he begins to beat the other slaves, men and women, and to eat and drink and get drunk, the master of that slave will come on a day when he does not expect him and at an hour that he does not know, and will cut him in pieces, and put him with the unfaithful."

- The parable shows Jesus' awareness that authority and power can be abused. God hears the cry of the poor who are being dominated. He will not "cut to pieces" such people, but their hearts will have to be torn open until they ask forgiveness of their victims and become reconciled.

- Bless my work, Lord. Together with all other members of the Sacred Space community, may I be just in all my dealings and never disrespectful.

Thursday 22nd October
Luke 12:49—53

Jesus said to the crowds, "I came to bring fire to the earth, and how I wish it were already kindled! I have a baptism with which to be baptized, and what stress I am under until it is completed! Do you think that I have come to bring peace to the earth? No, I tell you, but rather division! From now on, five in one household will be divided, three against two and two against three; they will be divided: father against son and son against father, mother against daughter and daughter against mother, mother-in-law against her daughter-in-law and daughter-in-law against mother-in-law."

- How am I living my faith today? Does it challenge others? For Jesus, here it means being "under stress." And his first disciples were called "disturbers of the peace" (see Acts 16:20).

- But there is also unhelpful stress that comes from anxiety. Let me then pray with St. Teresa of Avila: "Let nothing disturb you, let nothing frighten you, all things are passing away: God never changes. Patience obtains all things. Whoever has God lacks nothing; God alone suffices."

Friday 23rd October
Luke 12:54—59

Jesus also said to the crowds, "When you see a cloud rising in the west, you immediately say, 'It is going to rain'; and so it happens. And when you see the south wind blowing, you say, 'There will be scorching heat'; and it happens. You hypocrites! You know how to interpret the appearance of earth and sky, but why do you not know how to interpret the present time? And why do you not judge for yourselves what is right? Thus, when you go with your accuser before a magistrate, on the way make an effort to settle the case, or you may be dragged before the judge, and the judge hand you over to the officer, and the officer throw you in prison. I tell you, you will never get out until you have paid the very last penny."

- What are the present signs in my life telling me? Am I missing the point about something? For instance, I may be growing older, or perhaps I am nourishing dislike of another person. But how do I connect these facts with my relationship to God?

- Remove the cloud from my vision, Lord, and inspire me to act upon your truth.

Saturday 24th October
Luke 13:1—5

At that very time there were some present who told him about the Galileans whose blood Pilate had mingled with their sacrifices. He asked them, "Do you think that because these Galileans suffered in this way they were worse sinners than all other Galileans? No, I tell you; but unless you repent, you will all perish as they did. Or those eighteen who were killed when the tower of Siloam fell on them—do you think that they were worse offenders than all the others living in Jerusalem? No, I tell you; but unless you repent, you will all perish just as they did."

- Jewish belief was that whatever evil befell people was a punishment for sin. The more a person had to suffer, the greater his or her sin must be!

- Jesus rejects this simplistic notion. Instead, he emphasises repentance, which means a turning around toward God and one's neighbour.

October 25—31

Something to think and pray about each day this week:

Thin Places

The early Celts had an affinity for the spirit world. Gifted with imagination, they found the threshold between this and the unseen world easy to cross. They used to say that heaven and earth are only three feet apart and that, in the thin places, the distance is even smaller! The term "thin places" can put words on our own experiences of being drawn beyond ourselves into awesome yet kindly Mystery.

It is not strange that we have such experiences. Creation, after all, is intense with divinity. Divinity embraces us and reveals itself, if unpredictably, if we have eyes to see. The veil between God's world and what we call "our world" is often drawn back for a moment to give us a glimpse of the "beyond." Thomas Merton rightly says that the gate of heaven is everywhere. Places of beauty, wild landscapes, lonely mountains, magnificent sunsets, starry nights, or the roaring sea can enchant us. On other levels, falling in love can open up a transfigured world, as can the divine breakthroughs in a smile, a baby's tiny finger, human beauty, a kind remark, a bar of music. The beggar's face, the eyes of a starving child, or the hushed moment of death of someone we loved can also break open the door of the heart. Be alert for such "thin places," for God can be found in all things. And our Sacred Space points us daily to Jesus, in whom the human and divine blend perfectly to form one Person.

The Presence of God

As I sit here, the beating of my heart,
the ebb and flow of my breathing, the movements of my mind
are all signs of God's ongoing creation of me.
I pause for a moment and become aware
of this presence of God within me.

Freedom

Lord, grant me the grace to be free from the excesses of this life.
Let me not get caught up with the desire for wealth.
Keep my heart and mind free to love and serve you.

Consciousness

In God's loving presence, I unwind the past day,
starting from now and looking back, moment by moment.
I gather in all the goodness and light in gratitude.
I attend to the shadows and what they say to me,
seeking healing, courage, forgiveness.

The Word

God speaks to each one of us individually. I need to listen to what
he is saying to me. (Please turn to your scripture on the following
pages. Inspiration points are there should you need them. When you
are ready, return here to continue.)

Conversation

What is stirring in me as I pray?
Am I consoled, troubled, left cold?
I imagine Jesus himself standing or sitting at my side,
and I share my feelings with him.

Conclusion

Glory be to the Father, and to the Son, and to the Holy Spirit,
as it was in the beginning, is now, and ever shall be,
world without end. Amen.

October 2015

Sunday 25th October,
Thirtieth Sunday of Ordinary Time
Mark 10:46—52

They came to Jericho. As he and his disciples and a large crowd were leaving Jericho, Bartimaeus son of Timaeus, a blind beggar, was sitting by the roadside. When he heard that it was Jesus of Nazareth, he began to shout out and say, "Jesus, Son of David, have mercy on me!" Many sternly ordered him to be quiet, but he cried out even more loudly, "Son of David, have mercy on me!" Jesus stood still and said, "Call him here." And they called the blind man, saying to him, "Take heart; get up, he is calling you." So throwing off his cloak, he sprang up and came to Jesus. Then Jesus said to him, "What do you want me to do for you?" The blind man said to him, "My teacher, let me see again." Jesus said to him, "Go; your faith has made you well." Immediately he regained his sight and followed him on the way.

- People who live with disabilities such as blindness often show great courage, resourcefulness, and strength of character. Do I truly appreciate my own God-given ability to see and my other natural senses and abilities? Do I ever express gratitude for these wonderful gifts? And do I ever humbly ask God to help me to live well with my own disabilities and limitations?

- Bartimaeus becomes a joyous disciple. What difference does my own faith make in my life?

Monday 26th October
Luke 13:10—17

Now Jesus was teaching in one of the synagogues on the sabbath. And just then there appeared a woman with a spirit that had crippled her for eighteen years. She was bent over and was quite unable to stand up straight. When Jesus saw her, he called her over and said, "Woman, you are set free from your ailment." When he laid his hands on her, immediately she stood up straight and began praising God. But the leader of the synagogue, indignant because Jesus had cured on the sabbath, kept saying to the crowd, "There are six days on which work ought to be done; come on those days and be cured, and not on the sabbath day." But the Lord answered him and said, "You hypocrites! Does not each of you on the sabbath untie his ox or his donkey from the manger, and lead it away to give it water? And ought not this woman, a daughter of Abraham whom Satan bound for eighteen long years, be set free from this bondage on the sabbath day?" When he said this, all his opponents were put to shame; and the entire crowd was rejoicing at all the wonderful things that he was doing.

- This woman's appearance makes a statement in itself. She was crippled and bent over. This condition robbed her of her dignity and her rightful place in the community; she was "unable to stand up straight" and to face the world.

- Once again, Jesus' intervention made all the difference for her. Immediately she stood up straight and began a whole new way of being and living. As a person of faith, she praised God who had given her freedom again.

Tuesday 27th October
Luke 13:18–21

Jesus said to the crowds, "What is the kingdom of God like? And to what should I compare it? It is like a mustard seed that someone took and sowed in the garden; it grew and became a tree, and the birds of the air made nests in its branches." And again he said, "To what should I compare the kingdom of God? It is like yeast that a woman took and mixed in with three measures of flour until all of it was leavened."

- The kingdom of God is too wonderful to be described directly in human or worldly terms. We can only get glimpses of God's world. Do I belong to the surprising kingdom of God or to the predictable kingdom of this world?

- Something as small as a mustard seed or as little as a measure of yeast can, given the proper conditions, produce great growth and transformation. As the mustard tree shelters the birds of the air, the kingdom of God is hidden but quietly growing, and it has room for everyone who wishes to come.

Wednesday 28th October,
Ss. Simon and Jude, Apostles
Luke 6:12—16

Now during those days he went out to the mountain to pray; and he spent the night in prayer to God. And when day came, he called his disciples and chose twelve of them, whom he also named apostles: Simon, whom he named Peter, and his brother Andrew, and James, and John, and Philip, and Bartholomew, and Matthew, and Thomas, and James son of Alphaeus, and Simon, who was called the Zealot, and Judas son of James, and Judas Iscariot, who became a traitor.

- Whenever I see the names of the disciples listed, I dare to include mine among them, since I recognize that Jesus calls me to be a disciple, too. I am not being presumptuous or vain but ask again for the humility I need to be a follower of Jesus.

- I give thanks to God for those people upon whom I have relied, from whom I have received blessings; their discipleship has built me up in faith, and I pray that I may do likewise for others.

Thursday 29th October
Luke 13:31—34

At that very hour some Pharisees came and said to him, "Get away from here, for Herod wants to kill you." He said to them, "Go and tell that fox for me, 'Listen, I am casting out demons and performing cures today and tomorrow, and on the third day I finish my work. Yet today, tomorrow, and the next day I must be on my way, because it is impossible for a prophet to be killed away from Jerusalem.' Jerusalem, Jerusalem, the city that kills the prophets and stones those who are sent to it! How often have I desired to gather your children together as a hen gathers her brood under her wings, and you were not willing!"

- I sit with Jesus as he makes his moving lament over Jerusalem. I enter into his image of a tender God who is compared to a caring and protective mother hen. Perhaps the "brood" think that they have grown up and have no longer need of her. But we are in fact always totally in need of God to sustain us.

- As your beloved child, God, I am willing to have you gather me under your wings! I place my neediness and vulnerabilities before you.

Friday 30th October
Luke 14:1—6

On one occasion when Jesus was going to the house of a leader of the Pharisees to eat a meal on the sabbath, they were watching him closely. Just then, in front of him, there was a man who had dropsy. And Jesus asked the lawyers and Pharisees, "Is it lawful to cure people on the sabbath, or not?" But they were silent. So Jesus took him and healed him, and sent him away. Then he said to them, "If one of you has a child or an ox that has fallen into a well, will you not immediately pull it out on a sabbath day?" And they could not reply to this.

- Can I visualise the setting where Jesus meets the man suffering from dropsy and cures him with a hostile audience of lawyers and Pharisees looking on?

- What feelings and motivations are going on in the various characters? Why do the Pharisees react as they do? What does the man with dropsy make of it?

Saturday 31st October
Luke 14:1, 7—11

On one occasion when Jesus was going to the house of a leader of the Pharisees to eat a meal on the sabbath, they were watching him closely. . . . When he noticed how the guests chose the places of honour, he told them a parable. "When you are invited by someone to a wedding banquet, do not sit down at the place of honour, in case someone more distinguished than you has been invited by your host; and the host who invited both of you may come and say to you, 'Give this person your place,' and then in disgrace you would start to take the lowest place. But when you are invited, go and sit down at the lowest place, so that when your host comes, he may say to you, 'Friend, move up higher'; then you will be honoured in the presence of all who sit at the table with you. For all who exalt themselves will be humbled, and those who humble themselves will be exalted."

- How difficult it is to practise the art of humility! How difficult it is not to take the best seat, grab the best bargain, and be first in the queue for the concert I must see! Jesus asks us to think of others, be more aware of other's needs, step back a bit and allow others to be centre stage for a change.

- Heavenly Father, teach us how to follow in Jesus' footsteps, how to be compassionate, more understanding, more generous in our thinking and in our actions.

November 1—7

Something to think and pray about each day this week:

Lost and Gone Forever?

"Put my tears in your bottle. Are they not in your record?" (Ps 56:8). What a splendid demand this is! A variant translation is equally moving: "My tears are stored in your flask." While we weep for our friends who have died, God is watching with compassion. God respects our tears and gathers them up because they are precious.

The Bible is the Book of Tears. Jesus weeps over Jerusalem and over Lazarus. Tears are the concern of God: at the end "he will wipe every tear from our eyes" (Rev 21:4). So while death indeed brings tears, we believe that we do not weep before an uncaring universe. St. Paul says to his early converts: "Do not grieve as others do who have no hope" (1 Thes 4:13).

There is a lasting blessing attached to tears: "Blessed are you who weep now, for you will laugh" (Lk 6:21). Tears reveal our love for those who have died. But ours is not a lost love. Our tears are never wasted. Those who seem to be "gone" will be restored to us. Jesus says: "If I go and prepare a place for you, I will come again and will take you to myself, so that where I am, there you may be also" (Jn 14:3). He promises this reunion to his disciples, not as individuals only, but as a community. The whole Body of Christ will finally be gathered into one, and all of us will rejoice together.

The Presence of God

God is with me, but more, God is within me.
Let me dwell for a moment on God's life-giving presence
in my body, in my mind, in my heart
as I sit here right now.

Freedom

I need to rise above the noise—
the noise that interrupts and separates,
the noise that isolates.
I need to listen to God again.

Consciousness

I remind myself that I am in the presence of the Lord.
I will take refuge in his loving heart.
He is my strength in times of weakness.
He is my comforter in times of sorrow.

The Word

I read the Word of God slowly, a few times over, and I listen to what
God is saying to me. (Please turn to your scripture on the following
pages. Inspiration points are there should you need them. When you
are ready, return here to continue.)

Conversation

Do I notice myself reacting as I pray with the Word of God?
Do I feel challenged, comforted, angry?
Imagining Jesus sitting or standing by me,
I speak out my feelings as one trusted friend to another.

Conclusion

Glory be to the Father, and to the Son, and to the Holy Spirit,
as it was in the beginning, is now, and ever shall be,
world without end. Amen.

November 2015

Sunday 1st November,
Feast of All Saints
Matthew 5:1—12

When Jesus saw the crowds, he went up the mountain; and after he sat down, his disciples came to him. Then he began to speak, and taught them, saying: "Blessed are the poor in spirit, for theirs is the kingdom of heaven. Blessed are those who mourn, for they will be comforted. Blessed are the meek, for they will inherit the earth. Blessed are those who hunger and thirst for righteousness, for they will be filled. Blessed are the merciful, for they will receive mercy. Blessed are the pure in heart, for they will see God. Blessed are the peacemakers, for they will be called children of God. Blessed are those who are persecuted for righteousness' sake, for theirs is the kingdom of heaven. Blessed are you when people revile you and persecute you and utter all kinds of evil against you falsely on my account. Rejoice and be glad, for your reward is great in heaven, for in the same way they persecuted the prophets who were before you."

- Today, and always, Jesus is "sitting down" in the sacred space of my heart. I listen to him and his words of life. Which Beatitude do I find most affirming? Which gives me most encouragement for my life journey right now?

- Which of these Beatitudes challenges me the most? Whichever one I feel drawn to indicates my next step forward in my life's journey.

Monday 2nd November,
Feast of All Souls
Luke 7:11—17

Soon afterwards he went to a town called Nain, and his disciples and a large crowd went with him. As he approached the gate of the town, a man who had died was being carried out. He was his mother's only son, and she was a widow; and with her was a large crowd from the town. When the Lord saw her, he had compassion for her and said to her, "Do not weep." Then he came forward and touched the bier, and the bearers stood still. And he said, "Young man, I say to you, rise!" The dead man sat up and began to speak, and Jesus gave him to his mother. Fear seized all of them; and they glorified God, saying, "A great prophet has risen among us!" and "God has looked favourably on his people!" This word about him spread throughout Judea and all the surrounding country.

- Jesus had compassion for the woman bereft of her only son, who was the support of her life. In my bereavements, the Lord encounters me, also. Can I let the compassionate eyes of Jesus search mine with understanding and an offer of help?

- This passage contains a hint of the resurrection of those who have died. In God's eyes, there are no "dead" people. God is God of the living. If I think of those I miss as being now fully alive in divine company, it brings me hope and longing.

Tuesday 3rd November
Luke 14:15—24

One of the dinner guests . . . said to Jesus, "Blessed is anyone who will eat bread in the kingdom of God!" Then Jesus said to him, "Someone gave a great dinner and invited many. At the time for the dinner he sent his slave to say to those who had been invited, 'Come; for everything is ready now.' But they all alike began to make excuses. The first said to him, 'I have bought a piece of land, and I must go out and see it; please accept my apologies.' Another said, 'I have bought five yoke of oxen, and I am going to try them out; please accept my apologies.' Another said, 'I have just been married, and therefore I cannot come.' So the slave returned and reported this to his master. Then the owner of the house became angry and said to his slave, 'Go out at once into the streets and lanes of the town and bring in the poor, the crippled, the blind, and the lame.' And the slave said, 'Sir, what you ordered has been done, and there is still room.' Then the master said to the slave, 'Go out into the roads and lanes, and compel people to come in, so that my house may be filled. For I tell you, none of those who were invited will taste my dinner.'"

- It is easy to become familiar with comforts, to lose the savour of good things.

- I pray that I might have the generosity of the host who threw open the doors of the banquet hall, so that the hall was filled. I think of how I embody the welcome and freedom that offers the goodness of God to all.

Wednesday 4th November
Luke 14:25—27

Now large crowds were travelling with him; and he turned and said to them, "Whoever comes to me and does not hate father and mother, wife and children, brothers and sisters, yes, and even life itself, cannot be my disciple. Whoever does not carry the cross and follow me cannot be my disciple."

- My "possessions" and comfort zones are challenged by my growing relationship with Jesus. What would help me to loosen my grasp on these false securities?

- Let me ask his help so that I may trust him totally.

Thursday 5th November
Luke 15:1—7

Now all the tax-collectors and sinners were coming near to listen to him. And the Pharisees and the scribes were grumbling and saying, "This fellow welcomes sinners and eats with them." So he told them this parable: "Which one of you, having a hundred sheep and losing one of them, does not leave the ninety-nine in the wilderness and go after the one that is lost until he finds it? When he has found it, he lays it on his shoulders and rejoices. And when he comes home, he calls together his friends and neighbours, saying to them, 'Rejoice with me, for I have found my sheep that was lost.'

Just so, I tell you, there will be more joy in heaven over one sinner who repents than over ninety-nine righteous people who need no repentance."

- The Pharisees "were grumbling." Am I a grumbler, dissatisfied with the way God goes about things?

- My greatest difficulty may be that I cannot allow myself to be real and vulnerable with Jesus. Can I let him put me on his shoulders in my weakness? Can I pray, "Carry me, Lord"?

Friday 6th November
Luke 16:1—8

Then Jesus said to the disciples, "There was a rich man who had a manager, and charges were brought to him that this man was squandering his property. So he summoned him and said to him, 'What is this that I hear about you? Give me an accounting of your management, because you cannot be my manager any longer.' Then the manager said to himself, 'What will I do, now that my master is taking the position away from me? I am not strong enough to dig, and I am ashamed to beg. I have decided what to do so that, when I am dismissed as manager, people may welcome me into their homes.' So, summoning his master's debtors one by one, he asked the first, 'How much do you owe my master?' He answered, 'A hundred jugs of olive oil.' He said to him, 'Take your bill, sit down quickly, and make it fifty.' Then he asked another, 'And how much do you owe?' He replied, 'A hundred containers of wheat.' He said to him, 'Take your bill and make it eighty.' And his master commended the dishonest manager because he had acted shrewdly; for the children of this age are more shrewd in dealing with their own generation than are the children of light."

- If you are in debt, it would be such a relief to have the bank manager cut your debt. God has already cancelled my debt. I am now free before God and very grateful.

- How am I managing the gifts God has given me? They are meant to be at the service of those who are most needy.

Saturday 7th November
Luke 16:9—15

Jesus said to the disciples, "And I tell you, make friends for your-selves by means of dishonest wealth so that when it is gone, they may welcome you into the eternal homes. Whoever is faithful in a very little is faithful also in much; and whoever is dishonest in a very little is dishonest also in much. If then you have not been faithful with the dishonest wealth, who will entrust to you the true riches? And if you have not been faithful with what belongs to another, who will give you what is your own? No slave can serve two masters; for a slave will either hate the one and love the other, or be devoted to the one and despise the other. You cannot serve God and wealth." The Pharisees, who were lovers of money, heard all this, and they ridiculed him. So he said to them, "You are those who justify your-selves in the sight of others; but God knows your hearts; for what is prized by human beings is an abomination in the sight of God."

- "Whoever is faithful in little is faithful in much." How have I lived this?

- You ask us to believe in you, Lord, to trust in your goodness. Look into our hearts, Lord, and remove everything that causes us to stumble or fall. As we walk through life, help us keep our eyes on you.

November 8—14

Something to think and pray about each day this week:

Dare We Hope?

Early in his pontificate, Pope Francis created a stir when he suggested that atheists might be saved. On the other hand, Pope Benedict alarmed many people when he insisted on the translation "for you and for many" rather than "for you and for all." Clearly the question put to Jesus, "Will only a few be saved?" (Lk 13:23), has not lost its urgency over the past two thousand years.

The Jews believed that on Judgment Day the wicked will receive the punishment they richly deserve. This notion appeals to us if we think that we ourselves will be among the "good." But the Good News of Jesus upsets this. Paul puts it dramatically: "God gave up his Son for all of us. It is God who justifies. Who is to condemn?" (see Rom 8:31–34). This hope that all may be saved appeals to us when we think of ourselves as "sinners," which we are! The Lamb of God "takes away the sin of the world" (Jn 1:29); Jesus dies "to gather into one the dispersed children of God" (Jn 11:52). We can hope that, against all the odds, God will win a total victory over evil, and that the Body of Christ will lack none of its members. We must indeed dare to hope that God, for whom nothing is impossible, will achieve his purposes. We work, pray, and endure all things for this.

The Presence of God

What is present to me is what has a hold on my becoming.
I reflect on the presence of God always there in love,
amidst the many things that have a hold on me.
I pause and pray that I may let God
affect my becoming in this precise moment.

Freedom

If God were trying to tell me something, would I know?
If God were reassuring me or challenging me, would I notice?
I ask for the grace to be free of my own preoccupations
and open to what God may be saying to me.

Consciousness

Knowing that God loves me unconditionally,
I look honestly over the last day, its events and my feelings.
Do I have something to be grateful for? Then I give thanks.
Is there something I am sorry for? Then I ask forgiveness.

The Word

I take my time to read the Word of God, slowly, a few times, allowing myself to dwell on anything that strikes me. (Please turn to your
scripture on the following pages. Inspiration points are there should
you need them. When you are ready, return here to continue.)

Conversation

Remembering that I am still in God's presence,
I imagine Jesus himself standing or sitting beside me,
and I say whatever is on my mind, whatever is in my heart,
speaking as one friend to another.

Conclusion

Glory be to the Father, and to the Son, and to the Holy Spirit,
as it was in the beginning, is now, and ever shall be,
world without end. Amen.

November 2015

Sunday 8th November,
Thirty-Second Sunday of Ordinary Time
Mark 12:38—40

As he taught, Jesus said, "Beware of the scribes, who like to walk around in long robes, and to be greeted with respect in the market-places, and to have the best seats in the synagogues and places of honour at banquets! They devour widows' houses and for the sake of appearance say long prayers. They will receive the greater condemnation."

- Jesus reminds us once again how we are to treat each other. We are all sons and daughters of the Father, and so we must be aware of the dignity each of us carry within. Through baptism, we have been brought into the family of God, and so we are all connected through grace.

- No one is greater than another, and no one is more important than another; we are all equal in the sight of our Father in heaven.

Sunday 9th November,
Dedication of the Lateran Basilica
John 2:13—22

The Passover of the Jews was near, and Jesus went up to Jerusalem. In the temple he found people selling cattle, sheep, and doves, and the money-changers seated at their tables. Making a whip of cords, he drove all of them out of the temple, both the sheep and the cattle. He also poured out the coins of the money-changers and overturned their tables. He told those who were selling the doves, "Take these things out of here! Stop making my Father's house a market-place!" His disciples remembered that it was written, "Zeal for your house will consume me." The Jews then said to him, "What sign can you show us for doing this?" Jesus answered them, "Destroy this temple, and in three days I will raise it up." The Jews then said, "This temple has been under construction for forty-six years, and will you raise it up in three days?" But he was speaking of the temple of his body. After he was raised from the dead, his disciples remembered that he had said this; and they believed the scripture and the word that Jesus had spoken.

- There may be junk and clutter in the temple of my heart, too. How can I clear it to provide a sacred space for God today?

- Often it is only in hindsight that we see the meaning of an event. Can you recall having such an experience lately? Our Lady "treasured in her heart" the things about Jesus that she did not yet understand. Let me be like her.

Tuesday 10th November
Luke 17:7—10

Jesus said to his disciples, "Who among you would say to your slave who has just come in from ploughing or tending sheep in the field, 'Come here at once and take your place at the table'? Would you not rather say to him, 'Prepare supper for me, put on your apron and serve me while I eat and drink; later you may eat and drink'? Do you thank the slave for doing what was commanded? So you also, when you have done all that you were ordered to do, say, 'We are worthless slaves; we have done only what we ought to have done!'"

- This is a tough saying of Jesus. We know that a little gratitude and recognition of work well done can raise the spirits! So let me find an opportunity today to recognize and affirm someone whose life is filled with work.

- We can never boast or rest on our laurels in our search for God. There will always be new challenges opening up before us. But perhaps I take on too much myself? Then let me learn from a saint who said: "I will do these things in love and freedom, or leave them alone."

Wednesday 11th November
Luke 17:11—19

On the way to Jerusalem Jesus was going through the region between Samaria and Galilee. As he entered a village, ten lepers approached him. Keeping their distance, they called out, saying, "Jesus, Master, have mercy on us!" When he saw them, he said to them, "Go and show yourselves to the priests." And as they went, they were made clean. Then one of them, when he saw that he was healed, turned back, praising God with a loud voice. He prostrated himself at Jesus' feet and thanked him. And he was a Samaritan. Then Jesus asked, "Were not ten made clean? But the other nine, where are they? Was none of them found to return and give praise to God except this foreigner?" Then he said to him, "Get up and go on your way; your faith has made you well."

• Gratitude oils the wheels of life. What have I taken for granted this day for which I can now be grateful?

• The ten ordinary miracles of my life are health, my senses, family, love, friendship, meaning, nature, beauty, music, laughter. Let me thank God daily for them. Are there other little miracles I would add?

Thursday 12th November
Luke 17:20—25

Once Jesus was asked by the Pharisees when the kingdom of God was coming, and he answered, "The kingdom of God is not coming with things that can be observed; nor will they say, 'Look, here it is!' or 'There it is!' For, in fact, the kingdom of God is among you." Then he said to the disciples, "The days are coming when you will long to see one of the days of the Son of Man, and you will not see it. They will say to you, 'Look there!' or 'Look here!' Do not go, do not set off in pursuit. For as the lightning flashes and lights up the sky from one side to the other, so will the Son of Man be in his day. But first he must endure much suffering and be rejected by this generation."

- Your promise to us, Jesus, is that if we have you as Lord of our lives, everything we need will be ours.

- This is not to say that we will go through life without pain or hardship, but we will go through life with you at our side to guide and protect us and help us on our way.

Friday 13th November
Luke 17:26—36

Jesus said to the disciples, "Just as it was in the days of Noah, so too it will be in the days of the Son of Man. They were eating and drinking, and marrying and being given in marriage, until the day Noah entered the ark, and the flood came and destroyed all of them. Likewise, just as it was in the days of Lot: they were eating and drinking, buying and selling, planting and building, but on the day that Lot left Sodom, it rained fire and sulfur from heaven and destroyed all of them—it will be like that on the day that the Son of Man is revealed. On that day, anyone on the housetop who has belongings in the house must not come down to take them away; and likewise anyone in the field must not turn back. Remember Lot's wife. Those who try to make their life secure will lose it, but those who lose their life will keep it. I tell you, on that night there will be two in one bed; one will be taken and the other left. There will be two women grinding meal together; one will be taken and the other left."

- Today's reading is meant to shatter my complacency. Lord, keep my spirit keen in its search for you. Keep my faith strong in times of crisis.

- When doubt or fear weigh down my spirit, Lord, give me the grace to surrender to you in hope. May I trust in "the plans of your heart which endure from age to age" (see Ps 33:11).

Saturday 14th November
Luke 18:1—8

Then Jesus told them a parable about their need to pray always and not to lose heart. He said, "In a certain city there was a judge who neither feared God nor had respect for people. In that city there was a widow who kept coming to him and saying, 'Grant me justice against my opponent.' For a while he refused; but later he said to himself, 'Though I have no fear of God and no respect for anyone, yet because this widow keeps bothering me, I will grant her justice, so that she may not wear me out by continually coming.'" And the Lord said, "Listen to what the unjust judge says. And will not God grant justice to his chosen ones who cry to him day and night? Will he delay long in helping them? I tell you, he will quickly grant justice to them. And yet, when the Son of Man comes, will he find faith on earth?"

- Jesus, teach us to trust you and not lose heart when we call on you in prayer. The prayer of intercession will never go unanswered, but our ways are not your ways and our thoughts are not your thoughts.

- Keep us faithful in prayer, Lord, for you will never be outdone in generosity.

November 15–21

Something to think and pray about each day this week:

Love Awaits Us

An immense love awaits us as we step into eternal life. We do not know its details, but that does not matter. The God of Surprises is preparing for us everything that could make us uniquely happy. We were, after all, made to be loved, and at the end, Love itself will enfold us. With the three divine Persons will be all those who have gone before us, delighted that we have at last arrived. In this life we often feel like lonely marathon runners, but then we will find ourselves emerging into a great stadium with an immense crowd rising to applaud us. Surely, then, we will fall on our knees and cry, but our tears will be tears of joy, not of sadness. God will take us by the hand and present us to the gathered community in which everyone is totally on our side.

If this seems fanciful, recall the prodigal son. The father does not even wait for him to arrive. He runs to embrace him and carries him home. He clothes him in splendour and then presents him proudly at the great feast.

As we tend the dying, we can remind them that they are being drawn into the heart of love. Love comes to take them home, saying "Arise, my love, my fair one, and come away; for now the winter is past. . . . Let me see your face, let me hear your voice; for your voice is sweet, and your face is lovely" (Sg 2:10–14). Could we ask for more?

The Presence of God

At any time of the day or night we can call on Jesus.
He is always waiting, listening for our call.
What a wonderful blessing.
No phone needed, no e-mails—just a whisper.

Freedom

Lord, grant me the grace to be free from the excesses of this life.
Let me not get caught up with the desire for wealth.
Keep my heart and mind free to love and serve you.

Consciousness

I exist in a web of relationships—links to nature, people, God.
I trace out these links, giving thanks for the life that flows through them.
Some links are twisted or broken; I may feel regret, anger, disappointment.
I pray for the gift of acceptance and forgiveness.

The Word

I take my time to read the Word of God, slowly, a few times, allowing myself to dwell on anything that strikes me. (Please turn to your scripture on the following pages. Inspiration points are there should you need them. When you are ready, return here to continue.)

Conversation

Remembering that I am still in God's presence,
I imagine Jesus himself standing or sitting beside me,
and I say whatever is on my mind, whatever is in my heart,
speaking as one friend to another.

Conclusion

Glory be to the Father, and to the Son, and to the Holy Spirit,
as it was in the beginning, is now, and ever shall be,
world without end. Amen

November 2015

Sunday 15th November,
Thirty-Third Sunday of Ordinary Time
Mark 13:24—27

Jesus said to Peter, James, John, and Andrew, "But in those days, after that suffering, the sun will be darkened, and the moon will not give its light, and the stars will be falling from heaven, and the powers in the heavens will be shaken. Then they will see 'the Son of Man coming in clouds' with great power and glory. Then he will send out the angels, and gather his elect from the four winds, from the ends of the earth to the ends of heaven."

- Even in our darkest hour, the Lord does not abandon us. His eye always upon us, he watches over us night and day.

- But if we take his words to heart and stay close to him as we journey, we have nothing to fear. His gift to us is his presence with us till the end of the world.

Monday 16th November
Luke 18:35—43

As he approached Jericho, a blind man was sitting by the roadside begging. When he heard a crowd going by, he asked what was happening. They told him, "Jesus of Nazareth is passing by." Then he shouted, "Jesus, Son of David, have mercy on me!" Those who were in front sternly ordered him to be quiet; but he shouted even more loudly, "Son of David, have mercy on me!" Jesus stood still and ordered the man to be brought to him; and when he came near, he asked him, "What do you want me to do for you?" He said, "Lord, let me see again." Jesus said to him, "Receive your sight; your faith has saved you." Immediately he regained his sight and followed him, glorifying God; and all the people, when they saw it, praised God.

- Jesus asks me, "What is happening?" Is there anything of lasting importance happening in my life? May I be alert, Lord, as you pass by.

- "What do you want me to do for you?" Jesus asks me this every day! But do I want anything, or is my soul only half-alive?

Tuesday 17th November
Luke 19:1—10

Jesus entered Jericho and was passing through it. A man was there named Zacchaeus; he was a chief tax-collector and was rich. He was trying to see who Jesus was, but on account of the crowd he could not, because he was short in stature. So he ran ahead and climbed a sycamore tree to see him, because he was going to pass that way. When Jesus came to the place, he looked up and said to him, "Zacchaeus, hurry and come down; for I must stay at your house today." So he hurried down and was happy to welcome him. All who saw it began to grumble and said, "He has gone to be the guest of one who is a sinner." Zacchaeus stood there and said to the Lord, "Look, half of my possessions, Lord, I will give to the poor; and if I have defrauded anyone of anything, I will pay back four times as much." Then Jesus said to him, "Today salvation has come to this house, because he too is a son of Abraham. For the Son of Man came to seek out and to save the lost."

- Zacchaeus was a man of the world, wealthy and well connected, but not very popular in the community. Yet something stirred in him that caused him to find some way to see Jesus.

- Then Zacchaeus had a conversion experience when he looked into the eyes of Jesus, and his whole world turned around. I wonder what happened to him after Jesus left the village. .*. .

Wednesday 18th November
Luke 19:11—13, 15—24

As they were listening to this, he went on to tell a parable, because he was near Jerusalem, and because they supposed that the kingdom of God was to appear immediately. So he said,

"A nobleman went to a distant country to get royal power for himself and then return. He summoned ten of his slaves, and gave them ten pounds, and said to them, 'Do business with these until I come back.' . . . When he returned, having received royal power, he ordered these slaves, to whom he had given the money, to be summoned so that he might find out what they had gained by trading. The first came forward and said, 'Lord, your pound has made ten more pounds.' He said to him, 'Well done, good slave! Because you have been trustworthy in a very small thing, take charge of ten cities.' Then the second came, saying, 'Lord, your pound has made five pounds.' He said to him, 'And you, rule over five cities.' Then the other came, saying, 'Lord, here is your pound. I wrapped it up in a piece of cloth, for I was afraid of you, because you are a harsh man; you take what you did not deposit, and reap what you did not sow.' He said to him, 'I will judge you by your own words, you wicked slave! You knew, did you, that I was a harsh man, taking what I did not deposit and reaping what I did not sow? Why then did you not put my money into the bank? Then when I returned, I could have collected it with interest.' He said to the bystanders, 'Take the pound from him and give it to the one who has ten pounds.'"

- God takes risks for us, so let us take risks for God. By taking risks, we gain confidence, experience, and productivity.

- Grant me initiative and courage, Lord, on all levels of living. Let it be said of me that I tried to do great things for you.

Thursday 19th November
Luke 19:41—43

As Jesus came near and saw the city, he wept over it, saying, "If you, even you, had only recognized on this day the things that make for peace! But now they are hidden from your eyes. Indeed, the days will come upon you, when your enemies will set up ramparts around you and surround you, and hem you in on every side."

- Jesus weeps not for the destruction of bricks and mortar, but for the suffering of the people in the city and the destruction of peace.

- Today we remember all those who suffer in the midst of destruction.

Friday 20th November
Luke 19:45—48

Then Jesus entered the temple and began to drive out those who were selling things there; and he said, "It is written, 'My house shall be a house of prayer'; but you have made it a den of robbers." Every day he was teaching in the temple. The chief priests, the scribes, and the leaders of the people kept looking for a way to kill him; but they did not find anything they could do, for all the people were spellbound by what they heard.

- *Sacred Space* makes my poor heart a "house of prayer." God is active there, transforming me, even though I notice the changes only later.

- In praying *Sacred Space*, am I ever "spellbound" by what I read?

Saturday 21st November,
Presentation of the Blessed Virgin Mary
Matthew 12:46—50

While Jesus was still speaking to the crowds, his mother and his brothers were standing outside, wanting to speak to him. Someone told him, "Look, your mother and your brothers are standing outside, wanting to speak to you." But to the one who had told him this, Jesus replied, "Who is my mother, and who are my brothers?" And pointing to his disciples, he said, "Here are my mother and my brothers! For whoever does the will of my Father in heaven is my brother and sister and mother."

- When was the last time I felt I was left "standing outside"? When I feel this way, do I try to speak to Jesus?

- Because I at least try to do the will of God, I am a member of Jesus' inner family circle! Let this make me happy today.

November 22–28

Something to think and pray about each day this week:

Grace in Dying

I meet people in hospices and nursing homes who ask, "Is it wrong to pray to die?" They would wish the dull waiting period to be over. "God seems to have forgotten me," they will say. "Better to move on, even if I don't know what's ahead." Nursing staff and relatives can also harbour the same thoughts; there is the cost of maintenance, the shortage of beds, the tedium of visiting someone who can no longer converse well, if at all. It is no surprise, then, that in secular culture the push for euthanasia is gaining ground.

But while nothing seems to be happening on the outside, a great deal is going on within, and it is well-documented by authors such as K. D. Singh in *The Grace in Dying*. The process of dying is to be seen as the final stage of human growth. God is busy, hollowing us out so that we can "be filled with all the fullness of God" (Eph 3:19). All secondary issues are being set aside—health, possessions, money, status, opinions—and ultimately the effort to cling to one's very self becomes a distraction. God is working in the depths of our being, whether we know it or not. Made for God, we are being restored to the divine. Jesus said of Lazarus, "Unbind him, and let him go" (Jn 11:44). Perhaps our central task as carers is to support this divine process of unbinding the dying from what holds them back from God.

The Presence of God

I pause for a moment
and reflect on God's life-giving presence
in every part of my body, in everything around me,
in the whole of my life.

Freedom

God is not foreign to my freedom.
Instead, the Spirit breathes life into my most intimate desires,
gently nudging me toward all that is good.
I ask for the grace to let myself be enfolded by the Spirit.

Consciousness

I exist in a web of relationships—links to nature, people, God.
I trace out these links, giving thanks for the life that flows through them.
Some links are twisted or broken; I may feel regret, anger, disappointment.
I pray for the gift of acceptance and forgiveness.

The Word

God speaks to each one of us individually. I need to listen to what he is saying to me. (Please turn to your scripture on the following pages. Inspiration points are there should you need them. When you are ready, return here to continue.)

Conversation

How has God's Word moved me? Has it left me cold?
Has it consoled me or moved me to act in a new way?
I imagine Jesus standing or sitting beside me;
I turn and share my feelings with him.

Conclusion

Glory be to the Father, and to the Son, and to the Holy Spirit,
as it was in the beginning, is now, and ever shall be,
world without end. Amen.

November 2015

Sunday 22nd November,
Feast of Christ the King
John 18:33—37

Then Pilate entered the headquarters again, summoned Jesus, and asked him, "Are you the King of the Jews?" Jesus answered, "Do you ask this on your own, or did others tell you about me?" Pilate replied, "I am not a Jew, am I? Your own nation and the chief priests have handed you over to me. What have you done?" Jesus answered, "My kingdom is not from this world. If my kingdom were from this world, my followers would be fighting to keep me from being handed over to the Jews. But as it is, my kingdom is not from here." Pilate asked him, "So you are a king?" Jesus answered, "You say that I am a king. For this I was born, and for this I came into the world, to testify to the truth. Everyone who belongs to the truth listens to my voice."

- Pontius Pilate has gone down in history as the man who put Jesus to death. Yet Pilate did not find Jesus guilty; Pilate sent him to Herod for judgement. Jesus says his kingdom is not from this world but that those who believe in him will hear and listen to his voice.

- Jesus, in the midst of all the noise and distractions of this world, we find it hard to hear your voice. Open our ears, Lord, that we may hear and take account of your Word.

Monday 23rd November
Luke 21:1—4

Jesus looked up and saw rich people putting their gifts into the treasury; he also saw a poor widow put in two small copper coins. He said, "Truly I tell you, this poor widow has put in more than all of them; for all of them have contributed out of their abundance, but she out of her poverty has put in all she had to live on."

- It is not the amount which counts, but the heart with which it is given.

- "She, out of her poverty, has put in all she had to live on." I ask this unnamed woman to help me to put in at least something from my abundance.

Tuesday 24th November
Luke 21:5—11

When some were speaking about the temple, how it was adorned with beautiful stones and gifts dedicated to God, Jesus said, "As for these things that you see, the days will come when not one stone will be left upon another; all will be thrown down." They asked him, "Teacher, when will this be, and what will be the sign that this is about to take place?" And he said, "Beware that you are not led astray; for many will come in my name and say, 'I am he!' and, 'The time is near!' Do not go after them. When you hear of wars and insurrections, do not be terrified; for these things must take place first, but the end will not follow immediately." Then he said to them, "Nation will rise against nation, and kingdom against kingdom; there will be great earthquakes, and in various places famines and plagues; and there will be dreadful portents and great signs from heaven."

- Jesus' listeners are anxious to know what signs to look out for when the end times come. But the timing of such an event is God's secret! We see many of the signs written in this piece of scripture happen in our twenty-first-century world.

- Jesus, help us to remember that the future lies in your hands, and nothing can destroy or hurt us if we remain true to you as Lord of our lives.

Wednesday 25th November
Luke 21:12—19

Jesus said to his disciples, "But before all this occurs, they will arrest you and persecute you; they will hand you over to synagogues and prisons, and you will be brought before kings and governors because of my name. This will give you an opportunity to testify. So make up your minds not to prepare your defence in advance; for I will give you words and a wisdom that none of your opponents will be able to withstand or contradict. You will be betrayed even by parents and brothers, by relatives and friends; and they will put some of you to death. You will be hated by all because of my name. But not a hair of your head will perish. By your endurance you will gain your souls."

- "You will be betrayed" even by those closest to you. When relationships fail, I know the truth of this.

- At such times, do I believe that God is very close to me, watching over "the hair of my head"? Does this help me to retain my equilibrium and integrity?

Thursday 26th November
Luke 21:20—24

Jesus said to the disciples, "When you see Jerusalem surrounded by armies, then know that its desolation has come near. Then those in Judea must flee to the mountains, and those inside the city must leave it, and those out in the country must not enter it; for these are days of vengeance, as a fulfilment of all that is written. Woe to those who are pregnant and to those who are nursing infants in those days! For there will be great distress on the earth and wrath against this people; they will fall by the edge of the sword and be taken away as captives among all nations; and Jerusalem will be trampled on by the Gentiles, until the times of the Gentiles are fulfilled."

- Here Jesus speaks of the fall of Jerusalem and warns that the time of desolation is near and the people must flee to the mountains. There is sadness as Jesus thinks of those who may not be able to flee, the pregnant women, the very old, the most vulnerable. Isn't it usually these people who bear the brunt of most wars?

- Show us, Lord, how to become peace-filled people.

Friday 27th November
Luke 21:29—31

Then Jesus told them a parable: "Look at the fig tree and all the trees; as soon as they sprout leaves you can see for yourselves and know that summer is already near. So also, when you see these things taking place, you know that the kingdom of God is near."

- Jesus, you seem to have learned so much from nature! Grant me the same awareness so that I may learn the presence, action, and care of God in my life.

- Mention of this fig tree reminds me of the other fig tree which was given a second chance to bear fruit (see Lk 13:6—9). Do I have the courage to start again when things don't work out the first time?

Saturday 28th November
Luke 21:34—36

Jesus said to his disciples, "Be on guard so that your hearts are not weighed down with dissipation and drunkenness and the worries of this life, and that day does not catch you unexpectedly, like a trap. For it will come upon all who live on the face of the whole earth. Be alert at all times, praying that you may have the strength to escape all these things that will take place, and to stand before the Son of Man."

- Is there something that weighs down my heart? Dissipation, drunkenness, the worries of this life, or is there something else?

- How do I feel about the day of the Lord? Do I live with fear of being caught out? Am I looking forward to meeting him? Is my praying now a preparation to meet the Son of Man with confidence?

The Irish Jesuits are engaged in a wide range of ministries both at home and throughout the world. They serve as teachers, caregivers for homeless youth, parish priests, academics, artists, and administrators. Their website, *Sacred Space*, attracts more than six million visits annually and is produced in some twenty languages.

Founded in 1865, Ave Maria Press,
a ministry of the Congregation of
Holy Cross, is a Catholic publishing
company that serves the spiritual and
formative needs of the Church and its
schools, institutions, and ministers;
Christian individuals and families; and
others seeking spiritual nourishment.

———

For a complete listing of titles from

Ave Maria Press

Sorin Books

Forest of Peace

Christian Classics

visit www.avemariapress.com

ave maria press® / Notre Dame, IN 46556
A Ministry of the United States Province of Holy Cross